# SAXIFRAGES

## *and related genera*

# SAXIFRAGES

## *and related genera*

FRITZ KÖHLEIN

*Translated from the German by*
**DAVID WINSTANLEY**

Timber Press · Portland

# *Contents*

# *Foreword*

The original edition of this work, *Saxifragen*, was the first book on saxifrages to be published in German, and claims to be the most comprehensive work on the subject. It appears now in English, slightly adapted to meet the needs of readers in the English-speaking world. Here is an attempt to present the enormous genus *Saxifraga* in a clear and comprehensible shape. It is worth doing, for saxifrages are ideal plants for the 'modern' garden. They are small enough to fit into any space and are among the few plants which are decorative all the year round.

The book has been planned so as to provide the specialist with as much as possible of the information he may need, and also to guide the beginner who is taking his first steps in these broad territories; the detailed index is intended to direct them both.

No author can write a book on saxifrages without remembering three gardeners who were among the pioneers. They are Franz Sündermann, collector and grower; George Arends, an enthusiastic cultivator; and Karl Foerster, whose books helped to create wider enthusiasm for saxifrages.

All of us build on the work and experience of others, and depend on their help. I owe a particular debt of gratitude to Dr Encke, who gave me unstinted help in devising the plan of the book and in answering so many questions. I have also enjoyed generous advice and support from nurserymen who offer large collections of saxifrages, including Dr Hans Simon (Markt-heidenfeld), Ferdinand Franz Sündermann (Lindau), Jacob Eschmann (Emmen, Switzerland) and Hans Frei (Wildensbuch, Switzerland). For help on the bergenias I am indebted to Frau Helene von Stein-Zeppelin (Lauffen/Baden). Last but not least, I must thank my wife Annemarie for the important contribution which she has made to this book.

*Fritz Köhlein*

# · O N E ·

# *Botanical introduction*

This is a book for gardeners, not a botanical monograph. Nevertheless, botanical knowledge and horticultural practice are so closely interwoven that certain botanical facts have to be explained.

The genus *Saxifraga* is very large and contains more than 300 species. Counting natural hybrids and local varieties there must be nearly 500 different saxifrages. This does not include hybrids of garden origin and the numerous cultivars. Morphologically, many of the species are so diverse that the beginner may find it hard to believe that they are all members of one and the same genus.

## Names and distinguishing characters

The name 'saxifrage' (in German, *Steinbrech*) is simply the botanical term *saxifraga* anglicized. The word is derived from the Latin *saxum* ( = rock) and *frangere* ( = to break). To say that saxifrages break stones is of course an exaggeration. Most of these plants are small and none of them is really capable of breaking stones, though they may sometimes give this impression. However, their dust-like seeds find their way into the narrowest crevices, giving rise to plants which flourish under difficult conditions. There is another explanation for the name, alleged to go back to the use of *Saxifraga granulata* in herbal medicine. In the Middle Ages this widely distributed plant was used for the treatment of bladder stones, and was believed to have the power of breaking them into pieces.

The nomenclature used in this book – with very few exceptions – is based on Zander's *Handwörterbuch der Pflanzennamen* ('Dictionary of Plant Names', 11th edition, 1979) and on *Flora Europaea*, Vol. 1 (1964).

The genus *Saxifraga* is enormously diverse. They are small plants, some of them dwarf and none more than moderate in size. They are predominantly perennial, but there are a few annuals and biennials among them. Most of them have small leaves often arranged in rosettes and form cushions, in some cases hard and encrusted, in others mosslike. But there are some small herbaceous perennials with deciduous leaves. The leaves are alternate or less often opposite, thick and fleshy, leathery or thin and membranous, entire or more or less palmate. The flowers are arranged singly or in small numbers or in richly floriferous panicles, racemes or pseudoumbels. Most species have white flowers, but some are yellow or pink and a few are red. The calyx and corolla are usually divided into five, though occasionally up to nine, sepals or petals, and the calyx segments form a covering for the bud. The stamens – usually ten in number – are divided into an outer ring inserted opposite the petals, and an inner ring between them. The stamens are filamentous, club-shaped or awl-shaped, and the anthers are divided into two lobes. The ovary has two, or occasionally up to five, chambers and may be free, or in the case of species with a definite receptacle, fused to the latter. Saxifrages produce numerous minute seeds.

Classification of the 'Engleria' saxifrages has always presented difficulties. Though closely related to Section Porophyllum ('Kabschia'), they form a group distinct from them. In this book they are dealt with under Section Porophyllum. Attempts have recently been made to unite the latter with Section Tetrameridium, a group comprising a few Himalayan species. This seems unreasonable, as the plants in Section Tetrameridium have flowers with four petals, otherwise found only in Section Diptera; all other sections have flowers with five petals. For the time being it might be best to regard the 'Engleria' saxifrages as a subsection of Porophyllum, with which they cross readily but from which they are clearly distinguished by the coloured calyx.

Another difficulty arises from the allocation of *Saxifraga caesia* and *S. squarrosa* to Section Porophyllum ('Kabschia'). It is impossible to understand why the botanists have kept them there for nearly a century. These two species obviously belong to Section Euaizoonia. Neither of them crosses with any 'Kabschia' saxifrage. In this book these two species will be found at the end of Section Euaizoonia.

As regards nomenclature it is still disputed whether *S. paniculata* or *S. aizoon* is the correct name. *Flora Europaea* and Zander give *S. paniculata* as the valid name and I have followed these works, although Landolt says that it should be changed back to *S. aizoon*.


## Geographical distribution

The genus *Saxifraga* consists mainly of mountain plants, many of which are extremely resistant to adverse climatic conditions. Those species which grow in the Arctic extend as far as the borders of the perpetual snow, while the high alpine species growing in exposed places defy all assaults of the weather.

Saxifrages are plants of the northern temperate zone, but there are a few outliers in the Andes. These belong to Section Dactyloides and are related to *S. cespitosa*; the best known is *S. magellanica*. Saxifrages extend towards the North Pole as far as any flowering plant can survive. Some two dozen species belong to these pioneers.

In the Old World there are a few southerly outposts, with species in Madeira, in the Atlas mountains, in Ethiopia and in the Yemen. In Asia, the Himalayas and the mountains of south China form the southern boundary. In North America there is one species which extends into the alpine zone of Mexico. These frontiers represent an enormous area of distribution, but saxifrages are confined to certain regions within them, where they find the right climatic conditions. One important group is restricted to the mountains and there is a smaller group which, though not entirely confined to high altitudes, nevertheless shuns the continental plains and marshy lowlands.

The alpine species extend to the highest altitudes. In the Himalayas a few saxifrages are found as high as 6000 metres. Their preference for mountains is shown by the fact that of the 45 species occurring in central Europe only three are found in the plains (*S. bulbifera, S. granulata* and *S. tridactylites*). The Alps are a favourite territory of saxifrages, which often grow in detritus or scree. They are also found on rocks and in mountain woods. Some grow on the banks of small streams and others are found in wet grassland around springs.

Some sections are confined to relatively small areas. For example, Section Robertsoniana is found in the mountains of north Spain, in the west and central Pyrenees and also in south-west Ireland. There is also a locality in the Vosges, though here the plants are not wild but relics of cultivation. All occurrences elsewhere are garden escapes.

Section Micranthes is found mainly in eastern Asia and Pacific North America, there being only four species in Europe (*S. hieracifolia, S. nivalis, S. stellaris* and *S. clusii*). Section Hirculus, containing more than 100 species, is almost entirely restricted to the Himalayas and the mountains of western China. Only one species in the section is endemic to Pacific North America. The only ones which reach Europe are the circumpolar species *S. hirculus* and *S. flagellaris*.

Section Euaizoonia, important to gardeners, is confined to the mountains of central and southern Europe and the equally important Section Porophyllum ('Kabschia') occurs mainly in the Alps, the Balkan ranges and the Caucasus.

There are, however, some species which grow in Iran, Turkestan, the Himalayas and south-west China. Section Dactyloides is indigenous to Spain, North Africa, Madeira and also western and central Europe.

# · T W O ·

# *Saxifrages in the garden*

This huge and varied genus is an almost inexhaustible treasure chest for the gardener. Though not all the 300 + species are garden-worthy, it is surprising how many of them are. In addition there are numerous garden hybrids. Certain groups call for special conditions to show them at their best; as Karl Foerster said: 'Even if you grow no other alpines, it is worth having a rock garden for saxifrages alone.'

There are three sections of special value to the gardener: Dactyloides (mossy saxifrages), Euaizoonia (silver or encrusted saxifrages) and Porophyllum ( = 'Kabschia'). There are six further sections which have some horticultural importance, but not as much as the first three; they are Hirculus, Robertsoniana, Cymbalaria, Nephrophyllum, Porphyrion and Diptera. Sections Micranthes, Miscopetalum, Tridactylites, Trachyphyllum, Xanthizoon and Tetrameridium are of little importance to the ordinary gardener though they are of interest to collectors and are grown in botanical gardens.

Cultural requirements are dealt with in this book at the end of each section and special hints are given where necessary for individual species, but certain general recommendations will be given here. Beginners should start with the easily grown species listed in the Tables at the end of the book.

Saxifrage species are always grown for sale in pots and can therefore be planted at any time of year except when the ground is frozen. Spring and autumn both have their advantages as planting times. If autumn is chosen, care must be taken that plants in holes or crevices are firmly wedged in place so that the frost cannot dislodge them. Spring planting may coincide with the flowering time of certain species, notably the 'Kabschia' saxifrages. Holiday-makers who visit an alpine plant nursery can safely buy saxifrages in pots even if they are only just starting their journey. However, the plants should be given as much fresh air as possible and should be kept on the balcony, not in the hotel room. If necessary, plastic film can be used to keep the air moist.

A word about the delicate question of collecting plants from the wild. Silver saxifrages and 'Kabschia' species are protected in most countries and should never be collected. They can be obtained from nurseries. However, if a rambler in the mountains encounters a particularly fine local variety or natural hybrid, no one can possibly object to his taking one or two rosettes or offsets, which will easily root if treated as cuttings at home. There are many species of lesser garden value but of interest to the collector which are not under protection, but here too moderation should be the watchword.

The gardener who brings home a new saxifrage must take great care not to bring weeds with it. Liverworts and annuals find conditions to their liking in pots and it is all too easy to bring home nursery-garden weeds. This can be avoided as follows. If the plants are in pots, unpot them cautiously. Remove the uppermost layer of soil (1 cm) from each root ball. Look closely at the neck of the plant and make sure that every weed has been extracted. Then check the rest of the root ball and remove any perennial weeds which may have crept in. Even in the resting state, they can be recognized from the presence of two different kinds of roots. In this case, the perennial weeds must be removed by pulling the roots apart. Preparation of the soil is described elsewhere, but firm planting and thorough watering are of course essential.

Saxifrages demand little in the way of special care, provided they are given the right place in the garden and the soil has been properly prepared. The main routine task is removal of dead blooms after flowering. Among silver saxifrages each rosette which has flowered will die and can be plucked out. Mossy saxifrages can be trimmed with scissors, or for larger areas a pair of shears. 'Kabschia' saxifrages can be pinched out with finger and thumb. The autumn-flowering saxifrages of Section Diptera are not evergreen, and the dead leaves should be cleared away in the spring. Certain species will sometimes need trimming with scissors during the growing period if they threaten to overwhelm their neighbours. Watering may sometimes be necessary during droughts. A general-purpose fertilizer, sparingly applied in the spring, will benefit plants of various sections, in particular the dwarf 'Kabschia' saxifrages.

There need be no worries about hardiness. Though there are certain tender species, e.g. *Saxifraga maderensis*, they are not in commerce. The species and hybrids ordinarily offered need little or no protection in winter. However, until the new plants are established it is a good idea to give them a thin covering of conifer branches, if only to protect the frozen plants from desiccation.

# · T H R E E ·

# *Ways of using saxifrages*

There are so many different ways of using saxifrages in the garden that no book could possibly describe them all. However, the widest possible range of ideas is set out in the following pages. These ideas can be modified to suit individual gardens. Saxifrages retain their pleasing appearance all the year round and it is worth taking some trouble to devise the best possible ways of presenting them.

## Sunny areas of the rock garden

The silver saxifrages ('encrusted saxifrages') of Section Euaizoonia will tolerate the most exposure to sun. Many species and hybrids are also highly resistant to dryness, though none of them have the same drought-resistance as succulents such as sempervivum, sedum or opuntia. Atmospheric humidity is another factor. In gardens which enjoy high atmospheric humidity plants will tolerate greater exposure. Many of these saxifrages will survive a period of drought; the leaves of the rosette will become limp and will curve inwards, but when rain comes the plant will usually recover rapidly.

The cushions of silvery green or silvery grey rosettes harmonize with any other colour, as do their white flowers. The risk of colour clashes arises only in the few instances where the flowers are pale yellow or pink.

The silver saxifrages begin to flower at a time when conventional rock garden plants such as aubretia and alyssum have finished their vivid or even gaudy display. The season for campanula and dianthus is here, sempervivums are putting up their flowering spikes and many sedums are covered with bloom. When planning mixed plantings the gardener must choose plants of comparable vigour and size. Anyone who plants *Saxifraga valdensis* next to *Dianthus deltoides* or *Campanula poscharskyana* will lose the saxifrage, as it will soon be overwhelmed by such partners.

Silver saxifrages are not fussy about the position in which they are planted. They will grow well in crevices, in narrow strips of soil between rocks, on flat surfaces or gentle slopes. On a slope it is a good plan to build steps or terraces 40–50 cm wide. Instead of being completely horizontal they should be given a slight backward slope so as to retain rainwater and to keep the back of the terrace moist. Silver saxifrages will do well here, while dianthus and campanulas should be planted near the front so that they can hang down over the edge of the stones. The spaces between the stones at the front of the terrace are the driest spots and are the right places for sempervivum and sedum. All these saxifrages harmonize well with other plants and are equally tolerant of different rocks. Their natural setting is a calcareous sedimentary rock such as shell limestone. The white, grey or beige tones of the stone are neutral and go well with the plants. On the other hand, dark igneous rock or grey slate can offer splendid contrasts. Red sandstone is equally suitable. In shape, too, silver saxifrages fit into every kind of rock garden from natural layouts to strictly formal compositions with drystone walls, steps and ledges. *Saxifraga paniculata* (syn. *S. aizoon*) is the right size for small intimate plantings or larger schemes. It should be partnered by plants of comparable size such as *Campanula garganica* or *C. portenschlagiana* 'B. Prövis'. The latter variety is somewhat more miniature than the species. For an even more natural effect it is worth trying *Campanula cochleariifolia* and its white form. This dwarf alpine campanula spreads by means of fine underground runners into every crevice and also of course between the rosettes of saxifrages. Among the pinks there are plants of moderate size and vigour such as *Dianthus subacaulis* or the different varieties of *Dianthus gratianopolitanus* (syn. *D. caesius*). Varieties such as 'Nordstjernen' are too vigorous and should be excluded in favour of those of restrained growth. As partners for saxifrages I am especially fond of *Dianthus* 'Pink Jewel' and 'Pummelchen'. These varieties of campanula and dianthus can also be used side by side with other species and hybrids of Section Euaizoonia. Other perennials which go well with saxifrages include the rock-garden penstemon species, in particular those with pink or red flowers, such as *Penstemon pinifolius, P. scouleri* 'Red Form' (this grows somewhat larger) and *P. rupicola*. Various mat-forming species of sedum (*Sedum album*) can also be used, although they tend to spread widely; other possibilities include *Sedum forsteranum* ssp. *elegans, S. kamtschaticum* var. *middendorfianum, S. oreganum, S. reflexum* and *S. sieboldii*.

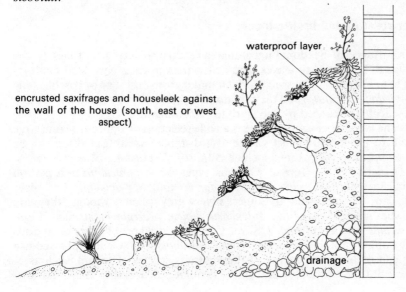

waterproof layer

encrusted saxifrages and houseleek against the wall of the house (south, east or west aspect)

drainage

*Fig. 1*

It would be impossible to list all the suitable sempervivum partners, but for the sake of pleasing contrasts those with light green rosettes should be used sparingly. Among suitable varieties are: *Sempervivum arachnoideum* 'Topas', *S. calcareum* 'Alpha', 'Gamma', 'Jubilee', 'Othello', *S. marmoreum* 'Rubrifolium', 'Rubin', 'Atroviolaceum', 'Noir', 'Patrician', 'Garnet', 'Mercury', 'Zirkon', 'Pilatus', and *Jovibarba heuffelii* 'Xanthoheuff'. There are gaps in every rock garden, but they can be filled by summer-flowering annuals or bedding plants, such as *Verbena peruviana, Portulaca grandiflora* or *Dorotheanthus bellidiformis*. Perennial species such as *Delosperma cooperi* or *Mesembryanthemum othonna* are also appropriate. Ornamental grasses (*Festuca cinerea* and *F. ovina*) and sedges (*Carex morrowii* 'Ingwersen', *C. morrowii* 'Old Gold', *C. ornithopoda* 'Variegata'), mosquito grass (*Bouteloua gracilis*), bulbs and dwarf shrubs round off the picture.

Various other species and varieties of saxifrage can be grown in sunny areas of the rock garden. Even among the mossy saxifrages (Section Dactyloides) there are some which will stand sun, though most of them prefer half-shade and moisture. One species which will stand dryness is *Saxifraga trifurcata*, a vigorous plant originating from Spain. The hybrids sold under the name *S. muscoides* 'Findling' ('Foundling') will tolerate a good deal of sun, as will the small hybrid 'Elegantissima'. London Pride, *S. × urbium* (also sold as *S. umbrosa*), is tolerably sun-resistant, as is the miniature form 'Clarence Elliott'. The variegated form displays its contrasting colours to best advantage in a sunny spot, though if grown in such conditions it will require reasonably moist soil. The moister the soil, the greater the range of mossy saxifrages which can be planted in full sun. Atmospheric humidity is also an important factor; in moist valley bottoms some of the more vigorous 'Kabschia' saxifrages will stand full sun.

## Silver rosettes and bronze tones

The saxifrages of Section Euaizoonia owe their silvery grey tones to the deposits of lime on their leaves (and hence are known as encrusted saxifrages). There are only a few species which make green cushions or rosettes (e.g. *S. cotyledon, S. mutata*) and they are not relevant to our present purpose. The silver effect is enhanced by exposure to full sunlight.

For the larger rock garden there is a wide selection of vigorous plants large enough to produce an effect visible at a distance. Saxifrages which can be used to produce silver tones include *S. hostii, S. crustata, S. cochlearis, S. callosa* in its various forms, vigorous types of *S. paniculata* and certain hybrids including *S. × churchillii, S. × farreri* and *S. × gaudinii*. The silver effect can be reinforced by other silvery-grey plants, though they are somewhat space-demanding: *Antennaria dioica, Marrubium supinum, Veronica incana, Stachys olympica* 'Silver Carpet' and vigorous types or hybrids of the cobweb houseleek (*Sempervivum arachnoideum*). Contrasting reddish tones can be provided by any of the vigorous species of sedum, such as *S. spurium* 'Purple Carpet', 'Fuldaglut', 'Erdblut', 'Schorbuser Blut' and low-growing but vigorous species such as *S. album* 'Murale', *S. album* 'Coral Carpet', or *S. divergens* 'Atropurpureum'. Bugle (*Ajuga reptans* 'Purpurea') tolerates dryness and can be planted in such places.

The red-leaved sempervivum hybrids must not be forgotten. Many of them display enhanced coloration in May and June. Suitable cultivars include 'Alpha', 'Gamma', 'Rubin', 'Mahagoni', *S. tectorum* 'Atropurpureum', *S. tectorum* 'Triste', 'Granat', 'Purple Giant', 'El Toro', 'Patrician', etc. All these plants spread vigorously and will have to be cut back from time to time.

The most delicate nuances of silver and bronze are provided by miniature plants. Planted *en masse*, they will produce sheets of colour, but the individual plant and often the individual rosette are equally effective. They need to be sited at a higher level, on the southerly aspect of a sunken pathway in the rock garden, in a trough, or simply around a large rock. Among the smaller saxifrages the most notable forms are *Saxifraga valdensis, S. cochlearis* 'Minor', or 'Vreny', *S. paniculata* 'Minutifolia' and other compact forms of that species. A special favourite is *S. paniculata* 'Baldensis', though it is not greatly different from *S. paniculata* 'Minutifolia'. Somewhat larger, though remaining reasonably small, is *S. paniculata* var. *brevifolia* (also known as *S. aizoon* 'Minor'). Suitable partners can be found among the smaller species of sempervivum (*S. arachnoideum* 'Standsfieldii', 'Shootrolds Triumph'). Other dwarfs include *Antennaria dioica* 'Minima', *Achillea × kolbiana, A. umbellata* var. *argenta, A. × kellereri*, the low-growing *Alyssum alpestre, Helianthemum scardicum, Helichrysum milfordiae*, the New Zealand counterpart of the edelweiss (*Leucogenes leontopodium*), *Plantago nivalis, Raoulia hookeri* and *R. lutescens* from New Zealand, *Sedum spathulifolium* 'Cape Blanco' and *Veronica incana* 'Candidissima'. The last-named must be grown in poor soil if it is to remain small and compact.

There is a wide choice of miniature plants with red or bronze leaves. My favourite sedum is *S. spathulifolium* var. *purpureum*. Though somewhat more difficult, *S. rubrotinctum* sometimes displays fantastic coloration. Some of the vigorous species and varieties of sempervivum mentioned above may be tried. If they spread too rapidly there should be no difficulty in restraining them. However, the ideal partners for small silver saxifrages are the red species of *Jovibarba* which have recently become available. Closely resembling Sempervivum, these plants have well-formed rosettes which do not spread widely, forming instead compact heads or clumps of rosettes. The propagation of *Jovibarba* is considerably more difficult than that of Sempervivum, which produces daughter rosettes freely. Within the rosettes of *Jovibarba* individual crowns or whorls emerge and develop into independent rosettes. Varieties having particularly beautiful reddish or brown rosettes include *Jovibarba heuffelii* 'Bronze Ingot', 'Chocoleto', 'Purple Haze', 'Cameo', 'Giuseppi Spiny' and 'Tan'. Seed from these bronze-toned varieties of *Jovibarba* gives seedlings 80–90% of which retain the same coloration. Sown in January, it will produce vigorous single rosettes by the autumn, ready for planting out. Mention should be made of two other varieties of Sempervivum which make suitable partners for saxifrages: *Sempervivum* 'Zackenkrone', which is somewhat larger and has a colour combination of purple and yellowish-green (unfortunately it is somewhat tender); and the new variety 'Black Prince', deep reddish-black in colour.

The combination of bronze tones and silvery rosettes can be enhanced by planting a few blue or silver-grey grasses. A suitable plant for large areas is *Helictotrichon sempervirens*, syn. *Avena sempervirens*. In some places it may be too large and other blue-grey grasses such as *Festuca cinerea, F. ovina* or *Koeleria glauca* may be more suitable. A favourite for small intimate plantings is the dwarf grass *Festuca valesiaca* 'Glaucantha'. There are many other ornamental grasses with coloured or variegated leaves, but care must be taken in their selection and planting if a natural effect is to be achieved.

## Drystone walls

Drystone walling is a feature of the formal rock garden, but stretches of low drystone wall do not look out of place in natural rock gardens and can be made to resemble the strata of sedimentary rocks. Plants can be grown on the top of the wall and in the joints between the stones.

Drystone bank with saxifrages (cross-section)

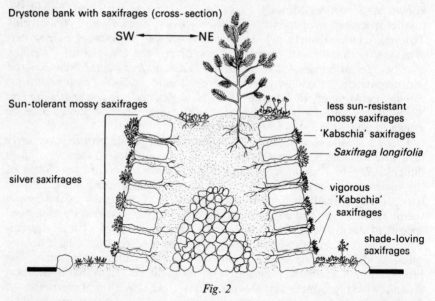

SW ◄——— ►NE

Sun-tolerant mossy saxifrages

less sun-resistant
mossy saxifrages

'Kabschia' saxifrages

*Saxifraga longifolia*

silver saxifrages

vigorous
'Kabschia'
saxifrages

shade-loving
saxifrages

*Fig. 2*

For walls in full sun the only suitable saxifrages are the species and hybrids of Section Euaizoonia. The forms with small rosettes listed on page 17 should be reserved for favoured sites. Of the forms with large or medium-sized rosettes all those which need moisture or partial shade such as *Saxifraga cotyledon, S. mutata, S. longifolia* and *S. florulenta* are ruled out. On the whole, medium-sized compact forms look better than those with large or sprawling rosettes.

Species suitable for spaces between stones include *S. paniculata* (syn. *S.*

*aizoon*) in all its forms except those with dwarf rosettes, *S. cochlearis*, which makes dense cushions, and *S. crustata*. Among the best hybrids for the purpose are *S. × burnatii*, *S. × churchillii* and *S. × farreri*. All of them will need watering in prolonged dry spells.

The top of the wall is the best place for the larger species and hybrids, most of which form somewhat looser cushions. Examples are *S. callosa* (syn. *S. lingulata*), *S. hostii* and their hybrids.

Ideally, a drystone wall should be planted while being built, so that the plants can be given plenty of soil and their special needs can be provided for. In practice, however, the gardener is often faced with an existing wall. In such an event it is important to use plants which have been grown in pots and which have a good soil ball thoroughly permeated by roots. Spring is the right season for planting; plants put in just before the winter are likely to be destroyed by frost before they have had time to establish themselves.

Using a narrow trowel, make a hole sloping backwards and slightly downwards, but do not remove all the earth between the stones. Mould the potball carefully to fit the space. Plants grown in deep narrow pots ('long toms') are best. Wedge the potball in place with a few small stones. Take care to choose suitable neighbours and avoid plants which grow into enormous mats. Appropriate partner plants, notably campanula and dianthus, were suggested in the previous section. Various species of sedum, such as *S. cauticolum*, *S. cyaneum* and *S. tatarinowii* look well on drystone walls.

## Freestanding walls

Two-sided drystone banks, as shown in Fig. 2, have an earth filling and a broad top. If possible, they should run east and west so as to have a sunny side and a shady side. Such a bank will enable the enthusiast to grow a comprehensive range of silver saxifrages.

The joints on the south side can be planted with the saxifrages listed in the foregoing section. Suitable plants for the north side are *S. cotyledon* and its cultivars 'Caterhamensis', 'Montavonensis', 'Pyramidalis', 'Somerset Seedling', etc., *S. mutata*, *S. longifolia* and their hybrids, *Saxifraga* 'Southside Seedling' and *S. calabrica* 'Tumbling Waters'.

The choice of stone may present difficulties since *S. mutata*, *S. cotyledon* and their hybrids are not limelovers and prefer an acid soil. By suitable preparation of the soil surrounding the rootball they can be planted even in limestone walls. It is of course simpler to use sandstone and to add lime (Nitrochalk) or limestone chippings to meet the needs of silver saxifrages. The top of the bank is reserved for less compact forms with large rosettes (*S. callosa*, *S. hostii*), but any of the dwarf encrusted saxifrages can be grown there.

Other plants suitable for the top of the bank are the bronze-leaved sempervivums listed on page 17. Along the foot of the north face the soil will be moister and will make a good home for plants from Section Robertsoniana. They are easily grown and enjoy shade.

## Miniature rock gardens or rock beds

There are many alpines which are displayed to their best advantage against the horizontal and vertical surfaces of a well-planned rock garden, but this option is not open to every gardener. The drystone bank is a possible alternative, but not one which appeals to everyone. The compromise solution is the miniature rock garden or rock bed.

Having chosen the site, the first step is to lay down a core of drainage material (gravel, hardcore, etc.). A layer of good garden soil should be piled on top of it. The bed should not be too high; 0.5 m is quite enough. Some carefully chosen rocks should be laid on the surface – a few good-sized stones look better than a lot of little ones. Saxifrages which prefer half-shade can be planted behind the bigger rocks and in small depressions. Rock beds can be of any size, but large ones will need stepping stones to allow the gardener to get at the plants.

Miniature rock garden

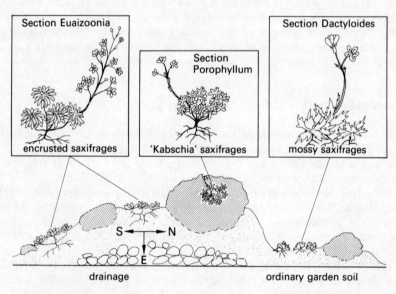

*Fig. 3*

As rock beds are usually placed in sunny positions, silver saxifrages flourish on them. Representatives of Section Robertsoniana (such as London Pride or its 'Primuloides' cultivars) can be planted in shaded depressions. Mossy saxifrages, if not too invasive, are also appropriate, as is the double form of *Saxifraga granulata* ('Fair Maids of France'). Rock beds should have a few dwarf shrubs, and some rocks with interesting crystals can enhance the overall effect.

# Terraces

Terraces are usually in sunny positions, and the choice is therefore restricted to the silver saxifrages of Section Euaizoonia. There is, nevertheless, quite a range of possibilities. The edge of the paved area can merge into a rock bed, but the paving stones must harmonize with the rock used in it, though they need not be identical. It is best not to surround the whole of the paved area with beds. In some parts the terrace should pass directly into lawn.

Another way is to build a drystone wall between terrace and lawn. Provided it is not too high – not more than 0.75 m (30 ins) – the effect can be very pleasing.

Silver saxifrages – more than most herbaceous perennials – give pleasure the whole year round. At winter's end, when so many plants are still below ground and when so many evergreens look bedraggled, the mats of saxifrage rosettes are still impeccably neat and tidy. A few weeks later, a closer look will show how the innermost leaves in each rosette are beginning to expand and the flower scape is developing. It is fascinating to follow their development day by day. If the saxifrages are scattered throughout the garden, the effect is much less impressive. Then comes the full spendour of their flowering. The panicles are surprisingly varied – tall and slender, stiffly erect or elegantly drooping, small and compact, often verging on umbels or in other cases strictly pyramidal. Some branch quite low down, while others form close-set heads of flowers. Their white blossoms vary in size and number, and many have spots at the base of the petals. Sulphur-yellow and pale-pink flowers add a touch of variety.

After flowering the scape should be removed by pulling it out with its rosette, holding down the neighbouring rosettes with the other hand outspread. There are so many rosettes that a few will not be missed. New rosettes now grow outwards from the margins and the cushion becomes larger and denser. The silver effect reaches its zenith in high summer, since this is the time when the chalk glands secrete the largest amounts of lime to protect the leaves against loss by evaporation. Even in autumn, when so many other plants look scruffy, silver saxifrages retain their charm. After the first cold night the rosettes sparkle with hoarfrost.

Then comes winter, bringing with it hard frosts which injure so many plants unless protected by a blanket of snow. The saxifrages do not turn a hair; if anything, their beauty is enhanced. The green and silver rosettes take on red and bronze hues, some turning carmine and a few almost vermilion.

Designers of labour-saving gardens tend to believe that perennials are too much bother. This does not apply to silver saxifrages; there are no plants that need less maintenance.

In large terraces a few spaces can be left unpaved for planting with silver saxifrages. Don't be content with two or three varieties: if the space is big enough plant six or seven different kinds. Don't be mean with them. Plant 5–10 of each kind, depending on the space available. Any gaps can be filled in with stones at first. The red sempervivums are useful partners. Brilliant colours look well in such positions. Empty spaces can be filled with *Verbena peruviana*; its scarlet umbels make a pleasing contrast. If the spaces between the paving stones are big enough, try groups of *Lobelia fulgens* 'Queen Victoria'. The reddish stems and leaves produce a fine effect, heightened by the scarlet flowers. The contrasting horizontals and verticals give added interest. These combinations of low-growing and taller plants can be developed still further, but always with restraint, as it is the silver saxifrages that must set the tone. *V. peruviana* and *L. fulgens* 'Queen Victoria' will survive the winter in mild areas, but elsewhere must be renewed from cuttings taken from stock plants overwintered in a cellar.

Terraces are often surrounded by low walls on which you can put trays and small troughs. These make good sites for small saxifrages of Section Euaizoonia. Sometimes it is possible to build up both sides of the wall leaving a space one brick deep between them. Saxifrages and sempervivums can be planted here, and even a few hardy cacti.

If the terrace is in half-shade saxifrages of Sections Dactyloides and Robertsoniana can be grown, or portable miniature gardens can be used to accommodate 'Kabschia' and 'Engleria' saxifrages.

## All about tufa, waterworn limestone, troughs and pans

In a book about saxifrages the materials and containers for planting are of special interest. Such 'accessories' are not to be found in every garden centre. In recent years the growing interest in alpine plants has caused a shortage of various natural materials, and substitutes have to be found.

### Tufa

There is no other genus for which tufa is so valuable as it is for the genus *Saxifraga*, and in particular for the 'Kabschia' saxifrages. Some amateurs confuse tufa with waterworn limestone (page 23). Tufa consists of calcium carbonate, as do shell, limestone, waterworn limestone, chalk cliffs, marble and other forms of limestone rock. Tufa is mostly of recent date and is formed from plant remains. Even today, it is still possible to find recently formed lime tufa. Grasses, twigs and miscellaneous plant remains collect in certain places in streams where the water contains large amounts of lime. This lime is deposited on their surfaces in the form of calcium carbonate. The layer of lime becomes thicker and thicker, and in time the organic plant material decomposes leaving highly porous limestone. Tufa is a rock permeated by innumerable pores and may be compared with a petrified sponge.

Tufa offers various advantages. Because it is so light, large pieces can be easily moved. Its surface is soft, and if suitable holes for planting are not already present, they can be easily made with hammer and chisel or with a drill. Because of its absorbent structure the rock stores water while allowing any excess to drain rapidly away. Water evaporates in large quantities from the porous surface, so that there is always a high level of atmospheric humidity round the plants. During dry periods the rock stores moisture from the nightly dews.

*Saxifraga*×irvingii 'His Majesty'

waterworn limestone and tufa make ideal homes for 'Kabschia' saxifrages

*Fig. 4*

Two disadvantages must be mentioned. Tufa is readily colonized by liverworts, and a careful watch should be kept for them. Secondly, good tufa is scarce and correspondingly dear. At one time tufa was used to build 'grottoes' in villa gardens. Happy the gardener who finds himself on the spot when such a building is being pulled down.

Volcanic tufa is not so well known but is equally suitable. It is available in lumps and in granular form. The latter can be used for adding to composts and as a surface dressing in troughs, pans and other containers.

### Waterworn limestone

Unlike tufa, waterworn limestone forms solid compact masses of rock. Through centuries of exposure to the weather the surface is irregularly modelled, with depressions and small holes which may even go right through the rock.

Care must be taken to choose pieces with plenty of natural hollows, as it is difficult to reproduce them convincingly with chisel or drill. However, by setting irregular stones side by side it is not difficult to make plenty of hollows for planting.

### Hollow bricks

Dwellers in the lowlands need not despair. Saxifrages can be planted in joints or crevices in other kinds of rock. Broken pieces of hollow brick are ideal. A load of such material can be dumped on a sunny slope and its surface covered with a mixture of sieved hollow brick rubble and earth. The resulting mass is full of channels which hold moisture while at the same time providing good drainage and a supply of air to the roots.

### Natural stone troughs

Owing to the great demand, these are now seldom to be found, even in the remotest villages, and the prices demanded in the trade are enormous.

Substitutes are available, but they lack the charm of a genuine old trough of natural stone.

### Concrete troughs

Most of us have no alternative but to resort to artificial stone. Gardeners can build their own troughs of concrete. To speed up the formation of a satisfactory patina, the concrete can be painted with a weak mixture of loam and cow dung.

Reproductions of sandstone troughs, made of concrete with a suitable surface covering, are now available in Germany (Helmut Gimmler KG). After they have been in use for a short time they are indistinguishable from natural stone troughs. The drawback, as with all troughs, is their weight.

### Asbestos cement

Troughs and pans of this material are light, inexpensive and available in a wide range of shapes and sizes. They can be recommended for miniature gardens planted with 'Kabschia' saxifrages. It is important to provide adequate drainage.

### Table gardens

A table garden is in effect a trough garden covering a larger area. The base is a large concrete paving slab supported on brick columns. A wall 10–20 cm high is built round the edges with breeze blocks or suitable material and the outer surface painted with cement paint so as to conceal the edge of the paving stone. To provide insulation against frost, the floor and inner walls should be lined with sheets of expanded polystyrene 2 cm thick.

### Hypertufa

Inventive gardeners have devised effective substitutes for tufa from combinations of peat, sand and cement. 'Rocks' for planting can be made from the following mixture: two buckets of finely sieved peat, one bucket of river sand or washed sharp sand and one bucket of cement. Mix the dry ingredients thoroughly and then add water, but not too much. This mix can be modelled with hands (protected with rubber gloves) into the shapes of waterworn limestone. Niches and cavities for planting can be made with a spoon. Even after the cement has set the material can be worked like tufa.

When required in large numbers such 'rocks' can be mass-produced. An original is made from plaster and the necessary holes are bored in it. The plaster model is coated with varnish or wax. A layer of silicone rubber is now applied over the entire surface including the planting holes. After a short time the silicone rubber hardens and can be stripped off. This elastic mould can then be filled with the hypertufa mixture as often as desired, but the proportion of water must be greater, so that the material is fluid. When the hypertufa has hardened the elastic mould is stripped off.

Saxifrages do well on hypertufa, as most of them like an alkaline medium.

Nevertheless, freshly made stones should be left out of doors for some time before planting to allow the humic acids in the peat to be neutralized and surplus alkali to be washed away from the surface. Furthermore, the 'rock' will look better when it has been colonized by moss.

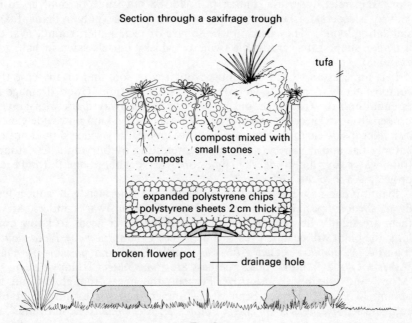

Section through a saxifrage trough

tufa

compost mixed with small stones

compost

expanded polystyrene chips
polystyrene sheets 2 cm thick

broken flower pot

drainage hole

*Fig. 5*

Hypertufa can also be used to make troughs, but for this purpose a much stronger mixture is needed, e.g. two buckets of finely sieved peat, three buckets of river sand or washed sharp sand and three buckets of cement. There is no great difficulty in making a mould from planks, but it is important to keep the weight of the trough within reasonable limits. Such troughs can be made with or without a bottom. For the first kind the bottom is made first by casting it in an oblong mould made of battens resting on a level surface covered with newspaper or plastic film. Drainage holes are 'preprogrammed' with corks. The side walls are then constructed in turn. If you have screw clamps at least 0.5 m long you can simply clamp the boards for the ends between those for the sides. If you want a 'rustic' appearance you can nail hammered sheet metal on to the inner surface of the outer mould. The inner mould will then have to be somewhat smaller, so as to maintain adequate wall thickness. Just enough water should be added to the mixture to allow it to flow. Colouring with cement pigments (red iron oxide, etc.) is not a good idea; the resulting troughs look like coloured paving stones, the colours alter and the whole thing looks 'kitsch'. The corners at least should be reinforced with thin rods or thick wire and it is best to reinforce the whole trough.

## Troughs in sunshine

The material from which the trough is made is much less important than the choice and arrangement of the plants. Troughs may be made of natural stone, concrete, hypertufa, timber (a hollowed out trunk or built up from railway sleepers), asbestos cement or even plastic (polyurethane foam simulating wood). They need not be square or rectangular; round, oval or irregular shapes are permissible (wine or whisky barrels sawn in half, for example).

It is unnecessary to fill the whole trough with soil, and in any case the compost tends to pack down with the passage of time. Good drainage is essential and the trough should be filled to the halfway mark with gravel, broken stone or pieces of expanded polystyrene of the kind now widely used as a filler inside cartons. Next comes the compost. Its surface should not be entirely flat and it can be made more interesting by burying a few stones (tufa, waterworn limestone, shell limestone), leaving about one-third of each projecting above the surface.

Planting can now be started. Even saxifrage enthusiasts will want a few dwarf shrubs. Special care is needed in the choice of dwarf conifers. All of them are small when young, but the trough gardener needs to know how large the plant will be in ten years' time. Among the spruces are *Picea glauca* 'Laurin', *P. pumila* 'Glauca', *P. abies* 'Little Gem' and possibly *P. abies* 'Alberta Globe'. Among pines the best are *Pinus mugo* 'Humpy', *P. mugo* 'Mops' and possibly *P. silvestris* 'Perkeo'; the finest, though difficult to obtain, is *P. leucodermis* 'Schmidtii'. Junipers call for caution. Suitable cultivars are *Juniperus communis* 'Compressa', *J. communis* 'Echiniformis', *J. procumbens* 'Nana' and with certain reservations *J. squamata* 'Blue Star', though the last is not as slow-growing as was originally thought; however, it tolerates cutting back and can be trained into a natural bonsai by careful pruning of the lower branches. The false cypruses offer a wide choice but many of them, even the dwarfs, soon outgrow the available space. *Chamae-cyparis obtusa* 'Rigida', *C. pisifera* 'Plumosa Compressa', *C. lawsoniana* 'Gnome', *C. pisifera* 'Nana', *C. lawsoniana* 'Ellwoodii Pygmy' form small bright green pyramids, and *C. obtusa* 'Nana Gracilis' might be added to the list, as it grows slowly, though ultimately reaching greater dimensions. Among cedars there is the very slow-growing *Cedrus libani* 'Sargenti', which will live for many years before becoming too large. Also worth mentioning are the juvenile form of *Thuiopsis dolobrata* 'Nana', *Podocarpus nivalis* from New Zealand and *Cryptomeria japonica* 'Vilmoriniana'. Others could no doubt be found, but these I have grown myself for many years.

Among broad-leaved shrubs there are a few true dwarfs: *Ilex crenata* 'Mariesii', *Daphne cneorum* 'Pygmaea', *Cotoneaster adpressus* 'Little Gem', *Cotoneaster* 'Schneideri', *Euonymus fortunei* 'Minimus', *Genista dalmatica*.

Let us now turn to the central theme, the saxifrages. Only one special group of silver saxifrages will thrive in full sun, but they are extremely decorative. The upper limit of size is set by *Saxifraga paniculata*, but it might be permissible to plant a large rosette saxifrage occasionally. If it grows too vigorously a few rosettes can be easily removed. Even the monocarpic *Saxifraga longifolia* is not out of place. Everything depends on the size of the trough. Nevertheless, the trough in sunshine is the ideal place for silver saxifrages with small rosettes such as *Saxifraga valdensis, S. cochlearis* 'Minor', *S. paniculata* var. *sturmiana, S. paniculata* 'Minutifolia', *S. paniculata* ssp. *brevifolia, Saxifraga* 'Vreny', and others, perhaps somewhat larger, such as the varieties and forms of *S. paniculata.* The dwarf hybrid of *Saxifraga longifolia* known as 'Type Kober' is also worthy of a place.

Though saxifrages should predominate, there will be room for a few other treasures. There is no space here to enumerate the numerous species of *Jovibarba, Sempervivum* and *Sedum.* However, it may be worth drawing attention to a dwarf sedum which has recently appeared: *Sedum acre* 'Cristata'. Dwarf plants of other kinds may be chosen: *Dryas octopetala* 'Nana', *Erodium reichardii, Arenaria tetraquetra, Helichrysum milfordiae, Ajuga crispa, Leucogenes leontopodium, Armeria cespitosa* 'Bevan's Variety', *Dianthus freynii, D. simulans, D. pavonius, D. alpinus, Scleranthus uniflorus, Dodecatheon* 'Red Wings', *Rosularia spathulata, Sempervivella sedoides, Silene acaulis* 'Plena', *Campanula sartori, Globularia repens* 'Pygmaea', *Iris attica, I. melitta* 'Rubromarginata', *I. arenaria, Saponaria pulvinaris, Hutchinsia alpina* ssp. *auerswaldii, Draba* × *suendermannii, Penstemon pygmaeus,* and dwarf species of *Festuca.*

A few dwarf bulbs will add interest, but as bulbs are susceptible to violent temperature changes it is important that the interior of the trough should be lined with sheets of expanded polystyrene not less than 2 cm thick. There is a wide range of low-growing fritillaries, e.g. *Fritillaria pontica, F. gracilis, F. elwesii, F. pudica,* but they are not all easy to obtain. Also suitable are the dwarf species of *Allium* and the miniature narcissi and tulips.

There is no lack of suitable plants – indeed, the main danger is overcrowding. For a medium-sized trough 1.5 m long, two or three dwarf shrubs are quite enough, and smaller troughs have room for one only. The main emphasis should be placed on *Saxifraga* and *Sempervivum.* They give pleasure all the year round, and look neat and tidy even when covered with hoarfrost. Other species should not make up more than one-third of the planting.

## Plantings in tufa and waterworn limestone rock in sunny positions

The advantages of tufa have already been underlined: there is no genus better suited for planting in this porous rock than saxifrages. For sunny situations the silver saxifrages (Section Euaizoonia) are ideal. Nearly 50 kinds are available. In half-shade the 'Kabschia' saxifrages are at home. Experts use species from both sections, since the silver saxifrages will do well in half-shade, while many 'Kabschia' and 'Engleria' saxifrages, given adequate humidity, will tolerate more sun.

The larger the pieces of tufa, the more elaborate the planting scheme can be. However, tufa in any form is scarce and large pieces are even scarcer. A large rock can be built up from several small ones. The impression of a large rock can often be created by packing smaller pieces close together, especially when the joints have been hidden by plants. There is another way of making large rocks. Choose a flat patch of ground and dig a hole to serve as a mould; it can be of any size or shape. Line the hole with tufa fragments packed closely together. Using a rather wet mix, place dabs of cement to make bridges between the stones, strengthening them with wire if necessary. When the cement has set lift this large hollow rock out of the hole and put it in its permanent place. If it is not too large, fill the cavity with earth and cover it with a large sheet or board. Then turn the whole thing right-way-up and

**Construction of a large composite rock from small pieces of tufa or waterworn limestone**

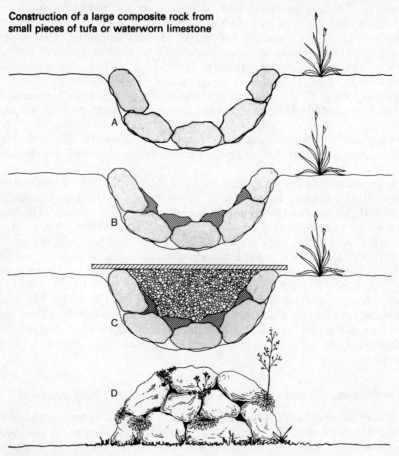

A. Dig a hole having the size and shape of the rock desired and line it with pieces of stone
B. Fix the stones together with dabs of cement
C. When the cement has set, fill the cavity with earth and cover it with a board
D. Turn the rock over, move it to its intended place and carefully pull out the board. The rock is now ready for planting

*Fig. 6*

carefully pull the board out. The earth filling can also be introduced from above through the spaces between the stones, but this is troublesome and time-consuming. If the job is properly done, the cement bridges in the interior of the composite tufa rock will not be visible from outside. The joints between the small stones provide plenty of places for planting. Similar constructions can be made from small pieces of waterworn limestone, but the bonding between stone and cement is less secure as limestone has a smoother surface than tufa.

Large tufa rocks often lack sufficient planting holes. This can be overcome by drilling holes as required. Modern DIY drills are quite powerful and can be used if they have a chuck which will take large drills. A drill of 2.5 cm is usually enough. The holes should not be too shallow. It is very important that the stone be firmly held otherwise the drill may pull it out of place and whirl it round. For this reason, do not press too hard. The tufa dust which collects in the drill holes is then washed out with a hose. At the bottom of the hole put some gravel, broken pot or similar material, so that the plant will not get 'wet feet' during heavy rain. Tufa will absorb any amount of moisture, but it needs a little time. (Everything said here about natural tufa rock applies equally to artificial rocks made of hypertufa.)

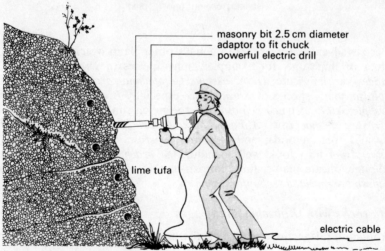

Drilling holes in lime tufa for planting 'Kabschia' saxifrages

*Fig. 7*

The silver saxifrages can now be planted. The choice is not restricted to the smallest forms; in these confined planting holes larger varieties will remain tolerably compact. If any plant displays too much vigour, surplus rosettes can easily be removed. For autumn planting, plants with a good pot ball should be chosen, provided it is not too large. In spring, however, plants with bare roots can be planted safely. The compost is packed round the roots with a small stick and the mouth of the hole wedged with a few small stones, so that the plant will not be washed out by heavy rain.

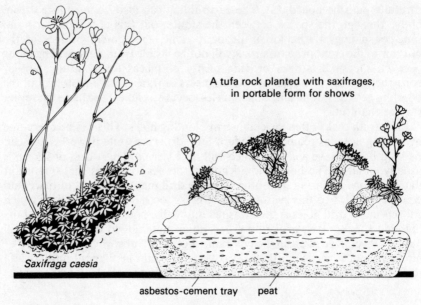

A tufa rock planted with saxifrages,
in portable form for shows

Saxifraga caesia

asbestos-cement tray      peat

Fig. 8

Besides silver saxifrages there are many other plants which flourish in holes in tufa or limestone, for example: many species of *Draba*, especially *D. bryoides* var. *imbricata*, *D. mollissima*; *Campulana zoysii*, *C. morettiana*, *C. cespitosa*; many species of *Edraianthus*, especially *E. pumilio*, *E. tenuifolius*; *Physoplexis (Phyteuma) comosa* (not too much sun); *Petrocallis pyrenaica*; *Androsace chamaejasme*, *A. hausmannii*, *A. hirtella*, *A. mathildae*, *A. pubescens* and their hybrids; and *Asperula suberosa*. Many small species of *Sempervivum* also look well including *S. arachnoideum* and its hybrids (although silicate plants, they flourish in tufa), *S. minus*, and *S. ciliosum*; *Jovibarba arenaria*, *J. sobolifera*, etc.

### Tufa rocks with 'Kabschia' saxifrages

Throughout this section the term 'Kabschia' includes the 'Engleria' saxifrages.

There are many saxifrages with beautiful flowers but the 'Kabschia' saxifrages excel. One asset is their earliness. In mild winters and favourable situations they may begin to flower at the end of January. The main flowering period is March to April, but there are some late flowerers which show blossom well into May. A tufa rock thickly planted with 'Kabschia' saxifrages can be a masterpiece! In the years before the war one of the best known enthusiasts for this form of gardening was Dr Rosenstingl of Gmunden in Austria. He built miniature gardens of tufa rocks packed together in wooden boxes, all the gaps between the rocks being planted with alpines, chiefly 'Kabschia' saxifrages.

Dr Rosenstingl came from Enns in upper Austria and also from this area came Arnold Chilarz, who carried on the tradition after 1945. Arnold Chilarz, who now lives in Vienna, built an alpine garden from fragments of shelly limestone, which is to be found on the southern outskirts of Vienna. He built his first miniature gardens in wooden frames but later turned to asbestos-cement seed trays measuring 22 × 28 cm or 25 × 50 cm. He used lime tufa and planted them mainly with small saxifrages and truly dwarf conifers. The Austrian Horticultural Society is a focal point for gardeners in this region and the 'Alpengarten Belvedere', some 150 years old, is a model. It is situated in the southern part of Vienna and built of shelly limestone, largely derived from the foundations of old houses which have been demolished. Arnold Chilarz has an enormous knowledge of saxifrages and in his lectures he shares it with a wider audience.

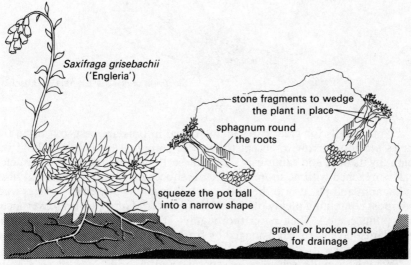

details of planting in tufa rocks

*Fig. 9*

The construction and planting of such miniature gardens has been dealt with in the previous section. The particular consideration here is their siting. The special needs of 'Kabschia' saxifrages must always be remembered; they must never be exposed to full sun and they should preferably be given an easterly aspect or a half-shaded but well-lit place. They need moderate soil moisture with good drainage and high atmospheric humidity. In half-shade, given ample light, the entire rock can be planted with 'Kabschia' saxifrages, though the south-facing side will require some of the more robust species and hybrids. Given high atmospheric humidity, all varieties will tolerate more sun. In my garden, 'Kabschia' saxifrages, even those in tufa, flourish in a south-facing site beneath a pergola made of wooden beams.

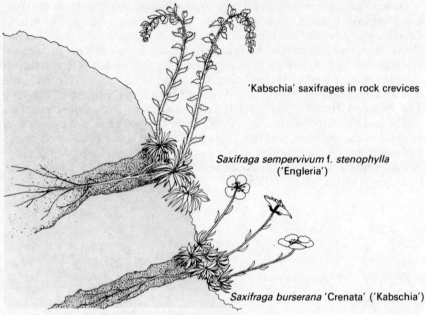

'Kabschia' saxifrages in rock crevices

*Saxifraga sempervivum* f. *stenophylla*
('Engleria')

*Saxifraga burserana* 'Crenata' ('Kabschia')

Fig. 10

Planting calls for great care. Plants raised in pots are best, but often the holes are too narrow to accept the ball of compost. In this event hold the plant by its neck and cautiously shake the earth off until the desired diameter can be reached with no more than gentle squeezing. Wrap the ball in a little sphagnum and put it into the hole, carefully packing any empty spaces with compost containing plenty of air-retaining material (crushed brick, vermiculite, pumice, etc.). Then water thoroughly. The following spring, check that the plants have not been damaged by frost, because if so they will not stand more than a few days' dryness.

There is a wide selection of species and hybrids (see page 87). In addition, there are many plants other than saxifrages which grow in shady or sunless crevices, for example all the forms and hybrids of *Primula auricula*. The various species of *Haberlea* and *Ramonda* are very fine, but in time they form fairly large rosettes: *Haberlea rhodopensis, H. rhodopensis* 'Virginalis', *H. ferdinandi-coburgii, Ramonda nathaliae, R. myconi* (syn. *R. pyrenaica*) and its white and pink colour forms. *Chiastophyllum oppositifolium* also looks well and sometimes produces self-sown seedlings on tufa. If the tufa is lime-free, lewisias will make attractive partner plants.

Properly planted tufa rocks require little care. 'Kabschia' saxifrages are extremely hardy, and even asbestos-cement trays with plantings in tufa require little or no winter protection when well established. When newly planted, however, they need a little protection so that the plants are not lifted out of their holes by frost. The compost in the holes and the rocks themselves must never dry out entirely, and in midsummer watering will be needed every two days in the absence of rain. It is a mistake to think that these dwarfs should never be fed; after flowering they should be watered with a weak solution of a complete fertilizer.

## Rock ledges in shade

The sun-loving section Euaizoonia is also very valuable for half-shaded and sunless places in the rock garden. Good drainage must be ensured, as standing water combined with heavy shade encourages fungus diseases. There are some species which prefer positions where they get little or no sun, in particular *Saxifraga cotyledon* and its hybrids (e.g. 'Southside Seedling', 'Montafonensis'). All three monocarpic species of this section have similar requirements (*Saxifraga longifolia, S. mutata, S. florulenta*). *S. longifolia* likes lime, while *S. cotyledon* and *S. mutata* will tolerate small amounts. *S. florulenta* is unfortunately almost unavailable.

*S. cotyledon* and its hybrids have tall pyramidal inflorescences, as does *S. longifolia*, not for nothing known as the 'king of saxifrages'. They produce their finest effects in a vertical planting. Crevices and narrow rock ledges in shade are ideal for this purpose. In such positions the rosettes are seen to best advantage. They look well all the year round and in the spring their flowering spikes shoot up obliquely like rockets. Plants in such positions require little or no care. However, it is important to use pot-grown plants with well developed root balls. These monocarpic species form a single large rosette, and several years will pass before they flower. After flowering the whole plant dies, but the far-sighted gardener will have raised new ones to replace it.

## Troughs and table gardens in full or half-shade

Troughs need not always be in full sun. A wide range of saxifrages can be grown in full or half-shade and there are indeed many of the sun-loving species of Section Euaizoonia which will flourish in less sunny spots. All of them like moisture but not standing water.

The daintiest saxifrages – the 'Kabschias' – are of course favourites for troughs. They look best when the surface is given some relief by embedding a few rocks in the compost. There is no need to drill holes; the saxifrages can be planted in the gaps between the rocks. The compost for 'Kabschia' saxifrages must be freely permeable and yet water-retentive. Though such troughs are exposed to repeated freezing and thawing, 'Kabschia' and 'Engleria' saxifrages seldom come to harm.

Vigorous species and hybrids should be placed at the edges of the trough so as not to crowd out smaller plants forming cushions perhaps only 5 cm across. Thought must be given to flower colour and flowering time. Avoid having too many yellow flowers close together and try to make the flowering season as long as possible.

Besides 'Kabschia' saxifrages there are plenty of species from other sections which are not too vigorous and which remain small. Other dwarf alpines can be used, such as miniature aquilegias (*A. akitensis* 'Kurilensis', *A. discolor, A. einseleana*), dwarf thrift (*Armeria cespitosa* 'Bevan's Variety'),

*Helichrysum milfordiae*, various small gentians, *Globularia repens* 'Pygmaea', and *Hutchinsia alpina*; edelweiss flourishes better in such places than in full sun. Lewisias fit in very well, and the low-growing *Mentha requienii* is also suitable, though it does not always survive hard winters. Other species include Grass of Parnassus (*Parnassia palustris*), dwarf primulas of Section Auricula, the alpine crowfoot (*Ranunculus alpestris*) and its varieties, *Scleranthus uniflorus, Solidago minutissima* and *Thalictrum kiusianum*. Space should be found for a few small ferns such as *Adiantum pedatum* 'Imbricatum', *Asplenium trichomanes, A. viride, Athyrium filix-femina* 'Bornholmensis'. Among suitable grasses *Carex baldensis* is a possibility, or perhaps better *Carex firma* from the Alps and its variety 'Variegata'.

Saxifrages from other sections, provided they remain small, do well in troughs in partial shade. Low-growing mossy saxifrages from Section Dactyloides flourish in such conditions, though they are not yet so commonly grown in Germany as they are in Great Britain. They include the Arendsii hybrids 'Luschtinez' and 'Rosenzwerg' and others such as 'Elegantissima', 'Darlington Double', 'Elf', 'Gnome', 'Mrs Pipe', 'Pearly King', 'Peter Pan', 'Pixie' and 'White Pixie'. There are many members of Section Robertsoniana which can be planted here, especially those with small rosettes. The low-growing mossy saxifrages and the small rosette saxifrages from Section Robertsoniana are more vigorous than the 'Kabschias', a point which should be remembered when planting them side by side.

A table garden with saxifrages

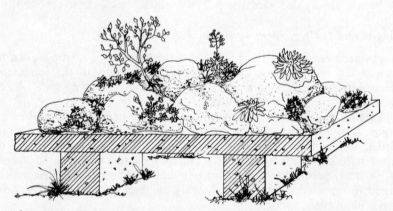

tufa or waterworn limestone rocks are cemented to the concrete slab with lime mortar and all the spaces between them are filled with compost

*Fig. 11*

Table gardens for 'Kabschia' saxifrages can be planted in much the same way as troughs. The first step is to make one or more pillars of reinforced concrete. The slab is then cast from the same material. The framework or shuttering must be solidly constructed. Suitable slabs can often be found in precast concrete factories. It is even possible to buy ready-made slabs intended for pingpong tables; these of course require several supports. Once the slab is in position, pieces of tufa or waterworn limestone can be cemented to it in such a way as to leave plenty of spaces which can subsequently be filled with compost. Lime–sand–cement mortar should be used, but the work should be done in such a way that it is hidden. Holes can be bored in the tufa as already described. More elaborate structures often need to be filled with compost during their construction and in such cases a drainage layer should be provided. Table gardens without a raised border seldom have drainage holes. As the slab will never be perfectly level, however carefully it has been laid in place, the run-off from heavy rainstorms will form a small drainage stream on one side. The gardener can make a virtue of necessity and construct a small drainage channel concealed with gravel and planted with a few moisture-loving perennials.

## Saxifrages in sunken paths

When a house has been built on a slope the subsoil from the foundations is usually banked up on the lower side and it is an easy matter to cut paths through this embankment, raising their sides with the soil dug out. Piled up on both sides, the soil from a cutting only 50 cm deep will be enough to make a planting area 80–90 cm in extent. The soil must of course be consolidated with rocks, not necessarily waterworn limestone or tufa; indeed almost any rock will serve. Stratified rock is easier to handle, but sandstone or even granite will do.

If a deeper path is feasible, the sides can be made more interesting. Instead of letting them slope uniformly, the banks on either side can be broken by one or two horizontal ledges. The path is floored with irregular paving stones laid in sand. They can be interplanted with saxifrages of Section Robertsoniana, especially the easy ones such as *Saxifraga × urbium* and *S. × geum*. A sunken path offers everything from dry sunny spots to moist shady areas. Small saxifrages, of whatever species, can be easily seen thanks to their elevated position. Defence against pests (blackbirds) can be concentrated on a relatively small area.

The path should not begin or end abruptly, but should merge gently and naturally into its surroundings. Dwarf shrubs should be planted generously, the selection available being wider than that suggested for troughs. Sunny spots provide homes for silver saxifrages, possibly combined with Sempervivums. East-facing slopes will accommodate 'Kabschia' saxifrages, forms of *Saxifraga cotyledon* and monocarpic single-rosette species. Mossy saxifrages will grow on the moist shady ledges, and saxifrages of Sections Diptera and Robertsoniana in the deepest shade.

Species from the sections of lesser horticultural interest can find a home here, and their special needs can be more easily satisfied. When choosing other alpines to go with the saxifrages, take care to avoid unduly vigorous plants.

A few suitable plants for the sunny areas of the sunken path: *Acantholimon albanicum, A. androsaceum, A. glumaceum, A. oliveri; Achillea umbellata* var.

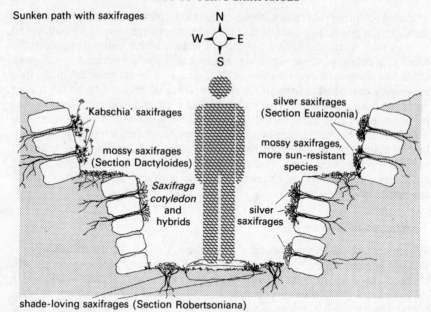

*Fig. 12*

*argentea*; *Aethionema armenum* 'Warley Rose'; *Ptilotrichium spinosum*; *Androsace*, many species; *Astragalus angustifolius*; *Campanula cochlearifolia* 'Warleyense', *C. fenestrellata, C. garganica* var. *hirsuta, C. × pulloides* 'G. F. Wilson', *C. tommasiniana, C. × wockei*; *Dianthus alpinus, D. arenarius, D. microlepis* var. *musalaea, D. subacaulis*; *Draba*, many species; *Edraianthus*; *Erysimum kotschyanum*; *Geranium dalmaticum, G. sanguineum* 'Lancastriense'; *Gypsophila aretioides, G. repens*; *Helianthemum oleandicum* ssp. *alpestre, H. scardicum*; *Iberis pygmaea, I. saxatilis*; *Leontopodium alpinum* ssp. *nivale* and other selected forms; *Lithodora diffusa* 'Heavenly Blue'; *Penstemon cardwellii, P. pinifolius, P. rupicola*; cushion phloxes especially the small flowered forms such as 'Nivea', 'Ronsdorfer'; *Saponaria × olivana, S. × boissieri*; *Sedum cauticolum, S. pluricaule* 'Rose Carpet', *S. tatarinovii*; *Thymus serpyllum* 'Pygmaeus'; *Trachelium jacquinii* ssp. *rumelianum* and many others including sempervivums.

A few suggestions for less sunny places: *Chiastophyllum oppositifolium*; *Haberlea*; *Hosta ventricosa* 'Minor'; *Lewisia*; primulas of Section Auricula; *Ramonda myconi, R. nathaliae, R. serbica*.


## Automatic humidification

Nearly all species of saxifrage love high atmospheric humidity, as indeed do all alpine plants, being accustomed to such conditions in nature. Some will of course tolerate the much lower humidity of most gardens (e.g. the encrusted saxifrages of Section Euaizoonia). But there are others which must have a high degree of atmospheric humidity for optimal development, for example the mossy saxifrages (Section Dactyloides) and the 'Kabschia' saxifrages. Many plants which grow at high altitudes fully exposed to sun prefer half-shade or full shade in the garden. Most saxifrages do not like too much moisture at their roots. For this reason gentle sprinkling in the mornings and evenings is enough; if the area is not too large this can be done with a watering-can though larger areas will need a hose with a spray nozzle. There are also inexpensive sprinkler heads for insertion into the ground.

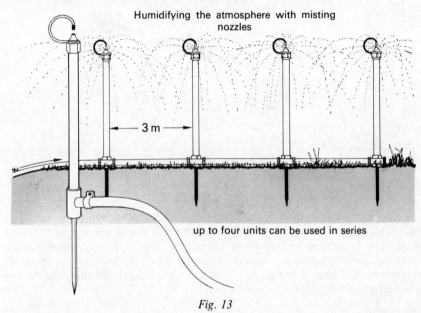

*Fig. 13*

The entire sprinkler system can of course be constructed as a permanent fixture. Hoses have their disadvantages, and it is all too easy to damage valuable plants when dragging the hose to and fro. There is a wide choice of automatic sprinkler systems commercially available. Rigid PVC tubing or high-pressure hose (nylon-reinforced) can be laid in the ground out of sight and spray nozzles can be installed at intervals close enough to give complete coverage. The installation is operated simply by turning on the water. It is important to provide a drain cock at the lowest point so that the system can be emptied before the onset of frosty weather.

A typical sprinkler head, 30 cm high, is made of brass tubing and has a connector for half-inch hose. The diameter of the area typically covered by the sprinkler is about 4.2 m. Up to four such sprinkler heads can be connected in series. The interval from one to the next should then be 3 m. The hose can of course be buried, and the sprinkler head will then project only some 25 cm above the ground. The lower end of the spray tube is pointed so that it can easily be pushed into the earth.

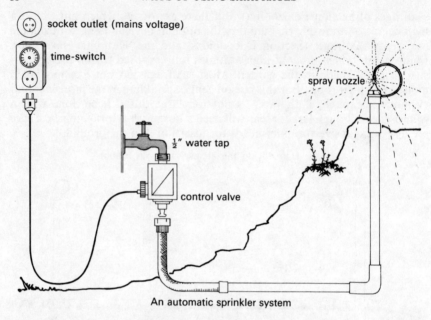

socket outlet (mains voltage)

time-switch

spray nozzle

½″ water tap

control valve

An automatic sprinkler system

*Fig. 14*

Fully automatic control can be provided whatever system is chosen. The electrically operated control valve, screwed on to the water tap, is operated by a time-switch or programmer connected to the power supply. Such systems can provide any desired watering schedule and can even cover prolonged absences on the part of their owners. Full electrical safety precautions are of course essential.

## The rock garden in half-shade

Mention has already been made of spots which enjoy less than full sun, but nothing has yet been said about the ordinary rock garden in half-shade having substantial areas available for planting. Here the gardener is no longer restricted to dwarf plants and can use the well-known species and varieties of saxifrage available in nearly every nursery.

Among these are the large mossy saxifrage hybrids such as 'Flower Carpet', 'Snow Carpet', 'Flowers of Sulphur', 'Triumph' and others. They require a certain minimum of soil moisture and if the soil is light it should therefore be enriched with peat, ground bark, bentonite meal or clay to increase its water-holding powers. Even out of flower, the large mossy cushions are highly decorative. Where space is available these plants should be used on a large scale, in groups of threes or fives. Well-rooted pot-grown plants should be used, so as to avoid the untidy appearance produced by planting large areas with small scrappy growths. In smaller areas the gardener can use the hybrids distributed under the name *Saxifraga muscoides* 'Findling' ('Foundling') and other small species and varieties described in the reference section, including *Saxifraga hypnoides* var. *egemmulosa*. At the boundaries, where it can romp about, the gardener can plant *Saxifraga trifurcata*, though this will also tolerate more sun.

Nor must the encrusted saxifrages of Section Euaizoonia be forgotten. Many of them will tolerate half-shade and some of them even prefer it, notably *Saxifraga cotyledon* in its regional varieties and garden forms. The monocarpic single-rosette saxifrages will also do well, although they prefer crevices.

These areas of half-shade or full shade are the best places for saxifrages of Section Robertsoniana. Their leader is *S.* × *urbium*, a natural hybrid, listed in nearly all catalogues as *S. umbrosa*. The true *S. umbrosa* is seldom met with. *S.* × *urbium* is a well known garden plant which looks presentable at all times of year. It forms large mats of dark green rosettes, and in May and June it produces small white or pale pink flowers on 30 cm scapes. Much neater and more decorative is 'Elliott's Variety'. Another widely grown hybrid is *S.* × *geum*. There is also a golden variegated form of *S.* × *urbium* which is seen to advantage in somewhat less subdued light.

These parts of the rock garden are suitable for the autumn-flowering species of Section Diptera, in particular *S. cortusifolia* var. *fortunei*. This and other varieties need shelter from early frosts which would spoil their flowers. Another important point is that the soil must not dry out during prolonged drought. *Saxifraga rotundifolia* is an undemanding plant for half shade. Though not of outstanding beauty, it is pleasing in a quiet way.

The choice of other species to accompany the saxifrages will depend on the gardener's tastes. Those who like to see bright colours will plant primroses, starting with the pink form (*P. vulgaris* ssp. *sibthorpii*) and going on to the new F1 hybrids. In April the brightly coloured drumsticks of *P. denticulata* look well against the dark green mats of mossy saxifrages. Cultivars of the cowslip and oxlip are available in many strains, notably the new single 'Crescendo', an F1 hybrid offered in six colours. Later in the season come *P. japonica* and the other candelabra primulas, *P. sikkimensis* and *P. florindae*.

Gardeners who prefer wild species of primula can choose from an enormous selection. Among the best of them is *Primula sieboldii*, available in many varieties.

Other plants for shady places include *Epimedium* (though its spreading tendency must not be forgotten), *Gentiana asclepiadea*, *Liriope* and the low-growing blue-flowered *Mertensia primuloides*.

## Flat beds in half-shade

Such areas offer enormous opportunities for the gardener who wishes to grow Saxifragaceae. The term 'half-shade' must not be rigidly interpreted; some spots will have more sun and others less. However, all these plants require a modicum of moisture and the gardener must take care that the sunnier spots are never allowed to dry out. Thorough preparation of the ground will save a great deal of work later on. The soil must be moist but well drained, for these plants cannot abide standing water.

Level parts of the garden should not present a flat or monotonous collection of plants. The horizontal plantings should be interrupted by scattered vertical motifs. Flowers and colour combinations are important, but of equal significance is the overall composition created by careful planning.

After eradicating perennial weeds, the next step is to ensure the correct soil structure. In most gardens the humus content is too low and more humus must be added. As the ideal soil pH is neutral or weakly acid, it is hardly possible to go wrong by using peat. Generous application of bark compost is also recommended. The coarser pieces promote soil aeration, particularly appreciated by ferns. Home-made compost may be used, but is likely to bring a crop of annual weeds. Leaf mould can be used if available. Artificial fertilizers are unsuitable but organic manures are valuable. Heavy clay soils can be lightened by digging in gravel or river sand. For sandy soils bentonite meal is beneficial, and as its pH is on the alkaline side it will help to neutralize excessive soil acidity.

If the area is substantial a few stepping stones should be provided. When first laid these should be at least 10 cm above the soil level. Repeated treading will soon compress the soil beneath them.

All the saxifrages mentioned in the previous section can be grown here, with the exception of the encrusted saxifrages which look out of place. The larger and more vigorous mossy saxifrages are suitable, as are the members of Sections Robertsoniana, Diptera and Miscopetalum.

Other genera of Saxifragaceae look well in shady places. The large leaves of the bergenias make a pleasing contrast, though some of them are perhaps unduly vigorous. Low-growing astilbes can also be used, with a taller one here and there. However, the upright varieties with brilliant red flowers look out of place. Other suitable genera include *Heuchera, Mitella, Tellima, Tiarella* and *Tolmiea*.

A shade garden of this kind would not be complete without ferns. Suitable species include *Adiantum pedatum, Athyrium filix-femina, Dryopteris borreri* and its narrow-leaved form *D. borreri* 'Pinderi', *D. erythrosora, D. filix-mas, Osmunda regalis, Polystichum setiferum* and its forms 'Proliferum' and 'Plumosum Densum'. The choice of sedges and grasses is not so wide, but among species worth considering are *Carex pendula, Deschampsia cespitosa* and *Festuca gigantea*. Bamboos deserve a place, but not all of them are hardy and some grow too tall. The low-growing species spread too vigorously and should be enclosed in a bucket with the bottom knocked out or in some similar restraint.

Many other plants can be grown under these conditions. One possibility is Solomon's Seal, ranging from the tiny mat-forming *Polygonatum hookeri* to the Japanese giant *P. macranthum* 'Weihenstephan'. *Hepatica nobilis* blooms early in the spring and is available in lilac, white, pink and red as well as the ordinary blue form. Pulmonarias are also offered in several different colours.

The maintenance of a shade garden is not too burdensome. Occasional watering will be needed in dry weather and from time to time the gardener will have to cut back vigorous growers which threaten to swamp weaker plants, although such 'internecine broils' often produce delightfully natural impressions. Annual top dressing with humus in some form supplemented with natural manure is beneficial. Where there are taller trees or shrubs it may be difficult to cover the ground in their vicinity because many plants cannot compete with their roots. The answer to this problem is to plant hostas, available in wide variety.

## Edgings

Although saxifrages are generally used in natural plantings, there are circumstances in which they can be arranged in strictly geometrical patterns. Certain species are entirely suitable for edgings, provided that their needs are satisfied. Saxifrages are not really appropriate for edgings in full sun, especially if they are steeply sloping, unless special measures are taken to meet their increased water requirements. For sunny places only the silver saxifrages will serve, especially the more vigorous species and forms with large rosettes. However, their tall scapes sometimes make an unwanted three-dimensional element. In gardens with high atmospheric humidity the saxifrages mentioned below may tolerate sunnier places.

In half-shade and full shade Sections Dactyloides (mossy saxifrages) and Robertsoniana include a few species which make good edging plants. Among the mossy saxifrages there is one species – *Saxifraga trifurcata* – which tolerates more sun, is very vigorous and rapidly coalesces to form an unbroken edging. Other options include the *Saxifraga* 'Arendsii' hybrids, *S. muscoides* 'Findling' ('Foundling') and the various forms of *S. hypnoides*.

The shade-loving saxifrages of Section Robertsoniana also make good edging plants, and look tidy after their flowering time. The best of the species is *S. cuneifolia*, while among the hybrids *S. × geum* and *S. × urbium* and its forms may be useful. The intersectional hybrid *S. × andrewsii* can also be used.

The number of plants required depends on the time available for them to grow into an unbroken edging. The gardener can use well-rooted pot-grown plants or mere divisions. The latter must of course be well-watered until they have taken root. In general an interval of 25 cm between plants is appropriate, but impatient gardeners can plant them closer. Once the plants have coalesced the edges can be straightened with scissors or any other suitable tool; this will not harm the plants. Because the plants are so close together they will exhaust the soil quickly and it is therefore advisable to give them some powdered manure from time to time; this can be mixed with water and applied between the rosettes with a watering can. The only other maintenance task is to cut off the scapes after flowering. In large borders this can be done with electric edging shears.

## Graves

The planting of graves is undergoing a revolution in taste. There are not so many orgies of summer flowers, and there is a growing preference for quieter and more natural compositions.

Saxifrages are ideal for grave plantings, even for those in full sun. Easy maintenance is ensured by using silver saxifrages in combination with bronze and cobweb sempervivums. A dwarf shrub may form the focal point. One obvious choice is the compact steel-blue juniper *Juniperus squamata* 'Blue Star'. Two or three medium-sized rocks will enhance the effect, especially if they have a reddish tinge or a crystalline appearance.

The red sempervivums should not make up more than 25 per cent of the area. They should be planted first, distributed irregularly over the area, and followed by a few plants of the Cobweb Sempervivum (*Sempervivum arachnoideum*) or its hybrids. Lastly, there should be a few medium-sized silver-rosette saxifrages such as *S. paniculata* 'Lutea' and 'Rosea', *S.* × *burnatii, S. cochlearis, Saxifraga* 'Whitehill', *S. crustata, S.* × *farreri, S.* × *fritschiana*. Though they are not all equally vigorous they seldom need restraint and if the restricted space causes one of them to bulge up into a round hillock this will enhance the general effect.

Urns can be planted along the same lines though varieties with small rosettes should of course be chosen. A list of suitable plants will be found on page 17. If the designer prefers the theme green and silver, the reddish sempervivums can be replaced by light green varieties.

For graves in full or half-shade the species and hybrids of Section Robertsoniana, listed previously, are more suitable. London Pride is one of the oldest edging plants and has long been used on graves. Here again a vertical motif in the form of a dwarf shrub is required. One example is the dwarf spruce 'Laurin', which grows only 1–2 cm a year.

Mossy saxifrages also look well, including the *Saxifraga* 'Arendsii' hybrids, but they will need watering more often. The other species mentioned earlier under the heading 'Edgings' are also appropriate. Unfortunately, there is still a shortage of good examples. Once it becomes more widely realized how easily the maintenance of such graves is, they will soon become more popular.

## Saxifrages in pots

A collection of saxifrages in pots may extend to 300 different species and varieties.

The first question is where to keep them. One solution is a cold frame, for example a concrete forcing frame, one of the commercial frames made of transparent plastic, or a do-it-yourself frame of boards covered with reinforced plastic sheet. The position is not crucial, as such a collection can easily be shaded and watered. Pots in a frame should be sunk in coarse sand or gravel, as saxifrages like a cool root run. Good drainage is essential, though in the event of prolonged rain the plants can be protected by an old window frame or something similar.

Small collections of pots can be accommodated on balconies. A southerly aspect will be too hot for 'Kabschia' and 'Engleria' saxifrages; the ideal is an east- or north-east-facing wall. Fairly frequent spraying with water will create the necessary humidity.

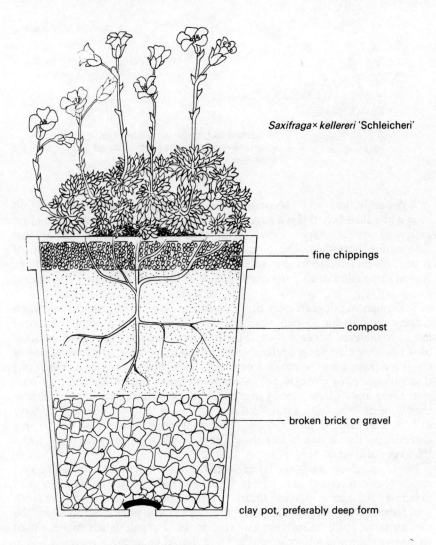

*Saxifraga× kellereri* 'Schleicheri'

fine chippings

compost

broken brick or gravel

clay pot, preferably deep form

Growing 'Kabschia' saxifrages in pots

*Fig. 15*

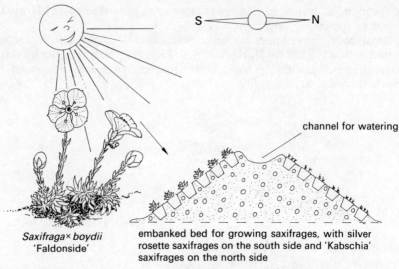

S━━━━◯━━━N

channel for watering

*Saxifraga× boydii*
'Faldonside'

embanked bed for growing saxifrages, with silver
rosette saxifrages on the south side and 'Kabschia'
saxifrages on the north side

*Fig. 16*

A pot collection can be accommodated without a cold frame. One solution
is an embanked bed: this is a narrow bed built up from both sides into a more
or less pyramidal shape. It should run north–south so that it offers an east
face and a west face. The core of the embankment should be made of
permeable material so as to ensure good drainage. Ideally, the pots should be
placed in position during the construction of the bed. To instal them later is
more difficult.

Saxifrages in pots can even be accommodated on level ground, but when
sinking the pots the gardener must make sure that there is plenty of coarse
drainage material beneath them. For long-term plantings in sunken pots the
old-fashioned clay pot is preferable to the modern plastic article. The size of
the pot depends on the plant. For small 'Kabschia' saxifrages a 3-inch pot
(8 cm) is quite big enough, but larger species may need a $3\frac{1}{2}$-inch or 4-inch
pot. Deep pots ('long toms') are best. Before planting the drainage hole
should be covered with a potsherd and the lower third of the pot filled with
grit, broken brick or sintered clay. The remainder is filled with the correct
compost for the section in question. The pot is then topped with one finger's
thickness of coarse chippings.

Proper labelling must not be neglected. Labels must be easily visible (yet
not too conspicuous) and legible. Industry has not yet found the ideal
material. One course is to use ordinary oblong plastic labels, written on with
a waterproof felt-tip pen. However, they have to be pulled out to allow the
writing to be read. More practical are the small plastic labels with an oval
writing surface and a narrow spike. They should be made of material which
does not become brittle on exposure to light. It is unfortunate that such
labels are so often white or yellow. A sober green would be much better, and
can sometimes be obtained.

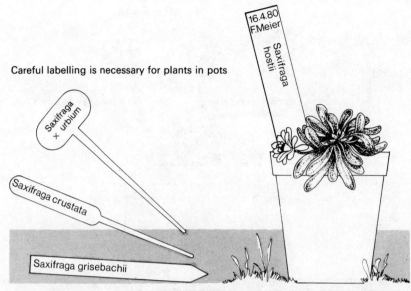

Careful labelling is necessary for plants in pots

*Fig. 17*

A collection of saxifrages in pots can be arranged in various ways, but it is best to keep all the species from each section together, if only because they need the same treatment. Close juxtaposition of similar species often makes it easier to recognize the minor distinctions which separate them. In Section Porophyllum it is a good idea to keep the wild species together. When there are many forms, as in the case of *Saxifraga burserana*, it may be worth making a special subcollection. Hybrids can be classified in accordance with the new nomenclature of Dr Horny, Dr Sojak and Dr Webr (Prague), who put all the hybrids of the same parentage in groups under a single designation; for example, all hybrids between *S. burserana* and *S. ferdinandi-coburgii* are put under the heading of *S. × paulinae* and distinguished by varietal names such as 'Franzii', 'Kolbiana', 'Paula', 'Pseudopaulinae'. Saxifrages of Section Porphyrion (*S. oppositifolia* in its various forms and related species) have much the same requirements as the 'Kabschia' and 'Engleria' saxifrages and can be accommodated beside them.

Most of the encrusted saxifrages are suitable for pot cultures, but some vigorous species with large rosettes require a big pot and must be divided more frequently. This part of the collection will stand full sun. The mossy saxifrages of Section Dactyloides are suitable for pot culture, but the vigorous *Saxifraga* Arendsii hybrids may present difficulties. Other sections of less importance to the gardener contain a few species which can be included in such a collection.

Most of the saxifrages suitable for cultivation in pots are fully frost-hardy, but there are a few species of mossy saxifrage from North Africa and Southern Spain which cannot stand northern winters and need the protection of an alpine house.

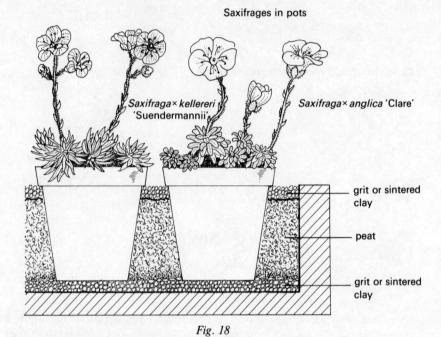

Fig. 18

## Saxifrages in the alpine house

An alpine house is an unheated greenhouse with provision for extra ventilation. It is used to cultivate the more difficult alpines which would not survive in the open or those which require protection if they are to be seen at their best. Most of them are plants susceptible to wet or plants which have a life cycle out of keeping with the climate of lowland Europe or equivalent areas of North America. An alpine house is of great value to the saxifrage enthusiast.

Ordinary small greenhouses are quite unsuitable. They get far too hot and any plants left inside them will soon die. There are some plants which enjoy dryness at the right time of year, but at the same time they require plenty of fresh air. This means that there must be abundant ventilation, both in the sides and the roof. An alpine house should be situated in full sun. If it contains plants which do not require full sun they can always be protected by shading.

Most of the plants grown in an alpine house do not require any heat during the winter. However, the gardener who wishes to grow tender plants will need a heating system to keep the temperature above freezing point. For saxifrages this is not necessary but an electrical installation is useful for lighting, ventilation, automatic misting and so on.

The plants are accommodated on staging which must be strong enough to carry the weight of rocks and earth. This staging can be built of brickwork or

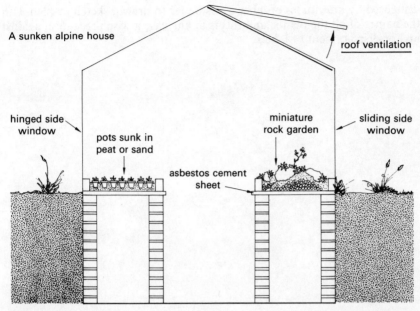

A sunken alpine house

roof ventilation

hinged side window

pots sunk in peat or sand

miniature rock garden

sliding side window

asbestos cement sheet

*Fig. 19*

constructed from angle iron. Thick sheets of asbestos cement make the best covering. They should slope gently backwards so as to carry off surplus water.

A collection of saxifrages in pots can be accommodated in an alpine house. An alternative is to build a miniature rock garden of tufa or waterworn limestone. It can be planted in the way described for tufa rock gardens out-of-doors. Good drainage is essential.

Which saxifrages are best for the alpine house? The 'Kabschia' and 'Engleria' saxifrages are favourites because they start to flower early in the year. The smaller silver saxifrages and the monocarpic species also make good alpine house plants, their silver encrustation being seen at its best when they are protected from excessive wet. In Section Dactyloides there are several species from Southern Spain and North Africa which do not like wet winters and do well in the alpine house. Though none of them is out-standingly beautiful, they are of interest to the collector. Examples are *S. pedemontana, S. pentadactylis, S. corbariensis, S. canaliculata, S. camposii, S. demnatensis, S. portosanctana, S. oranensis, S. erioblasta, S. maweana.* Section Hirculus contains *S. brunoniana* and *S. flagellaris*, which develop their full beauty in the alpine house.

Inside the alpine house, plants with similar requirements should be kept side-by-side. In the spring all of them will require somewhat more watering, but after flowering the water supply should be cut down. Every effort should be made to maintain a high degree of humidity, especially when 'Kabschia' saxifrages are grown in large numbers. Miniature rock gardens are often disfigured by multitudes of labels. It is better to draw a sketch or plan with the names of all the plants, and this is in any case a wise precaution against loss or displacement of labels.

# ·FOUR·

# *Propagation*

The species are usually propagated by seed but vegetative propagation techniques are also useful, including simple division, cuttings or rooted offsets. The three sections of greatest horticultural importance will be dealt with separately as the techniques required are different for each.

## Section Euaizoonia

The silver saxifrages are easily raised from seed. In my own garden I have often found self-sown seedlings on tufa. The main problem is to obtain pure seed. Saxifrage seed is sometimes offered in the catalogues but its purchase is a gamble. The parent plants should be grown far away from any other species of Section Euaizoonia or alternatively the seed should be collected from the

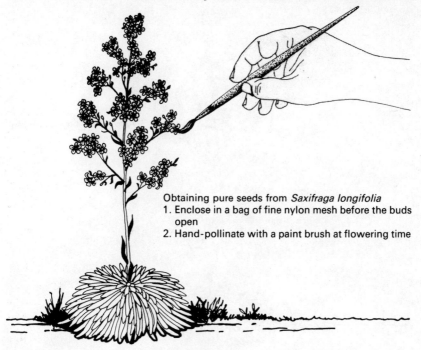

Obtaining pure seeds from *Saxifraga longifolia*
1. Enclose in a bag of fine nylon mesh before the buds open
2. Hand-pollinate with a paint brush at flowering time

*Fig. 20*

wild, though even this does not guarantee pure seed, as there are numerous natural hybrids. The gardener who just wants decorative silver cushions can safely buy such seed as there are hardly any hybrids which are not of pleasing appearance. The only way of ensuring pure seed is to collect it from plants in your own garden, after taking certain vital precautions. If there are no other saxifrages of Section Euaizoonia within 50 metres of the mother plant, the harvested seed will probably be free from hybrids – but even this cannot be guaranteed.

Many of the species of this section have the same chromosome numbers and hybridize readily. They must therefore be protected against pollination from other species. The inflorescences must be enclosed in a wrapping of gauze or moderately coarse nylon mesh. The flowers must be allowed to breathe and impermeable materials such as plastic film or greaseproof paper are quite unsuitable. The scape is usually too weak to carry the weight and must be supported with a cane. The covering must be applied and fixed with a tie before the buds open. When most of the flowers have opened, take a small sterilized watercolour brush and hand-pollinate the flowers; then put back the gauze and secure it. When the seeds are ripe, cut off the scape and lay it on a sheet of paper in a dry spot, free from draughts. The seed will fall out of its own accord or with the aid of gentle tapping. Transfer it to a paper envelope, label it carefully and keep it in a dry well ventilated place until you are ready to sow it. The seed should never be stored in sealed plastic boxes or similar containers.

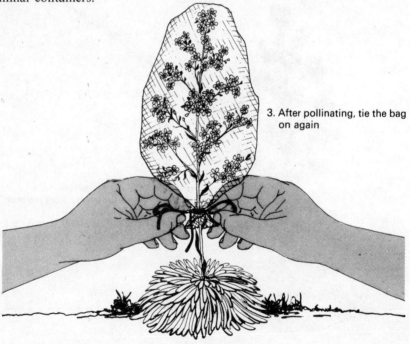

3. After pollinating, tie the bag on again

Fig. 21

Saxifrage seed is very fine. In the case of *S. paniculata* about 17,000 seeds weigh one gram. The average germination is around 50 per cent. The seeds of this section need exposure to low temperatures before they will germinate. The best results are obtained by exposing the seed pans to temperatures between 0° and +5° C for 4–6 weeks. Lower temperatures will do no harm. Snow is beneficial and it is a good idea to cover the seed pans with snow from time to time.

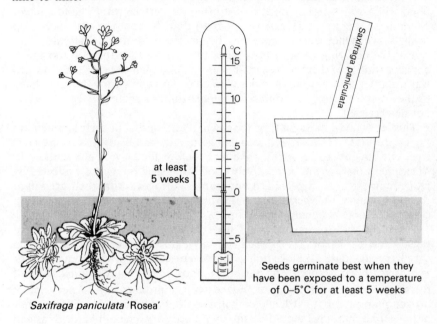

at least
5 weeks

Seeds germinate best when they
have been exposed to a temperature
of 0–5°C for at least 5 weeks

*Saxifraga paniculata* 'Rosea'

*Fig. 22*

The amateur seldom requires large numbers of seedlings, and clay pots or small seed boxes are big enough. Good drainage is essential. The nature of the seed compost is not as important as is sometimes thought, as the seedlings will spend only a short time in it. Much more important is that the compost should be sterilized, so that the seedlings will not be attacked by fungus diseases. The simplest plan is to use a peat-based seed compost without additives. An alternative is to mix John Innes seed compost and sharp sand in equal volumes, adding a little bentonite meal. My standard mixture consists of four buckets of moistened, sieved loam, four buckets of sharp sand (river sand or washed sand 0–3 mm), four buckets of peat and one-third to one-half bucket of bentonite meal. No fertilizers should be added except to peat-based compost. Organic manures are better avoided because they may carry fungus diseases. It is enough to give the seedlings a very weak liquid fertilizer after they have germinated.

Because saxifrage seed is so fine even the expert tends to sow it more thickly than might be desirable. It is a good idea to dilute the seed with fine silver sand or talc before sowing it. As a precaution against soil fungi a knife point of Orthocide may be added. All these can be put in a wide-mouthed glass jar and mixed by thorough shaking.

Leave the seeds uncovered or alternatively sieve the thinnest possible layer of compost over them. Press them down gently with a piece of wood. Cover the pot with a sheet of glass or plastic film so as to maintain humidity and prevent the surface from drying up. Never use a watering-can, as the sudden flood will wash the seeds together. Moisten the surface with a hand sprayer or immerse the pot in a basin of water so that the compost can suck it up from below. Once germination has begun these 'footbaths' should stop. Check the covering of seed pots from time to time. If there is too much condensation give them more air. It is not a good plan to bring the pots into warmth after they have been exposed to cold. This will switch the seeds back to the summer resting condition. A temperature of around $+15°$ C should not be exceeded.

This leads on to the right time for sowing. Late spring or early summer are not appropriate. Home-raised seed will germinate best if sown as soon as it is ripe, but bought seed is seldom available before January. From January to March germination will be relatively good but later it is adversely affected by rising temperatures. A peculiarity of many saxifrages is that their growth in the initial stages after germination is extremely slow. Only after they reach a certain size does the tempo speed up.

When the rosettes have reached fingertip size prick them out into small pots. These can be of clay or plastic; even yoghurt cartons will do provided they have adequate drainage holes. The rosettes can be pricked out singly or in groups of two or three. The potting compost must be well drained. Any of the seed composts can be used, mixed with approximately 25 per cent of broken pumice. Light garden loam will also do, but if it is acid a little pumice or limestone chippings should be added. If necessary lime can be used instead (ground calcium carbonate). After growing throughout the summer the young plants can be put out, but unless they have well developed root balls it is better to wait until the following spring.

The encrusted saxifrages can also be propagated vegetatively and in most cases, unless very large numbers are needed, this is preferable. The simplest method is division. Most species and hybrids of this section form large mats. The whole mat can be taken up and divided into pieces of any desired size, or alternatively the mat can be left in place and pieces can be taken from the outer margin. The divisions can be planted out immediately or grown on in medium-sized pots. The best times for division are spring and autumn.

Propagation by rooted offsets is another easy method. Dig up the mother plant and shake off the earth. Then take two or three rosettes at one edge and tear them off with a downward motion. There will usually be a few roots at the base of each offset. They can then be potted singly or in small groups in well-drained compost. Put the pots in a cold frame until growth begins; maintain humidity by covering with plastic film or closing the frame, and shade against strong sunshine. Offsets can be taken after flowering and again in autumn.

Propagation by cuttings is also feasible. Cuttings are taken in June as soon as the new growths are long enough. Remove the leaves from the lower half of each cutting and insert them in pots, using a rooting hormone if desired. Extra-good results can be achieved by using different layers of material in the pots. The lower third should be filled with drainage material (gravel, chippings, plastic foam, sintered clay), then follows a layer of potting compost as previously described and finally a covering of fine sand (silver sand) roughly one finger thick. On a large scale it is better to use multipot plates. The pots should be housed in a closed frame with adequate humidity until the cuttings have rooted. The young plants should not be planted out until the following spring.

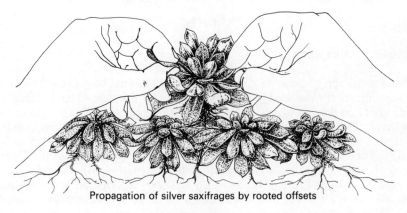

Propagation of silver saxifrages by rooted offsets

Fig. 23

Propagation by small divisions, offsets or cuttings is also practicable in late autumn. A cold frame or an unheated greenhouse can be used.

In recent years there has been some experimental work on the vegetative propagation of monocarpic saxifrages in the Botanic Garden, Tübingen, under the direction of A. Fessler. *Saxifraga longifolia* has been successfully propagated from leaf cuttings. However, it is not enough just to pull off the leaves and insert them. Though they will form roots, they will not develop into rosettes because the necessary eye is lacking. Because of this, the mother plant must be completely divided. The individual leaves are cut off with a knife in such a way that each carries a portion of stem together with the dormant eye in the leaf axil. The cuttings are treated with rooting hormone and inserted in sand. This method is suitable for amateurs but uneconomic for the nurseryman. The best time of year is still uncertain and further experiments are needed. *Saxifraga mutata* can be propagated from cuttings taken from the leaf axils by breaking off the flowering point of the plant. The plant will emit rosettes from the axils and they should then be treated in the same way as cuttings. This technique has not yet been tried for *Saxifraga longifolia*.

**Sowing saxifrage seeds**

1. Sow the fine seeds very thinly
2. Do not cover them with compost, just flatten the surface gently
3. Water from below, and moisten from above with a spray

*Fig. 24*

## Section Porophyllum

The propagation of these delightful miniatures presents no great difficulties, but raising them from seed is a very slow process. Like the silver saxifrages, their seeds need to be exposed to cold, and the technique of raising them is the same. Their germination is somewhat more capricious, but what really tries the gardener's patience is the sluggishness of their growth in the early stages. The species and hybrids cross freely. If pure seeds are required, the plant should be covered with a jam-jar before the buds open and hand-pollinated with a brush. Uncontrolled or open pollination is of course feasible and can be relied on to produce a wide range of beautiful plants. Seed from 'Kabschia' saxifrages is hardly ever offered for sale and gardeners must collect their own. Seedlings take at least three years to flower.

'Kabschia' saxifrages can also be divided. Choose a vigorous plant, dig it up soon after flowering and divide it into small pieces, each with a portion of root. Any compost can be used, provided it meets the basic requirements of 'Kabschia' saxifrages: moderate moisture with good drainage and good aeration in the upper layers. Most of them like a slightly alkaline soil. The basic compost usually consists of peat mixture No. 1 and sharp sand, with a proportion of bentonite meal. To ensure good aeration various materials can be added, such as granular pumice, sintered clay chips, Perlite or vermiculite, or broken brick. The slightly acid reaction of the peat will largely be neutralized by the bentonite meal. Garden soil of light texture with plenty of humus can also be used as the basis of the compost, but if possible some fine limestone chippings should be added. Cuttings offer the most rapid means of vegetative increase. Opinions differ as regards the correct method and time of year. Cuttings are usually taken in May or June. This gives good results, but March may be better. Though many species are in flower at this time the flowering spikes can easily be removed. Cuttings put in at this time will be well-rooted in six weeks. The rooted cuttings are then transferred to small pots. The advantage of taking cuttings early in the spring is that the plants have a full season ahead of them in which to grow and fill their pots with roots. If possible, they should not be planted out in the autumn, but in the early spring of the following year.

In my own garden, however, I propagate these species from winter cuttings alone. Take the cuttings in October, when the routine work of the garden is beginning to slacken. Remove the leaflets from the lower half of each cutting. Insert them singly or in groups of two or three. A rooting hormone will increase the yield. A simple peat–sand mixture can be used for the cuttings, but British gardeners recommend one part of fine loam, one part of silver sand, one part of fine peat and one part of chippings. The boxes of cuttings should be kept in a cold frame or an unheated greenhouse. During the winter they will need little or no attention and by May they will all be rooted.

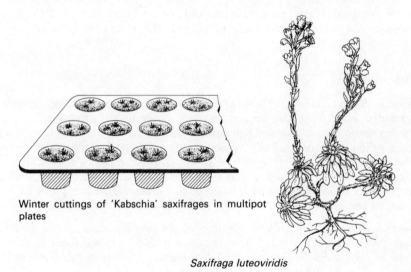

Winter cuttings of 'Kabschia' saxifrages in multipot plates

*Saxifraga luteoviridis*

*Fig. 25*

Cuttings from 'Kabschia' saxifrages can even be taken in midsummer, though they will require rather more attention. At this time of year pure sand is often used as the rooting medium. It must be uniformly watered, and the frame must be covered with glass or plastic film.

As regards vegetative propagation, the 'Engleria' saxifrages do not differ from the 'Kabschias', but the 'Englerias' can be relied on to produce plenty of seed. If sown directly after harvesting it will germinate readily, but stored seed from 'Engleria' saxifrages may lie dormant for a very long time.

## Section Dactyloides

It is hardly worth sowing seed collected from plants growing in the garden. Most of them are complex hybrids which cross readily. The seeds of mossy saxifrages are even finer than those of silver saxifrages, there being about

25,000 seeds to one gram. It is possible to buy seeds of certain strains which are genetically stabilized.

The seeds should be sown as described in the previous sections. Though some of the species require exposure to cold, for many of the garden hybrids this is no longer necessary.

Division is the best means of propagation, and is usually done in the autumn or even just after flowering. When plants are needed in large numbers, the bunches of rosettes can be planted out in a carefully prepared bed. This should be sited in a shady place and the young plants should be watered frequently until well-rooted. On a smaller scale, the divisions can be raised in pots.

Alternatively, cuttings can be taken in late autumn and inserted in loose sandy compost. If left in a cold greenhouse or under glass in a bed they will root over the winter. In the course of one year the single rosettes will develop into well-grown plants.

## Other sections

**Section Robertsoniana.**  These are best propagated by division in early spring or in autumn. Dig up a clump and divide it into small pieces, each having some fibrous roots. They can be planted directly where they are to grow or in a prepared bed of garden soil with added peat, and left there until they have made good growth and have adequate roots. This method of propagation is so productive that seed sowing is hardly necessary. Seed is abundantly produced, and in the case of *S. × urbium* there are about 15,000 seeds to one gram.

**Section Diptera.**  Division in spring presents no difficulties, provided that each piece has a few roots. These species can also be raised from seed, but even in mild areas *S. cortusifolia* and *S. cortusifolia* var. *fortunei* are often destroyed by frost before seed can be harvested.

**Section Porphyrion.**  Sections taken after flowering or in early summer will root readily in sandy compost in a closed frame, which should be lightly shaded. Large mats often have outgrowths with ready-formed roots; these can be cut off and planted in separate pots. Seed can be sown in autumn or winter, and requires exposure to cold.

**Other sections.**  Most of the plants in *Section Miscopetalum* can be propagated by seed, division or cuttings. *Section Cymbalaria* can be propagated by seed only, and *Section Hirculus* is usually increased in this way. Plants of *Section Nephrophyllum* often produce self-sown seedlings, and can also be propagated from underground bulblets or axillary bulbils.

## Sources of seed

The selection of saxifrage seed offered even by specialist seed merchants is not very wide. Besides the varieties of mossy saxifrages already noted, there are some species of Section Euaizoonia from which seed is sometimes offered, but the supply varies from year to year. Seed of *S.* × *urbium* 'Elliott' (*S. umbrosa* 'Elliott') is also available. The gardener who wants to raise a wide range of saxifrages from seed will have to join one of the specialist societies listed at the end of the book and take part in their annual seed exchange. For those with the right contacts, it is sometimes possible to obtain seed from botanic gardens.

# FIVE

# Diseases and pests

As compared with other perennial garden plants, saxifrages are seldom attacked by pests or diseases. Their worst enemy is the blackbird. Unfortunately, it is always the finest and most delicate 'Kabschia' saxifrages which attract their attentions. Most commonly in late summer or early autumn, the gardener may find that his collection of cushion saxifrages has been torn up and scattered to the four winds. All that remains is a pile of unidentifiable green or grey rosettes. The birds do this damage while searching for tiny worms, grubs and slugs which live in the interior or on the under-surface of the cushions. Anyone who feeds blackbirds during the winter must not be surprised if they visit his garden at other times of year, especially as a garden with a wide range of planting offers birds a temptingly varied menu. The only remedy is to instal bird scarers and during the danger season in late summer to cover the plants with green plastic netting. It is, alas, unlawful to shoot them in Britain.

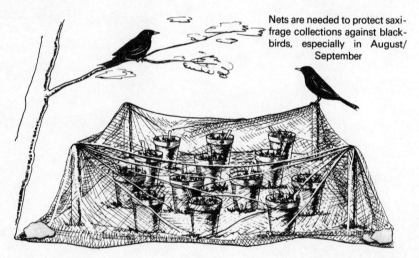

Nets are needed to protect saxifrage collections against blackbirds, especially in August/September

*Fig. 26*

Though there are various harmful fungi, these seem to attack saxifrages in the wild more often than in gardens. The encrusted saxifrages of Section Euaizoonia are perhaps the most vulnerable. In places which are too wet and where stagnant water tends to accumulate, plants of this section are often affected by the parasitic fungus *Exobasidium warmingii*. Single rosettes or large parts of the cushion may die. Rust fungi such as *Puccinia pazschkei* and *P. huteri* are occasionally seen. The affected parts should be removed and the entire plant transferred to a more suitable spot. For prevention it can be sprayed with Orthocide.

The 'Kabschia' saxifrages are occasionally attacked. Single rosettes or areas of the cushions turn brown or black and die. The cause is seldom clearly ascertainable. It may be inadequate aeration of the root ball due to excessive compaction of the soil or it may be a fungus disease; spraying with a mixture of Orthocide and Benlate will often help. In the wild, all alpine saxifrages are subject to attack by a parasitic fungus (*Pyrenophora chrysospora*).

Apart from blackbirds, the pests and diseases of saxifrages are of little significance. Of much greater importance for their healthy growth is the choice of a suitable position and the right soil mixture.

# ·SIX·

# Garden history and the raising of new varieties

Saxifrages are not among the plants, such as roses, lilies and irises, which date back to the beginnings of horticulture. Nevertheless, a few species are first mentioned very early. *Saxifraga cotyledon* was certainly grown in 1596, chiefly in monastery gardens. In the garden at Eichstätt this plant was known as *Cotyledon minus* and its German name was 'Klein lang schmalblätricht Nabel-Kraut'. There can be no doubt that this plant had long been cultivated in those parts of Europe where it occurs naturally; for example, Norwegian countryfolk used its sprays of flowers in bridal bouquets.

With the growth of interest in gardening among well-do-to citizens various species of saxifrage were brought into cultivation, but exact information is often lacking. From the beginning of the nineteenth century London Pride (*S.* × *urbium*) was widely used for edgings. Some of the mossy saxifrages were introduced about this time. *S. geranioides* was in cultivation as early as 1770, *S. trifurcata* is mentioned in 1804 and *S. pedemontana* followed in 1824. Even more remarkable is the mention of *S. maweana* from North Africa as being in cultivation in England as early as 1827. *S. cortusifolia* var. *fortunei* was introduced from Japan in 1815, though the species itself, *S. cortusifolia*, did not follow until 1883. *S. stolonifera* (syn. *S. sarmentosa*) was in cultivation in 1783. *S.* × *wildiana* originated as a random cross in the Botanic Garden, Dresden, in 1836; it is a hybrid between the species from two sections (*S. paniculata* × *S.* × *geum*).

As already mentioned, the first record of an encrusted saxifrage comes from the garden at Eichstätt. *S. paniculata* was in cultivation in 1731. Other species followed, for example, *S.* × *fritschiana* = *S. pectinata* 1870, *S.* × *zimmetrii* = *S. paniculata* × *S. cuneifolia* in the same year, *S. longifolia* 1871, *S. cochlearis* 1883. Reginald Farrer introduced *S. paniculata* var. *minutifolia* in 1911. The intersectional hybrid *S.* × *forsteri* was discovered in 1877 in North Tyrol.

The craze for building rock gardens and collecting plants for them brought a sharp increase in the demand for saxifrage species and natural hybrids. This cult began in the second half of the nineteenth century and spread swiftly. The most enthusiastic collectors, cultivators and, later, plant-breeders lived in Germany. The craze then spread to England, where numerous gardening enthusiasts were already at work. Somewhat later came the building up of large collections in Switzerland, Austria and France, in districts not far from the Alps.

In Germany the name of Franz Sündermann is closely linked with the genus *Saxifraga* and in particular the 'Kabschia' saxifrages. Some of these neat little cushion plants were introduced at early dates. *S. caesia* (now allocated to Section Euaizoonia) was mentioned in 1752. *S. diapensoides* followed in 1825, and *S. aretioides* and *S. burserana* in 1826. *S. sancta* was recorded in 1839, though its date of introduction is also given as 1882. The original introduction was probably lost. *S. marginata* was mentioned in 1883 but *S. lilacina* from the Himalayas was not introduced until 1900.

Franz Sündermann had an outstanding knowledge of alpine plants and was an expert cultivator. He was born in Würzburg on 17 November 1864 and worked there in the Botanic Garden after completing his apprenticeship. He then moved to the Botanic Gardens at Graz and Innsbruck, and was deeply impressed by the beauty of alpine plants in their natural surroundings. He met Kellerer, Director of the Royal Gardens, and they became life-long friends. He decided to start an alpine nursery, and before long established one in Lindau am Bodensee. He travelled through nearly all the mountain ranges of Europe in the search for new, garden-worthy alpines. He had close contacts with the best known systematic botanist of the time, Professor Engler, and collaborated with him in scientific studies of the genus *Saxifraga*. His travels in search of new alpines continued into old age and there are many species that bear his name.

The first printed catalogue of alpine plants was published by Franz Sündermann at Lindau am Bodensee in 1886. The English title is 'Catalogue of alpine plants, subalpine perennials, hardy ferns, terrestrial orchids and water plants'. Present-day enthusiasts sometimes imagine that alpine gardening is a hobby of recent origin. The 1886 catalogue offered a total of 94 different saxifrages, including 28 hybrids, mostly of natural origin. Most of the species were priced at between 30 and 60 pfennigs, which in comparison with contemporary incomes was not cheap. A few recently introduced species and natural hybrids cost as much as 3 marks, a very high price.

To return to the 'Kabschia' saxifrages: Franz Sündermann and Johann Kellerer scoured the mountains of Europe for further species. They were true plant-hunters and some of their reports still make most interesting reading. One of them, printed in the *Allgemeine Botanische Zeitung* in 1901, is reproduced below:

---

## *Saxifraga Ferdinandi Coburgi* nov. spec.

by Johann Kellerer, Sofia and F. Sündermann, Lindau i.B.

At the request of His Royal Highness Prince Ferdinand of Bulgaria, well known as an enthusiast for alpine plants, Johann Kellerer, of the Royal Botanic Garden in Sofia, undertook an extensive botanical collecting trip in Macedonia in 1897. Among other rare and beautiful plants he brought back an interesting *Saxifraga*, which we at first considered to be *S. scardica*. However, as it has now become apparent that *S. scardica* is entirely different in appearance, there can be no doubt that this is a new saxifrage and we have therefore chosen the above name.

Our *Saxifraga* forms dense rigid light grey-green cushions and seems to have some affinity with *S. aretioides*, having the same flower colour. It also displays many similarities with *S. tombeanensis*, but differs in that the leaflets are somewhat longer and narrower and have dense lime deposits which give them an ashen grey colour. Leaflets 4–6 mm long, 1 mm wide, the oldest and lowest leaflets not infrequently reaching a length of up to 1 cm, with fine hairs on the margin to almost half their length, narrowing slightly towards the apex. The rosette is conical, prolonged into a short point bent inwards. The leaflets unite to form a short columnar stem of 6–9 mm diameter and in time the branching of these stems gives rise to a dense medium-sized hemispherical cushion from which the flower spikes arise. In cultivation flowering starts at the beginning of March.

The densely glandular hairy flower scape is 4–6 cm long and is covered with 9–12 cauline leaflets; above it is divided into 4–5 short panicles with 1–3 flowers on each, usually making 8–12 flowers altogether. Petals bright yellow, 4 mm wide, 5–7 mm long, narrowing to 1 mm at the base and not touching one another.

This remarkable saxifrage grows on the Pirin Planina in Macedonia above Bansko on steep limestone rocks at an altitude of roughly 1400 m. It is accompanied by *Saxifraga luteo-viridis* and an apparently new arabis which forms dense low-growing mats.

---

Besides collecting various saxifrage species and introducing them into cultivation, F. Sündermann also distributed numerous garden hybrids originating in his own nursery, in particular 'Kabschia' saxifrages. The first 'Kabschia' hybrids arose at approximately the same time in Great Britain and Germany. *S. × faldonside* (now *S. × boydii* 'Faldonside') and *S. × boydii* (now *S. × boydii* 'William Boyd') originated in Kelso, Scotland, in 1890. In 1894 Sündermann introduced *S. × apiculata* (now *S. × apiculata* 'Gregor Mendel') and *S. × salamonii* (now *S. × salmonica* 'Salomonii'). From then on Sündermann introduced a large number of other hybrids, many of which are still fully worthy of a place in the garden. Even today, the range of saxifrages offered by specialist gardeners outside Germany still consists largely of plants bred by Sündermann. A few examples are listed here, together with the dates of their introduction:

| Old name: | Current name: |
|---|---|
| 1902 *Saxifraga × elisabethae* | *S. × elisabethae* 'Carmen' |

| 1905 *Saxifraga × paulinae* | *S. × paulinae* 'Paula' |
| 1906 *Saxifraga × eudoxiana* | *S. × eudoxiana* 'Eudoxia' |
| 1906 *Saxifraga × ochroleuca* | *S. × elisabethae* 'Ochroleuca' |
| 1907 *Saxifraga × bertolonii* | *S. × bertolonii* 'Antonio' |
| 1907 *Saxifraga × petraschii* | *S. × petraschii* 'Kaspar Maria Sternberg' |
| 1907 *Saxifraga × pungens* | *S. × apiculata* 'Pungens' |
| 1908 *Saxifraga × clarkei* | *S. × clarkei 'Sidonia'* |
| 1909 *Saxifraga × borisii* | *S. × borisii* 'Sofia' |
| 1912 *Saxifraga × bursiculata* | *S. × bursiculata* 'King Lear' |
| 1915 *Saxifraga × doerfleri* | *S. × doerfleri* 'Ignaz Dörfler' |
| 1915 *Saxifraga × fleischeri* | *S. × fleischeri* 'Mephisto' |

Among cultivars originating in England are:

| 1909 *Saxifraga × kewensis* | *S. × kewensis* 'Big Ben' |
| 1912 *Saxifraga × bursiculata* | *S. bursiculata* 'King Lear' |

Many fine hybrids were subsequently derived from crossings with the Himalayan *S. lilacina*. These include pale pink and carmine pink cultivars which have broadened the colour range of the 'Kabschia' saxifrages. At this time the most important breeders apart from Sündermann were Kellerer and Heinrich.

Sündermann also carried out crossings with other sections, for example *S. × rigescens = S. tricuspidata × S. tenella*. Interest in saxifrages flourished. One of Sündermann's catalogues published before the First World War lists over 180 different saxifrages, though many of them would nowadays be considered to be of purely botanical interest.

Another famous gardener whose name is linked with saxifrage-breeding is Georg Arends of Wuppertal-Ronsdorf. He was enormously successful in raising new perennials for the garden. His enthusiasm was not confined to the genus *Saxifraga* but extended to the whole family Saxifragaceae, notably the astilbes. A large hybrid complex, the *Astilbe* Arendsii hybrids, carries his name. His nursery later produced numerous hybrid bergenias, a group at that time included in the genus *Saxifraga*.

George Arends then turned his attention to the mossy saxifrages. A few species had been in cultivation since the beginning of the nineteenth century, and in the early years of the twentieth century there were one or two hybrids. To trace the ancestry of the *Saxifraga* Arendsii hybrids back to their ultimate origins would now probably be impossible. The plants which their raiser employed were often of hybrid origin or had names of doubtful validity. Some of his crossings are described as *Saxifraga cespitosa* hybrids, but it is uncertain whether this was the true *S. cespitosa* or whether it was *S. rosacea* Moench, which at that time passed under the name of *S. decipiens* but in garden circles was often confused with *S. cespitosa*. It seems probable that the plant in question was really *S. rosacea*.

For us today it is enough to know that the *Saxifraga* Arendsii hybrids are fine garden plants. According to the Arends firm, their ancestry is as follows: *S. rhei* × hybrid from *S. granulata* × *S. decipiens* and *S. hypnoides* 'Rosea' and *S. hypnoides* 'Purpurea'. The first of the new varieties – 'Blutenteppich' and 'Purpurmantel' – appeared in 1911. They were followed in 1912–13 by the cultivars 'Grandiflora Alba', 'Juwel', 'Splendens', 'Schöne von Ronsdorf', 'Magnifica', 'Rose Superba' and the very low-growing 'Teppichkönigin'. 'Triumph', probably the best of all, came in 1920. This cultivar is still offered by specialist alpine nurseries even in Britain. Last of all, in 1930, came 'Schneeteppich', 'Schwefelblüte' and 'Purpurteppich'. Another new introduction from the Arends firm was *S. muscoides* 'Findling', first offered in 1959. However, it should be noted that the parent was not the true species *S. muscoides* All., but a hybrid.

The breeding of cultivars from Section Dactyloides was also carried on with great success in Britain, where the climate is more favourable to these plants than on the continent. These British novelties need some care in cultivation and should be given a position with high humidity. Another German firm which has had some success in the breeding of mossy saxifrages is Riedel.

The First World War brought the breeding of saxifrages to a halt, but by 1925 Sündermann's catalogue was again offering some 125 saxifrages, 'Kabschias' and 'Englerias' figuring in larger numbers than ever. By 1936, the firm's 50th Jubilee, the saxifrage craze had reached a new peak. One amazing feature of the Jubilee catalogue is that many prices had not changed since the first catalogue in 1886. By then, of course, the nursery was in the hands of the next generation. Under the direction of Ferdinand Sündermann the company brought out several new 'Kabschia' cultivars and survived the Second World War, though not without grave difficulties.

The link between the name of Sündermann and the genus *Saxifraga* is recognized in the English-speaking world as well as in Germany. The Sündermann family have led the field, first as collectors and then as cultivators and raisers of new plants. The third generation deserve no less credit for their work in maintaining a huge selection of saxifrages, from which many other specialist nurseries have drawn their original stocks. The present representatives of the family are Ferdinand Franz Sündermann and his sister Rosemarie Paulmichl, a great saxifrage expert.

New 'Kabschia' hybrids are still emerging, especially in Great Britain. Czechoslovakia is another country where there is enormous interest in these plants. A large series of new hybrids has recently originated there, including *S.* × *borisii* 'Josef Manes', 'Karlstejn', 'Vesna', 'Vincent van Goch' and *S.* × *pragensis* 'Golden Prague'. Some new 'Kabschia' saxifrages have been introduced by the nursery of J. Eschmann in Emmen bei Luzern (Switzerland). This firm, together with Messrs Frei, Wildensbuch b. Schaffhausen (Switzerland) and Dr Simon, Marktheidenfeld a. Main, deserve credit for building up large selections, for selecting the best of them and for raising the species from seed collected in the wild.

Enthusiasm for alpine plants is worldwide. In the USA L. H. Foster has raised numerous new hybrids in Section Porophyllum ('Kabschia'), though they have not yet been widely distributed in Europe; among them are 'Clarissa', 'Cleo', 'Corona', 'Demeter', 'Diana', 'Dulcimer', 'Eliot Ford', 'Elisabeth Sinclair', 'Falstaff', 'Fanfare', 'Flush', 'Friar Tuck', 'Galahad', 'Ganymede', 'Helios', 'Icicle', 'Klondike', 'Lusanna', 'Midas', 'Millstream Cream', 'Nugget', 'Opalescent', 'Peach Blossom', 'Prospero' and 'Timmy Foster'.

## Section Euaizoonia (encrusted or silver saxifrages)

As regards their rosettes there is not much further scope for development; they are available in all sizes and shapes, with greater or lesser degrees of lime encrustation. What would be desirable is a wider range of flower colour. By crossings based on *S. paniculata* 'Rosea' and 'Lutea' this should not be too difficult. By large-scale sowing it might be possible to intensify the delicate pink and pale sulphur-yellow hues and ultimately to produce silver saxifrage hybrids with carmine-pink and bright yellow flowers. Several species – *S. paniculata, S. hostii, S. callosa* and *S. cotyledon* – have the same chromosome number ($2n = 26$) and there should therefore be no obstacle to crossing.

## Section Dactyloides (mossy saxifrages)

These hybrids still offer scope for improvement. Though they make superb cushions and flower very freely, most of them will not tolerate much sun. Certain cultivars with double flowers have recently emerged in Great Britain. As doubling prolongs the flowering period, attempts should be made to induce it in other varieties. There is already a wide range of dwarf varieties with very short scapes. There is a need for double-flowered dwarf varieties which will tolerate more sun. Such an improvement might be attained by raising large numbers of seedlings and selecting the more sun tolerant, or by crossing with various Spanish species which naturally possess greater sun resistance (dense hair covering). The range of available colours is by no means exhausted. Since the introduction of the Arends variety 'Schwefel-blüte' with its pale sulphur-yellow flowers there has been no progress among the yellows. This hue could certainly be deepened by breeding and selection. The aim should be a short-scaped dwarf variety for troughs, resistant to drought and full sun, with double flowers of deep yellow. The following chromosome numbers are known: *S. hypnoides* $2n = $ ca. 30, 48, 64, *S. cespitosa* $2n = 80$, *S. rosacea* ssp. *rosacea* $2n = 56$, *S. rosacea* ssp. *sponhemica* $2n = 50, 52$ (from *Flora Europaea*).

## Section Porophyllum ('Kabschia')

The range available is already very wide and does not leave much to be desired. However, when looking at certain varieties, the gardener sometimes wishes that they were somewhat more vigorous. Firm solid cushions with a diameter of 20 cm would be welcome, to say nothing of more abundant flowers. The flowering time might be somewhat longer. As regards flower colour there are still unrealized possibilities especially in intermediate nuances. Greater tolerance of sun is also an important aim. Not all the chromosome numbers are known, but the following have been established: *S. diapensioides* $2n = 25$, *S. vandellii* $2n = 26$, *S. burserana* $2n = 26$, *S. aretioides* $2n = 26$, *S. sancta* $2n = 26$.

Some of these objectives might be attained sooner than we expect. There is perhaps scope for crossing between species from different sections. Section Robertsoniana seems to offer a promising link.

# SEVEN

# Classification into sections

Let us begin by looking at the position of a Saxifrage species, e.g. *Saxifraga paniculata* (syn. *S. aizoon*), in the plant kingdom (from Engler, *Syllabus der Pflanzenfamilien*):

Class: Angiospermae (flowering plants)
   Subclass: Dicotyledoneae (plants with two seed leaves)
     Superorder: Archichlamydeae
       Order: Rosales
         Suborder: Saxifragineae
           Family: Saxifragaceae
             Genus: *Saxifraga*
               Species: *Saxifraga paniculata*

The genus *Saxifraga* is extremely large, containing well over 300 species. Botanists have therefore attempted to subdivide the genus into smaller groups, in this instance known as sections. Such subdivisions are subject to modification from time to time depending on the progress of research and sometimes even on the personal opinion of the botanist.

Fortunately, revisions of the sections of the genus *Saxifraga* have been moderate and restrained. Formerly the genus was more extensive and included a Section Peltiphyllum (now the separate genus *Peltiphyllum*) and Section Megasea (now the genus *Bergenia*).

The currently accepted classification into 15 sections goes back to the monograph on the genus *Saxifraga* published by Engler and Irmscher in 1916:

1. Micranthes (Haw) D. Don (formerly Borophila Engl.) (see page 167)
2. Hirculus (Haw) Tausch. (see page 155)
3. Robertsoniana (Haw) Ser. (see page 141)
4. Miscopetalum (Haw) Engl. (see page 166)
5. Cymbalaria Griseb. (see page 172)
6. Tridactylites (Haw) Engl. (see page 164)
7. Nephrophyllum Gaud. (now known as Section Saxifraga) (see page 150)
8. Dactyloides Tausch. (see page 117)
9. Trachyphyllum Gaud. (see page 160)
10. Xanthizoon Griseb. (see page 162)
11. Euaizoonia (Schott) Engl. (see page 72)
12. Porophyllum (formerly Kabschia) Engl. (see page 87)

13. Porphyrion Tausch. (see page 137)
14. Tetrameridium Engl. (see page 174)
15. Diptera Borkh. (see page 146).

Each of these sections is distinguished by clearly visible characteristics, though intermediate forms exist in some instances. However, the morphological differences within a section, e.g. Hirculus, are often so striking that the layman finds it hard to believe that he is looking at plants belonging to one and the same section. The principal characters of the sections are summarized below.

**1. Micranthes.**   Leaves toothed, notched or entire, forming a rosette with relatively few leaves. The flower stalks are leafless or have a few reduced stem leaves, obviously different from the basal leaves. Seeds elongated. Flowers white, sometimes with coloured dots, small and inconspicuous. Because of its size this section has been divided into subsections: Punctata, Davuricae, Nivali-virginenses, Melanocentrae, Integrifoliae, Stellares, Intermediae, Merkianae. As this section is of little horticultural importance the allocation of species to subsections will not be described.

**2. Hirculus.**   Leaves entire. Scapes with more or less numerous leaves. Do not form well defined rosettes. Flowers yellow or orange-yellow. More than 100 species of widely varying appearance. Sub-sections Hirculoideae, Gemmiparae, Sediformes, Flagellares, Hemisphaericae.

**3. Robertsoniana.**   Evergreen plants with overground runners. Scapes leafless or with a few weakly developed leaves. Rosette leaves more or less spoonshaped and leathery. Leaf margins more or less toothed. Petals radial, small, of equal length, white or pink or spotted. Hybridizes freely, even with members of other sections.

**4. Miscopetalum.**   Tufted plants with round or oval stalked leaves and variably toothed leaf edges. Upright scapes with few or many leaves. Loose inflorescence of small flowers, usually white, often spotted.

**5. Cymbalaria.**   Annuals with ivy-shaped leaves. Cupule insignificant or short, ovary hence completely superior or fused in lower third with cupule. Petals ovate to narrow obovate, narrowing towards the base and usually with a claw. Flowers yellow, rarely white.

**6. Tridactylites.**   Usually annuals or biennials. Basal rosettes with thin undivided three-pointed leaves. Scapes branching, more or less leafy, with small white flowers.

**7. Nephrophyllum.**   Most but not all species produce small bulbils at the base or in the leaf axils of the scape. Leaves usually kidney-shaped, relatively soft and notched. Flowers normally white. Many species disappear completely in winter. Sub-sections Arachnoideae, Irriguae, Granulatae, Sibiricae.

**8. Dactyloides.**   More or less dense cushions or mats consisting of rosettes of variously notched and forked leaves with hairs or glands. The soft leaved green rosettes do not die after flowering. Spread by overground lateral runners. Flowers numerous, white, pink or red or intermediate tints. Subsections:

1. Tenellae: *S. tenella*
2. Sedoideae: *S. sedoides*
3. Muscoideae: *S. muscoides, S. facchinii*
4. Aphyllae: *S. aphylla*
5. Androsaceae: *S. androsacea, S. coarctata, S. depressa, S. humilis, S. italica, S. presolanensis, S. seguieri.*
6. Glabellae: *S. glabella*
7. Axilliflorae: *S. praetermissa, S. wahlenbergii*
8. Aquaticae: *S. aquatica*
9. Ceratophyllae: *S. camposii, S. canaliculata, S. corbariensis, S. cuneata, S. demnatensis, S. geranioides, S. maderensis, S. moncayensis, S. pedemontana, S. pentadactylis, S. portosanctana, S. trifurcata, S. vayredana.*
10. Gemmiferae: *S. conifera, S. continentalis, S. erioblasta, S. globulifera, S. hypnoides, S. maweana, S. oranensis, S. reuterana, S. rigoi, S. spathulata, S. trabutiana.*
11. Cespitosae: *S. adenoides, S. boussingaultii, S. cespitosa, S. hartii, S. lactea, S. magellanica, S. pavonii, S. rosacea, S. seleniflora.*
12. Exarato-Moschatae: *S. cebennensis, S. exarata, S. hariotii, S. moschata, S. nervosa, S. nevadensis, S. pubescens.*

**9. Trachyphyllum.** Mostly small mat-forming species with narrow undivided entire linear lanceolate leaves. Scape with few branches, normally about 10 cm high. Flowers dirty white, pale or orange-yellow. Usually on lime-free soil. Not very decorative.

**10. Xanthizoon.** Loose mats of tangled stems, sparsely covered with narrow leaves; little tendency to rosette formation. Leaves undivided with notched or bristly edges. Flowers singly or in loose umbels, pale or deep yellow, orange, purple or deep red.

**11. Euaizoonia.** Rosettes with stiff, tongue-shaped or spade-shaped leaves more or less lime-encrusted, often giving a silvery effect. Flowers in spikes, panicles or convex umbels. Numerous flowers in early summer, usually white, often with red spots. Rosettes die after flowering, but thin overground runners arising from their centres produce new rosettes. Usually on lime-rich soil (except *S. cotyledon*). Subsections:

Crustatae: *S. callosa* (syn. *S. lingulata*), *S. cochlearis, S. crustata, S. valdensis, S. longifolia*
Peraizoonia: *S. paniculata* (syn. *S. aizon*), *S. hostii*
Cotyledoniae: *S. cotyledon*
Florulentae: *S. florulenta*
Mutatae: *S. mutata*

**12. Porophyllum.** Better known to gardeners under the name 'Kabschia'.

At one time Subsection Engleria was included in this section, but recently it has been allotted to Section Tetrameridium (see below). Firm dense evergreen cushions consisting of small rosettes which do not die after flowering. Small stiff leaflets, subulate, rounded or needle-sharp, covered with few or many lime pits. Short scapes carrying white, yellow or pink florets, singly or several. Flowers in early spring. Subsections:

Juniperifoliae: *S. juniperifolia, S. caucasica, S. sancta*
Kotschyanae: *S. kotschyi*
Marginatae: *S. lilacina, S. marginata, S. scardica, S. spruneri*
Squarrosae: *S. caesia, S. squarrosa* (now in Section Euaizoonia)
Rigidae: *S. burserana, S. diapensioides, S. tombeanensis, S. vandellii*
Aretioideae: *S. aretioides, S. ferdinandi-coburgii*

In addition there is Subsection Mediae which includes the 'Englerias' and contains the species *S. media, S. porophylla, S. grisebachii, S. stribrnyi, S. sempervivum* (syn. *S. thessalica*), *S. luteoviridis*.

**13. Porphyrion.**    Low mats with opposite leaves arranged crosswise. Lying close to the soil or rooting. Leaflets small, leathery and evergreen. Flowers on short pedicels, purple.

**14. Tetrameridium.**    All the species are Asiatic and only one has been in cultivation (*S. nana*). An attempt has been made to allocate 'Engleria' saxifrages to this section, but as the species of Section Tetrameridium have four-petalled flowers this is totally illogical.

**15. Diptera.**    Rounded, stalked leaves of leathery appearance. Characteristic of this section are the flowers with petals of unequal length. Flowers white with or without coloured spots. Flowering time late summer and autumn.

This book is based on the above sectional classification. As already mentioned, any such classification is to some extent fluid. Changes have been made in the past and others will be made in the future. As an example of another classification here is one from Gustav Hegi, *Illustrierte Flora von Mitteleuropa*:

Section I: Micranthes (Haw) D. Don
Section II: Hirculus Tausch
Section III: Gymnopera D. Don (= Robertsoniana Ser.)
Section IV: Diptera (Borkh.) Sternb.
Section V: Trachyphyllum Gaud.
Section VI: Xanthizoon Griseb.
Section VII: Aizoonia Tausch.
    1. Florulenta group
    2. Cotyledon group
Section VIII: Porophyllum Gaud.
    1. Media group (= 'Engleria' saxifrages)
    2. Juniperifolia group
    3. Marginata group

    4. Aretioides group
Section IX: Porphyrion Tausch
Section X: Miscopetalum (Haw) Sternb.
Section XI: Saxifraga
    1. Arachnoidea group
    2. Petraea-Tridactylites group
    3. Sibirica group
    4. Granulata group
    5. Ajugifolia group
    6. Aquatica group
    7. Cespitosa group
    8. Androsacea group
    9. Aphylla group
  10. Muscoides group
Section XII: Trachyphylloides H. Huber
Section XIII: Cymbalaria
Section XIV: Discogyne

To gardeners and plant-lovers a section is a group of plants with similar cultural requirements and horticultural uses; such people are not greatly interested in minor morphological distinctions or phylogenetic relationships. Taxonomic or nomenclatural changes do not greatly concern them and no one will be upset if they continue among themselves to speak of 'Kabschia' and 'Engleria' saxifrages.

# · E I G H T ·

# *Species, varieties and hybrids described*

In the pages which follow, the Sections are dealt with in order of horticultural importance.

### Section Euaizoonia
### (silver saxifrages, encrusted saxifrages)

This section contains some of the largest and most striking species and hybrids. The main features are the firm, well-developed rosettes with spathulate or tongue-shaped leaves, often lime-encrusted. The inflorescences are panicles or corymbs. The flowering time is May to June. The flowers are white, cream, pale yellow or pale pink, though the red spots which sometimes adorn the white flowers often give them an overall pink hue. The rosettes die after they have flowered. Unless seed is desired, the stem and its rosette should be removed immediately after the flowers have faded. So as not to uproot other non-flowering rosettes they should be held down with the outspread hand. In most cases an adequate supply of daughter rosettes is produced, but this is not true of the three monocarpic species *S. longifolia, S. florulenta* and *S. mutata*. They must be propagated by seed.

Although most of the encrusted saxifrages have highly attractive flowers, their main garden value lies in their beautiful mats and cushions. The rosettes range from the minute (*S. valdensis* forms) to the enormous (*S. longifolia* – over 15 cm in diameter). Most of them have a silvery appearance imparted by the lime encrustations on the rosette leaves. There are of course exceptions; for example, *S. cotyledon* has little or no lime encrustation, a feature transmitted to some of its hybrids.

The taller species and varieties can be used as cut flowers. In mixed flower arrangements they should be placed so as to overtop the other flowers.

Unlike the species of most other sections, many of the encrusted saxifrages will stand full sun, though they do not share the drought resistance of the houseleeks (*Sempervivum*). *S. mutata* and *S. cotyledon*, however, require some shade if they are to display their full beauty. There are many others which will flourish equally well in full sun or in half-shade. The amount of light required can be ascertained by observing the rosettes. If these are not sufficiently compact, the plant is not getting enough light. This can be put right by transplanting at any time of year.

*S. longifolia* grows best on steep east-facing slopes, just the spots that 'Kabschia' and 'Engleria' saxifrages love. Species and hybrids with dense lime encrustation like limestone chippings to be added to the soil, and this measure will promote the growth of densely packed cushions. Porous tufa gives equally good results. In contrast, *S. cotyledon* and some of its hybrids do not like lime in the soil, though they are not totally intolerant. *S. florulenta* must have absolutely lime-free soil, preferably derived from igneous rock. Good drainage is essential for all the species of this section; stagnant water will lead to diseases. Moderate soil moisture and air humidity are desirable. The plants will survive short periods of dryness without difficulty, but during prolonged drought the rosettes shrivel and turn yellowish. They usually recover when given water.

Apart from the few exceptions described in the previous paragraphs, most of the encrusted saxifrages are comparatively easy to grow, even in dry walls and rock crevices. Nearly every nursery offers one or two encrusted saxifrages and some of the specialists list 30 or more.

## Species

### Saxifraga callosa Sm. (syn. S. lingulata Bell.)

A vigorous and beautiful species found in the south-western Alps and Pyrenees. As might be expected from its wide distribution the species is extremely variable. The type grows in the Maritime Alps (*S. callosa* Sm. ssp. *callosa*). It forms tufted rosettes with grooved linear-spathulate blue-green leaves, up to 9 cm long and 0.4 cm wide, bent outwards and reddish at the base. The leaf edges are encrusted with lime to a greater and lesser degree depending on the origin of the plant. The arching inflorescences, cymes or corymbs, are up to 35 cm high. The petals are white with red spots at the base. It flowers in June and grows well in a sunny place if planted in loamy soil containing lime chippings, but it will not tolerate standing moisture. So many varieties and forms have come into cultivation that it is difficult to obtain the true plant.

**S. callosa** 'Albertii' (syn. *S.c.* var. *albertii*). Rosettes larger than the type, inflorescence more spreading, 25–30 cm high. It is uncertain whether this is a local form or an old hybrid.

**S. callosa** var. *australis* comes from central and southern Italy. Leaves linear and pointed (up to 4 cm long and 0.5 cm wide). Inflorescence 25 cm long. A beautiful form from Gran Sasso is available in the trade.

**S. callosa** var. *bellardii* (syn. *S. lingulata* var. *bellardii*) comes from the south-western Alps and has irregular rosettes. Leaves linear-spathulate, pointed, up to 10 cm long and 0.2 cm wide. Flowers pure white, scapes hairless.

**S. callosa** ssp. *catalaunica* (Boiss.) D. A. Webb (syn. *S. catalaunica* Boiss., *S. lingulata* var. *catalaunica*) from Catalonia and south-eastern France forms flat rosettes 7–8 cm in diameter, with dense lime encrustations. Leaves short, ovate-spathulate. Scapes up to 20 cm, glandular-hairy. It does not flower freely, but this is really an advantage as its main beauty lies in its superb rosettes. Flowers white to yellowish in June or July. Tolerates full sun.

*S. callosa* var. *lantoscana* occurs in the Maritime Alps. Distinguished by its short blunt spathulate leaves. Dense lime deposits on the indistinctly toothed leaf margins and under-surfaces. Rosettes very tight and firm. Dense curved inflorescences 20 cm tall, with white flowers in June. This is a genuine wild form and is more often seen in gardens than the type. There is another garden form known as *S.c.* var. *lantoscana* 'Superba'. It resembles var. *lantoscana* but has taller scapes. A form with large star-shaped rosettes and dense 25 cm tall racemes is offered in nurseries under the name *S. lantoscana* var. *Sündermann*.

*S. callosa* var. *latonica* has stocky rosettes and the whole plant is more compact than the type. Scapes 25 cm tall. Petals white with red dots. Flowering extends into July.

*S. callosa* 'Winterfeuer' (H.W.) (syn. *S. lingulata* 'Winterfeuer') is distinguished by its cinnabar-red winter colouring.

*S. callosa* var. *sancta-balmae* closely resembles *S.c.* ssp. *catalaunica*, but the rosettes are neater and the dark green leaves narrower and densely encrusted with lime. Scapes 15 cm, flowers white.

Other local variants are offered in the trade, such as *S. callosa* 'Judikar' which has very narrow rosette leaves. All these forms of *S. callosa* will tolerate a dry place in full light, but will do just as well in a shady position.

## *Saxifraga cochlearis* Reichenb.

Growing in the south-western Alps on both sides of the French Italian frontier, this species varies in size and characteristics from one locality to another and no one can truly assert that he has the genuine form. All the forms have small hemispherical rosettes with numerous short spoon-shaped untoothed leaves thickly encrusted with lime. These spoon-shaped leaves distinguish it from other species of this section, except the closely similar *S. valdensis*. The leaves vary in length from 0.6 to 2.5 cm and the rosettes in diameter from 1.3 to 2.8 cm. The numerous close-packed rosettes form small mounds. The scapes are up to 20 or even 25 cm high and the average diameter of the plant is much the same. The loose inflorescence has pearly buds and pure white flowers in May or June.

There is a type with large rosettes known as *S. cochlearis* 'Major'. Offered under the name *S. cochlearis* 'Minor' (syn. *S. probyni* Correv.) is a much smaller form, an ideal plant for small troughs. The scape is only 10 cm high and the white florets contrast prettily with the red stems. The congested silver-white rosettes form small cushions, though they take some time to reach their ultimate size of 12–13 cm. *S. cochlearis* 'Pseudo-valdensis' is even smaller, its scapes being only 8 cm tall.

## Saxifraga cotyledon L.

This is found on lime-free soil in the central Alps from Savoy eastwards as far as Vorarlberg and Graubünden. It also occurs in the Carpathians, in Norway, Sweden and Iceland, and in North America, usually on siliceous rocks in shady places.

The rosettes are flat, having a diameter of up to 12 or occasionally even 15 cm. It has broad strap-shaped leaves, 2–8 cm long and 0.6–1.7 cm wide. They are leathery or fleshy, finely toothed and glabrous, broadening towards the point. The rosettes die after flowering. The central stem puts out new rosettes so that the plant forms a small colony or even a mat. The scapes range from 15 to 80 cm in height, depending on the situation, though they are usually not more than 60 cm. They have numerous scattered stem leaves resembling the basal leaves, 1–3 cm long and having short glandular hairs. The inflorescence is a curved composite panicle of pyramidal shape with numerous florets. The five petals are obovate, blunt, white with reddish veins and occasionally red dots, 0.5–1.0 cm long. Flowering time is June–July. Flowering rosettes are more than two years old.

This is an old garden plant, cultivated in the garden at Eichstätt in 1613 under the name *Cotyledon minus*. In the garden it requires soil containing little or no lime and prefers complete or partial shade. The beautiful white panicles are seen to best advantage when the plant is grown high on a steeply sloping bank. It can also be cultivated in pots in the open air or the alpine house.

Like all species which have a wide distribution range, *S. cotyledon* exists in numerous natural forms, some of which have been selected by gardeners.

*S. cotyledon* 'Caterhamensis'. Selected from the northern forms, this grows more readily than the type and its flowers have conspicuous red spots.

*S. cotyledon* 'Montavonensis'. This broad-leaved form comes from the central Alps where it grows side by side with the typical form. Somewhat smaller in all its parts, especially the flowers.

*S. cotyledon* 'Norwegica'. A northern form, selected from the wild and widely grown, particularly in Britain. The difference from the typical form is easily seen in the leaves, which taper sharply to a short point. The flowering stem starts to branch about 8 cm above the base and may have up to 50 side branches each carrying up to 20 white flowers.

*S. cotyledon* 'Pyramidalis' is one of the most beautiful forms. Found in the central Alps and occasionally in the Savoy Alps, it has a superb pyramidal inflorescence, branching from the base of the flowering stem and almost as broad as it is tall. The rosette leaves are longer and narrower than those of the type and it prefers somewhat more moisture.

*S. cotyledon* 'Somerset Seedling'. The main difference is in the flowers, which have deep carmine red dots. It also has fine rosettes 12–15 cm in diameter. Inflorescence 50–60 cm high.

In nature this species is associated with *Androsace multiflora, Sempervivum arachnoideum, Asplenium septentrionale, Saxifrage paniculata* and *Draba dubia*.

### Saxifraga crustata Vest (syn. *S. incrustata* Vest)

This grows in the south-eastern limestone Alps from the Etsch into Carniolica, and from there southwards into Bosnia, Herzegovina and Western Serbia. It is found on dolomite and limestone and in stony, sparsely covered grasslands.

From *S. callosa* (syn. *S. lingulata*), a closely related species with a western distribution, it is distinguished chiefly by the width of its leaves, especially in the lower third, and also by its more abundant flowers. *S. crustata* forms dense cushions made up of tightly packed flat rosettes, 2–8 cm in diameter, which die after flowering. It has narrow linear leaves up to 5 cm long, bent outwards near the tip. They are stiff and leathery, having a narrow cartilaginous margin. The underlying colour is blue-green, but they are thickly encrusted with lime. The upright scape is 20 to 40 cm tall and densely covered with glandular hairs; it branches from the middle upwards to form a panicle. The stem leaves are few in number, smaller than the rosette leaves and serrated at their margins. The five petals are obovate, about 0.5 cm long and white or creamy in colour, very occasionally having red dots. The inflorescence is slenderer than that of *S. paniculata* (syn. *S. aizoon*). It grows readily in the garden and will tolerate full sun, preferring poor rather than rich soil.

It can be grown side by side with sempervivums. In nature it is associated with *Physoplexis comosa* (syn. *Phyteuma comosum*), *Saxifraga caesia, S. squarrosa* and *Potentilla nitida*. In nursery catalogues *Saxifraga incrustata* and *S. crustata* are sometimes offered separately. Though there are of course local differences, botanically these belong to the same species. Various local forms are also offered. The variety *rosea* mentioned by Wocke is probably no longer available.

### Saxifraga florulenta Moretti

Confined to an area some 50 km in diameter between Tende and Argenta in the Maritime Alps, this very uncommon species grows on igneous rock at an altitude of 2000–3250 m and is strictly calcifuge. It is regarded as a relict of bygone ages.

It has large flat rosettes, 12–16 cm in diameter, made up of regularly arranged dark-green leaves, 5–7.5 cm long, pointed and without lime encrustation. The rosettes take many years to grow to this size and as the species is monocarpic they die after flowering. The inflorescence is not as attractive as that of *S. longifolia* and in cultivation many years pass before the plant flowers. The compact inflorescence is 20–40 cm high, the individual flowers being well-shaped and muddy flesh-pink in colour. It is not an easy plant to grow and will not tolerate lime in any form.

## Saxifraga hostii Tausch (syn. *S. longifolia* Lap. var. *media* Sternb., *S. longifolia* Host.)

Widely distributed in the southern and eastern limestone Alps, extending westwards as far as Lake Como and eastwards to the Karawanken, it grows on rock ledges and on patches of limestone tufa in stony meadows. It forms handsome rosettes usually 4–10 cm in diameter but sometimes up to 15 cm. It spreads by offsets into large mats. The rosette leaves are spreading, strap-shaped or almost linear, and blunt to slightly pointed. They are 2–10 cm long and 0.3–0.9 cm wide, thick and leathery, with hairs at the base, notched and serrated at their margins, dark green in colour, with lime-secreting pits on the upper surface. There are numerous scattered stem leaves, smaller than the rosette leaves. The stiff scape rises to 50–60 cm. The inflorescence is a raceme or panicle, merging into a corymb at the apex. The five petals are elongated, obovate or elliptical with rounded apices. The flowers are milk-white, sometimes with purple spots. Flowering time is May–June.

This species grows vigorously and soon covers a considerable area. It is highly decorative even when out of flower. In the autumn it usually assumes a reddish tinge. It will tolerate considerable exposure to sun.

Several types are available.

**S. hostii** var. *altissima* (syn. *S. altissima*). Occurs in Styria and eastern Carniolica. It has larger, upright leaves and scapes over 60 cm high. Conspicuous white outlining of leaf margins. Plants in cultivation are often not genuine. Less vigorous than the type.

**S. hostii** var. *rhaetica* (syn. *S. rhaetica*) from the Judicarian Alps has narrower leaves (0.3–0.5 cm wide and 4–6 cm long), wine-red in colour at the base. About 30 cm tall.

The botanists distinguish two subspecies: *S. hostii* ssp. *hostii* (syn. *S. altissima* Kerner var. *altissima* (Kerner) Eng.) and *S. hostii* ssp. *rhaetica* (Kerner) Br.-Blanq.

In nature it is associated with *Asplenium viride, Carex baldensis, Silene saxifraga, Horminum pyrenaicum* and *Telekia speciosissima*.

## Saxifraga longifolia Lapeyr.

An unmistakable plant with a restricted area of distribution in the Pyrenees on both sides of the frontier and also in the adjacent mountains of eastern Spain. It grows on limestone rocks at altitudes of up to 2400 m. Though more constant than *S. callosa*, there are certain variations in leaf width. Over a number of years it forms a large rosette which finally throws up a magnificent panicle of flowers and dies as the seed ripens.

The rosettes attain a diameter of 15 cm, or occasionally even 20 or 25 cm. The stiff, close-set leaves are remarkably regular in their arrangement. The individual leaves are narrow, more than 10 cm long, untoothed, smooth and lime-encrusted. The non-flowering rosettes are of great beauty, especially when planted in vertical clefts or fissures. This species prefers half-shade, and if possible an easterly aspect. The scape, up to 70 cm tall, is stiff and has glandular hairs. The conical-cylindrical inflorescence consists of numerous white florets – up to 1000 have been counted. The plant is indeed worthy of its nickname 'the King of Saxifrages'.

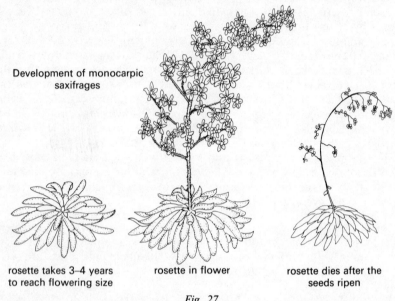

Development of monocarpic saxifrages

rosette takes 3–4 years to reach flowering size    rosette in flower    rosette dies after the seeds ripen

*Fig. 27*

As the rosette does not form daughter rosettes and as it dies after flowering, seed is the only means of propagation. *S. longifolia* crosses readily with other Euaizoonia saxifrages. To ensure the purity of the seed, the inflorescence must be enclosed in a bag of fine gauze so as to exclude insects carrying foreign pollen. The gardener must pollinate the flowers himself with a camelhair brush. The other expedient is to remove the flowers from all other Euaizoonia saxifrages in the garden before they open. Seedlings take 4–6 years to reach flowering size. Any plant which forms more than one rosette must be a hybrid.

### Saxifraga mutata L.

This saxifrage has green rosettes and grows in the Alps, the Carpathians and the Tatra. It is usually found on calcareous soil, in screes, river gravels or moist rock fissures but also occurs on moorland soils. It does not normally reach such high altitudes as other encrusted saxifrages.

In appearance it is unmistakable. It has uniform green rosettes without lime encrustation, each having a single short unbranched axis. The plants live for two or three years and die after flowering. Sometimes they produce offsets before flowering, but when this is not the case they must be propagated by seed. The well-proportioned rosettes range from 4 to 13 cm in diameter. The rosette leaves tend to curve upwards and are strap-shaped or spathulate, leathery, 3–7 cm long. Near the apex they are entire and in the middle inconspicuously indented. The numerous, scattered stem leaves are 1–3 cm long. The scape grows to 30–50 cm and has white glandular hairs. The loose panicle forms a narrow pyramid with several flowers on each branch. The 5–8 mm petals are linear-lanceolate, and yellow to orange in colour. Although the plant does not reach any great age, it is of interest to enthusiasts. It flowers in May–June and is best grown in half shade. Its cultivation does not present any great difficulty, but regular seed sowing is necessary if it is to be kept. In nature it is often associated with *Primula auricula*.

## *Saxifraga paniculata* Mill. (syn. *S. aizoon* Jacq.)

In many catalogues and books this is still listed as *S. aizoon*.

This species with its numerous subspecies and varieties is widely distributed throughout the mountain ranges of the northern hemisphere. It is found in northern Spain, the Pyrenees, the Vosges, the hills of the central Rhineland, the Black Forest, the Jura, the mountains of Bohemia and Moravia, in central Poland, in all parts of the Alps, the Apennines and Abruzzi, Corsica, the Carpathians, Yugoslavia, Bulgaria and Greece (except in the south), the Caucasus, Scandinavia, Greenland and north-eastern North America. Its range being so wide, it is not surprising that many different forms have evolved. Unfortunately, the cultivated forms are in a state of confusion and many of them can be identified only by comparing them with plants collected from the wild, a course which is not always feasible. *S. paniculata* is a lime-loving plant, though it sometimes occurs on lime-free soil. Its favourite habitats are rock clefts, ledges, stony pastures and thin grasslands. It often grows in places which are not covered with snow.

It is a perennial plant which forms cushions and small mats consisting of rosettes 0.8–6 cm in diameter. The flower scapes vary enormously in the different forms, being from 2 to 45 cm tall. They branch into panicles from the middle upwards and they sometimes have glandular hairs. The leaves are obovate to spathulate, stiff and leathery, with serrated margins and small white lime pits. The panicle, often merging into a corymb towards its apex, has branches with 1–3 florets, or occasionally up to 5. The five petals, 0.3–0.6 cm long, are obovate or elliptical. The colour varies in different geographical forms. Some are white and others yellowish-white, and they have purple dots of varying intensity.

Although some botanists have attempted to classify the subspecies and varieties, no satisfactory scheme has yet been put forward. In nurseries and botanic gardens one encounters plants which, though bearing identical labels, display obvious differences. Travellers who bring back a few rosettes from the wild should not attempt to pursue the botanical identification beyond the species. In such cases it is better simply to put the locality behind the species name, e.g. *S. paniculata* (Grossglockner).

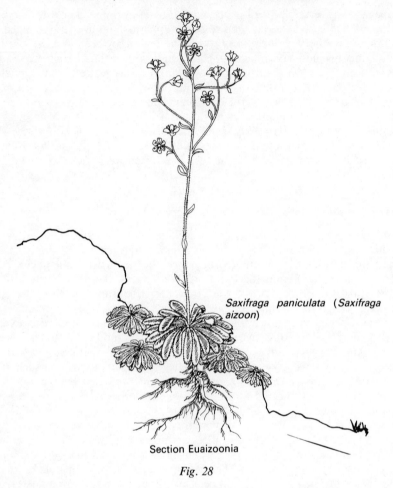

Saxifraga paniculata (*Saxifraga aizoon*)

Section Euaizoonia

*Fig. 28*

It would be pointless to review the vast range of forms from a purely botanical standpoint, especially as the botanists themselves are not in agreement.

The following forms are in cultivation:

**S. paniculata** 'Baldensis' (syn. *S. aizoon* var. *baldensis*). Has very small rosettes. Distinguished from *S. paniculata* var. *minutifolia* by its reddish scapes. Both are probably derived from the Monte Baldo region.

**S. paniculata** 'Balcana' (syn. *S. aizoon* 'Balcana'). A fairly small form with flat rosettes. The robust upright scapes are about 20 cm tall. White flowers with conspicuous red dots. There is a selected form with even heavier red spotting under the name *S. paniculata* 'Multipunctata'.

**S. paniculata** ssp. *brevifolia* (syn. *S. aizoon* ssp. *brevifolia, S. aizoon* var.

minor, S. aizoon 'Minor'). Fairly small rosettes with short leaves (1 cm long, 0.5 cm wide). Forms very beautiful cushions. Sparse white flowers on 15 cm scapes.

**S. paniculata** var. *carinthiaca* (syn. *S. aizoon* var. *carinthiaca, S. carinthiaca*). Occurs chiefly in Carinthia. The loose rosettes have fewer leaves than the other types. They are linear-spathulate (1.5 cm long, 0.4 cm wide), dark green and thickly encrusted with lime. Flowers creamy white, scapes 15–20 cm tall, without glandular hairs.

**S. paniculata** ssp. *cartilaginea* (Willd.) D. A. Webb (syn. *S. cartilaginea* Willd., *S. aizoon* var. *cartilaginea*). A form from the Caucasus which some botanists regard as a true species (*S. cartilaginea* Willd.). Distinguished by the rosette leaves, 2.5 cm long and 0.6 cm wide, narrowing to a point and having indented cartilaginous borders. Loose rosettes, free-flowering, white, about 30 cm tall. A robust grower.

**S. paniculata** ssp. *kolenatiana* (Regel) D. A. Webb (*S. kolenatiana*) Regel (syn. *S. aizoon* ssp. *kolenatiana*). Also from the Caucasus; distinguished from *S. paniculata* ssp. *cartilaginea* by its pink flowers and long narrow leaves. Vigorous, but not widely distributed. Likes more shade than other types. Sometimes listed in catalogues as *S. paniculata* ssp. *cartilaginea* var. *kolenatiana*.

**S. paniculata** 'Labradorica' (syn. *S. aizoon labradorica*). Compact cushions with rosettes 1.2–2.0 cm in diameter. Inflorescence only about 8 cm tall. The silver grey cushions are highly decorative.

**S. paniculata** 'Lutea' (syn. *S. aizoon* 'Lutea', *S. aizoon* f. *lutescens*). A widely distributed garden form with pale yellow flowers. Height 16–28 cm, depending on the site where it is grown. Looks particularly fine beside *S. paniculata* 'Rosea'.

**S. paniculata** var. *major* (syn. *S. aizoon* 'Malbyi'). In the mountains of central Europe, but rare in the Alps. Common in Dalmatia, though only at lower altitudes. An outstandingly vigorous form with tall inflorescences (30–45 cm). The scapes are reddish and the large rosettes (leaves 2–5 cm long) often have a reddish tinge, which deepens in winter. A deeply coloured selection is offered under the name 'Winterfeuer'. *S. paniculata* 'Atropurpurea' (syn. *S. aizoon* 'Atropurpurea') also comes under this heading.

**S. paniculata** var. *minutifolia*. Dwarf rosettes. Rosette leaves spathulate, 0.4–0.6 cm long and 0.12–0.15 cm wide. Dark brown scapes and white flowers, about 10 cm high. Not greatly different from *S. paniculata* 'Baldensis'.

**S. paniculata** 'Orientalis' (syn. *S. aizoon orientalis*). This plant, widely grown in England, comes from the Balkans but is not the same as *S. paniculata* 'Balcana'. Medium-sized rosettes, creamy white flowers with red spots on scapes 20–25 cm high. There are three local forms: 'Dormitor', 'Orjen' and 'Rhodope'.

**S. paniculata** 'Rex' (syn. *S. aizoon* 'Rex'). A selected form with beautiful silver-grey cushions and 25 cm scapes which assume a mahogany-red colour. A vigorous plant with unspotted creamy-white flowers. Discovered by Farrer on the Dossenhorn in 1903.

**S. paniculata** 'Rosea' (syn. *S. aizoon* 'Rosea'). A form from Bulgaria with pale pink flowers. A very beautiful plant with yellowish-green rosettes, varying in hue according to the position in which it is grown. Arends offered a more robust selection under the name *S. aizoon* var. *rosea* f. *splendens*.

**S. paniculata** 'Stabiana' (syn. *S. aizoon stabiana*). An Italian form with white flowers on scapes 15–20 cm tall.

**S. paniculata** var. *sturmiana* (syn. *S. aizoon* var. *sturmiana, S. sturmiana*). A type from the central Alps with small rosettes. Upwards-pointing, wedge-shaped leaves, 1.4 cm long by 0.4 cm wide, serrated, with hairs at the tips. The scape is 5–15 cm tall and brown in colour. Flowers white.

**S. paniculata** 'Venetia' (syn. *S. aizoon venetia*). A form from the south-eastern Alps, more commonly grown in England. This, too, is a miniature edition with flat cushions resembling those of *S. paniculata* var. *minutifolia*. White flowers borne on stems only 5 cm tall.

The following forms of this species are still found in nurseries:

*S. paniculata* 'Lagraveana' (syn. *S. aizoon* 'Lagraveana') from the French Alps near La Grave. Low cushions, white petals with rounded serrations. *S. paniculata* 'Portae' (syn. *S. aizoon* 'Portae') forms cushions made up of small rosettes. *S. paniculata* 'Rosularis' (syn. *S. aizoon* 'Rosularis') has larger leaves. *S. paniculata* 'Correvoniana' forms low cushions with scapes only 10 cm tall. *S. paniculata* 'Hirtella' has slightly hairy leaves and scapes 10 cm tall. *S. paniculata* 'Koprvnik' is much the same.

This list is by no means complete; an English collector describes some 30 different forms, some of which are closely similar. When grown in a place which suits it, *S. paniculata* often produces self-sown seedlings, especially on tufa. If there is sufficient range of types in the garden, this will lead to the emergence of new intermediate forms. *S. paniculata* is probably the best of the encrusted saxifrages and should be grown in every garden. Space can always be found for it and it associates happily with most other plants. In nature *S. paniculata* is often associated with *Sedum album, Draba aizoides, Primula auricula, Globularia cordifolia, Hieracium humile* and alpine grasses.

## Saxifraga valdensis D.C.

Grows in the south-western Alps near the French-Italian border (Savoy and Cottian Alps). It is widely distributed, but not common. Two of its classical localities are Mt Cenis and Mt Viso.

In nature it grows in clefts and fissures in limestone. It looks like a more compact form of *S. cochlearis* 'Minor', with which it is often confused. It can be distinguished by the rosette leaves, which are not so spoon-shaped as in *S. cochlearis* and its forms. The rosettes form hemispheres or firm cushions only 1–2 cm high. The narrow spathulate leaves, 0.4–0.6 cm long, are reflexed and thickly lime-encrusted. The scape is 6–15 cm high, depending on the situation where it grows, and has a reddish tinge. It carries comparatively few white flowers, about 5–10 in number. This species is not entirely easy in culture and grows slowly. It looks well in troughs or pans and will tolerate full sun. The average diameter of the cushions is 9 cm. *S. valdensis* has been assigned to the 'Kabschia' saxifrages, but this is incorrect, as it crosses with the encrusted saxifrages (*S. cochlearis* × *S.valdensis*) but not with any 'Kabschia'.

The next two species, *S. caesia* and *S. squarrosa*, have been quite unjustifiably assigned to the 'Kabschias'. Though they constitute a link between the sections Porophyllum ('Kabschia') and Euaizoonia, they clearly belong to the latter section. This is borne out by the fact that none of the 'Kabschia' or 'Engleria' saxifrages hybridize with either of these species, though they cross readily with other saxifrages.

## *Saxifraga caesia* L.

A widely distributed plant found in the Alps, east and central Pyrenees, and Apennines and in large areas of the Carpathians, in Bosnia, Herzegovina and Montenegro as far as the Albanian border. In Germany it is fairly common in the Bavarian Alps up to about 2400 metres. It is often found in alluvial sand. In the Dolomites it is extremely common, often associated with *S. squarrosa*. Nearly always on limestone or dolomite, it is usually growing in narrow clefts in scree or in patchy grasslands, often in exposed places where it does not enjoy prolonged snow covering. In nature it is associated with *Silene acaulis, Helianthemum alpestre, Gentiana verna, Minuartia verna, Globularia cordifolia, Dryas octopetala, Festuca pumila* and *Carex firma*.

   *S. caesia* forms firm dense cushions. The elongated spathulate blue-green leaflets are recurved outwards from their bases and cover the stems like tiles on a roof. Each leaf has 5–7 light green lime pits. The rosettes are among the smallest in the section. The scapes, 5–12 cm high depending on its situation, have only a few leaves and carry 2–5 white flowers in a short cluster. The species can be distinguished from *S. squarrosa* by the fact that in the latter the leaflets are recurved outwards not from the base but near their ends. Furthermore, in *S. caesia* the upper half of the scape has glandular hairs, in *S. squarrosa* the lower half.

   In connection with its wide distribution range there are two points which deserve attention. The first is that there are intermediate forms closely resembling *S. squarrosa*. In the neighbourhood of Innsbruck the only form is that described by the botanists as *S. caesia* f. *subacaulis*, which has practically no scapes and carries single flowers. The Swiss Alpine Plant Nursery of M. Frei offers a vigorous form under the name *S. caesia* 'Guggerbach'. Another fine and densely encrusted selected natural form is *S. caesia* 'Tremalzo' offered by the Alpine Plant Nursery of Jacques Eschmann. The second point is that, although it is so widely distributed and often occurs in large numbers, *S. caesia* is not an easy garden plant and is very difficult to keep for long. In nature, it is a pioneer plant which grows in exposed places, often bare of snow and unprotected from severe cold and wind. Mild damp winter weather may well be one of the main causes for its failure in the garden. The best results with *S. caesia* have been obtained by planting it in narrow holes bored in tufa, with some limestone chippings in the compost. The roots should be kept tolerably moist. Individual cushions seldom attain a diameter greater than 10 cm.

### Saxifraga squarrosa Sieber.

Closely related to *S. caesia* but smaller. It is also an endemic of the south-eastern limestone Alps, from the Judicarians as far as the Sarntaler Alps and the Karawanken. Widely distributed in the Dolomites, it grows on limestone in thin stony grassland, stony meadows and stabilized screes at altitudes of 1200–2500 m, usually in partial shade. It forms dense hemispherical grey-green cushions, 4–7 cm in diameter, which continue to grow after flowering. The stiff linear obtuse upright leaves are recurved only near their tips, and cover the stem like tiles on a roof. The scape is 5–7 cm high and carries a panicle or corymb of 2–7 flowers. It flowers in April or May and has rounded white petals.

In cultivation it is not easy and flourishes best in tufa. On flat sites it often fails to survive the winter, probably because of excessive wet. In nature it is associated with *Androsace helvetica, Salix serpyllifolia, Anemone baldensis, Draba aizoides, Potentilla nitida, Carex firma, Leontopodium alpina* and *Achillea clavenae*. When planting in crevices take care that the roots have enough space to extend downwards. Well-established cushions may be up to 10 cm in diameter. Botanists distinguish two types, *S. s.* f. *glandulosissima* and *S. s.* f. *glabrata*, based on the gland covering of the scape, but these are of no importance to gardeners.

### Saxifraga × tirolensis

A natural hybrid between *S. caesia* and *S. squarrosa*, found where its parents grow side-by-side. As they are much alike, the hybrid does not diverge widely from them. In cultivation it seems to be somewhat more vigorous.

### Hybrids

Besides the species and their numerous varieties, local forms and selected forms, there are numerous hybrids. Not all of them are necessarily more beautiful or more vigorous than their parent species though there are some treasures among them such as the cultivars 'Southside Seedling' and 'Tumbling Waters' which originated in England. One of the best of the newer hybrids is 'Vreny', raised by Eschmann in Switzerland. The species of this section cross so readily that numerous hybrids have arisen, collectors recognizing more than 50 types.

Hybrids are likely to arise spontaneously in gardens where several encrusted saxifrages are grown. Seedlings do not flourish in ordinary garden soil and there is no danger of their becoming weeds. Selfsown seedlings are most likely to arise on tufa. Spontaneous hybrids of this kind are often beautifully compact plants and even if they are not destined to become world champions they are worth propagating for personal pleasure.

**S. × burnatii** (*S. paniculata* × *S. cochlearis*). A natural hybrid from the Maritime Alps. Intermediate between the parents, though perhaps closer to *S. cochlearis*. White flowers on reddish stems 15–18 cm high. Narrow rosette leaves with attractive lime deposits.

**S. × canis-dalmatica** (*S. paniculata* 'Balcana' × *S. cotyledon*). A vigorous plant with grey-green rosettes, the leaves sharply incurved. Scape 25 cm high, flowers white with dark red spots.

**S. calabrica** 'Tumbling Waters' (*S. callosa* × *S. longifolia*). This cultivar is not widely grown, although it originated in 1913, *S. callosa* (*lingulata*) var. *lantoscana* being the seed parent and *S. longifolia* the pollen parent. The hybrid closely resembles *S. longifolia*, but, unlike the latter, produces daughter rosettes just before the mother rosette dies.

The symmetrical silvery rosettes are decorative even when out of flower. It has numerous white flowers in a loose inflorescence 50–75 cm high. If several are planted close together on a vertical rock face the arching inflorescences truly give the impression of a waterfall, especially as the plant is so free-flowering.

**S. × churchillii** (*S. hostii* × *S. paniculata*). A natural hybrid which has been in cultivation for many years. Resembles *S. paniculata*, but somewhat larger with deeply toothed leaf margins and a taller inflorescence. Also known as *S. × bellunensis*.

**Saxifraga** 'Esther' (*S. paniculata* 'Lutea' × *S. cochlearis*). A hybrid with pale yellowish flowers on 15 cm scapes.

**S. × farreri** (*S. cochlearis* × *S. callosa*). Another pretty hybrid with reddish stems and white flowers. Blooms in May or June, about 20 cm high.

**S. fritschiana** (*S. × pectinata*; *S. paniculata* × *S. crustata*). A natural hybrid and a reliable garden plant. Neat rosettes with long narrow leaves having dense lime deposits on their margins. Scape 12–18 cm with creamy white flowers.

**S. × gaudinii** (*S. paniculata* × *S. cotyledon* 'Pyramidalis'). Rosette leaves rather like those of *S. cotyledon*. White flowers with red spots, the 15–18 cm high scapes branching from the base upwards. A natural hybrid found in the Pyrenees and central Alps.

**Saxifraga** 'Kathleen Pinsent' (*S. callosa* × *S. paniculata* ssp. *kolenatiana*). A beautiful hybrid with pink flowers. Not as easy to cultivate as other encrusted saxifrages. The intensely silvery rosettes have spathulate leaves and the scape is about 20 cm high.

*Saxifraga* 'Kathrin'. Originated in Sündermann's nursery. Small spheroidal cushions. Scape only 15 cm. Red flowers.

*Saxifraga* 'Lindau'. Another hybrid from Sündermann with hemispherical cushions made up of round rosettes. Scape 30 cm, flowers white. Not to be confused with the 'Kabschia' 'Lindau'.

*Saxifraga longifolia* hybrids. Under this heading comes a large number of hybrids, most of which are of garden or nursery origin, as *S. longifolia* hybridizes readily and it is not easy to obtain pure seed. Any plant which produces more than one rosette must be a hybrid. Some beautiful cultivars raised and named in England are now in circulation in Germany.

'Cecil Davies' came from a cross between *S. longifolia* and *S. paniculata* or *S. cochlearis* – the exact parentage is unknown. It has compact silvery rosettes and reddish scapes with magnificent white flowers. Daughter rosettes are not generously produced.

'Dr Ramsey' (*S. longifolia* × *S. cochlearis*) is one of the best encrusted saxifrage hybrids. It has striking silvery rosettes with wide spoon-shaped leaves and elegant inflorescences some 25 cm high. The flowers are pure white and the rosettes turn reddish in the autumn, a change which can be intensified by growing the plant in poor soil.

A hybrid derived from *S. longifolia* and *S. cochlearis* or *S. callosa*, probably the latter, is offered under the name 'Francis Cade'. It has narrow rosette leaves and scapes 25 cm high.

*S. longifolia* 'Kober Type' is in circulation among saxifrage enthusiasts. The rosettes are rather small and have long narrow silver grey leaves. They are very compact and look well in tufa.

*S.* × *macnabiana* (*S. cotyledon* × *S. callosa*). An easily cultivated plant of elegant appearance with robust, much-branched scapes some 20 cm high. The white flowers have pink spots on the inner surfaces of the petals. The rosette leaves are wide and dark green. The true plant from the crossing made in the Edinburgh Botanic Garden has scapes about 45 cm high, but many of the plants offered under this name are not genuine.

*S.* × *paradoxa* (syn. *S. engleri*; *S. hostii* × *S. crustata*). A natural hybrid from the eastern Alps tending in appearance more towards *S. crustata*, especially in its flowers. The rosette leaves are very narrow and are covered with white lime deposits which give them a silvery look. The inflorescence is 15 cm high and the creamy white flowers make a striking contrast against the dark brown scapes.

*Saxifraga* 'Southside Seedling' (a hybrid of *S. cotyledon*). Among the finest garden plants. Everyone who sees the plants in flower in the rock garden at the Royal Botanic Garden, Edinburgh, is enchanted by them. They have splendid rosettes 12–15 cm in diameter. The generous sprays of blossom are beautifully shaped, and the white flowers have a deep red spot at the base of the petals. The flower stalks are covered with glandular hairs. The pollen parent is unknown. 'Southside Seedling' produces daughter rosettes more freely than *S. cotyledon*. It is very free-flowering and the sprays reach a height of some 40 cm. It grows vigorously, but does not like full sun.

**Saxifraga** 'Vreny'. A novelty from the nursery of Eschmann, Emmen, Switzerland, with beautiful flat rosettes having a diameter of 2.5–3 cm. The leaf margins are deeply toothed and are thickly encrusted with silvery lime deposits. It has white flowers on 15 cm scapes in May–June. Suitable for troughs.

**Saxifraga** 'Whitehill' (*S. paniculata* × *S. cochlearis* (?)). A small hybrid for favoured spots, it has creamy white flowers on stems 12–15 cm high. The blue-green rosette leaves have a faint reddish tinge at the base.

## SECTION POROPHYLLUM
('Kabschia' and 'Engleria' saxifrages)

It is regrettable that this section has had to be renamed, especially as gardeners and botanists alike have used the names 'Kabschia' and 'Engleria' for over 100 years. In this book the sections are given their scientifically correct names, but in the text the old names 'Kabschia' and 'Engleria' are still used (in quotation marks because of their special status).

For good and sufficient reasons the two groups are treated as one, and they certainly do not differ in their cultivation or their uses in the garden. The 'Kabschias' are in the majority, only the following belonging to the 'Englerias': *S. media, S. porophylla, S. grisebachii, S. stribrnyi, S. sempervivum* (syn. *S. thessalica*) and *S. luteoviridis*. Their close relationship is reflected in the multitude of hybrids.

Together with the encrusted and the mossy saxifrages, the 'Kabschias' and 'Englerias' are horticulturally the most important sections of the genus. They are delightful plants, but in cultivation they are somewhat more demanding than other alpines. It would be fair to say that most of them are plants for the grower who has already acquired some experience, but this does not mean that the beginner should be discouraged. It is not so much their management which is so exacting, but the choice of the right place and the right conditions. The requirements of the 'Kabschia' saxifrages must be borne in mind from the outset: shade from midday sun, good drainage but moist soil, and the highest possible atmospheric humidity. Simple as these needs may sound, it is far from easy in practice to meet them all. Nevertheless, the beginner can take heart from the fact that there is a considerable range of robust species and hybrids which will put up with less-than-perfect conditions.

Let us turn to the first requirement, namely protection from direct midday sun. It is simply not feasible to plant them on level ground or on south-facing slopes together with *Sempervivum* and encrusted saxifrages. Older gardening books often recommend plantings on steep, east-facing slopes. This advice is entirely correct. 'Kabschia' saxifrages flourish in crevices and spaces in rock gardens facing east or north-east, yet there are many other suitable situations. A west-facing site will do or even a fully exposed place, provided there are bushes to give it some shade from the hottest midday sun. On the other hand, these saxifrages will also thrive in places where they get very little sun, provided that they get plenty of light. In my garden I have a fair-sized collection in a trough made of U-shaped concrete blocks in an exposed site beneath a wooden pergola. The morning sun shines directly on the plants, but towards midday they are shaded by the wooden beams. The result is a pattern of one-third shade and two-thirds sunlight, constantly shifting as the sun moves across the sky. In mid-afternoon the sun disappears behind a large bush of *Viburnum rhytidophyllum*. Protection from scorching midday sun is even more important for plantings of 'Kabschia' saxifrages in troughs. The higher the atmospheric humidity, be it natural or artificial (automatic misting), the greater their tolerance of sunshine.

Once a suitable place has been chosen, their other needs must be considered. Provided all their wishes have been satisfied, the plants will grow on a flat surface, but this does not show off their full beauty. They look far better in narrow crevices, in holes in tufa or waterworn limestone, or in narrow layers of soil between horizontal stones.

Tufa is perhaps the best for the purpose, though they can be planted in narrow gaps between horizontal layers of sedimentary rock, such as shelly limestone, slate or conglomerate. Nevertheless, 'Kabschia' saxifrages grow particularly well in holes and clefts in tufa. In the first place this guarantees good drainage, and secondly the porous structure of the rock holds an adequate water supply for a long time.

When choosing planting sites the gardener must bear in mind the ultimate size of the species or variety. In this respect they differ enormously. All the 'Englerias' remain small, and among the 'Kabschia' saxifrages there are some which do not exceed 5 or 10 cm in diameter. On the other hand there are some vigorous plants which reach a size of 25 cm, such as *S. × apiculata* 'Gregor Mendel', *S. × elisabethae* 'Carmen', *S. × paulinae* 'Franzii', *S. × eudoxiana* 'Haagii', *S. × elisabethae* 'Ochroleuca', *S. sancta* spp. *pseudosancta* var. *macedonica* and *S. × stormonthii* 'Stella'.

The dimensions given in this book for species and hybrids are inevitably only approximate. It is most unwise to plant fast-growing varieties close to delicate dwarfs. The choicest places should be reserved for the smallest species and hybrids.

The right compost is essential. One English authority of the past recommends that the soil should be mixed with broken limestone, mortar rubble and broken tile to a depth of 20–25 cm. Next comes a layer of peaty soil, and on top an 8 cm layer of loam, leaf mould and stone chippings. The upper layer is enriched by mixing in broken limestone and crushed brick. Though this mixture is highly recommended, there is no need to follow such directions slavishly.

The basic principle is that the soil should be well drained and yet slightly moist. Though this may seem a contradiction, the two requirements are in fact compatible. The drainage material for the lower layer can consist of whatever is most easily available: builders' rubble, broken bricks, gravel, expanded-polystyrene packing material chopped into small pieces or anything of the kind. The pieces can be fairly coarse, and if good drainage is to be ensured, the spaces between them should not be filled up with fine earth. A special intermediate layer is not absolutely necessary, and the compost can be laid directly on top in a layer 10–15 cm thick. The only compost which is totally unsuitable is pure peat. Though it holds water well, it does not allow any drainage.

Possible ingredients for the compost include: soil-less peat compost No. 1, peat manure, loam, Bentonite meal, steam-sterilized garden compost, fine expanded polystyrene chips (Styrofoam), granulated pumice, sintered clay, crushed brick, Lavalite, Vermiculite, sharp sand, fine tufa chips, leaf mould, weed-free garden soil, earth from molehills etc. In my own garden I generally use a basic mixture of one-third steam-sterilized compost, one-third sharp sand and one-third peat with fertilizers, to which I add Bentonite meal, pulverized sintered clay and a small amount of crushed tufa. As nearly all the 'Kabschia' and 'Engleria' saxifrages are lime-lovers, with a few exceptions such as *S. lilacina*, lime should be added, preferably in the form of limestone chippings. Except in the case of vertical plantings, the surface of the soil should be partially covered with fist-sized stone fragments buried to two-thirds of their depth. Tufa has proved of great value for this purpose.

High soil-moisture levels are particularly dangerous during the winter months, when wet is combined with cold. There are some enthusiasts who cover large areas of their gardens with frames or sheets of plastic to keep off excessive winter wet. Covers of this kind must of course be firmly secured if they are to resist wind. Usually it is enough to protect a few individual susceptible plants with a sheet of glass on a wire frame.

The last requirement is high atmospheric humidity. In the wild this is generally provided by the constantly changing weather. High mountains are frequently enveloped in cloud, and melting snow makes a further contribution, often lasting well into the summer. In the garden these conditions are not easily simulated. During prolonged heat it is often helpful to sprinkle the plants with a watering-can every evening and early every morning. They should be given only just enough to moisten the surface. From time to time they will of course need a thorough soaking and this can be done with a hose. A better expedient is a spray which emits a fine mist, and the ideal is a fully automatic air humidifying installation.

It is wrong to suppose that 'Kabschia' saxifrages do not require any feeding or manuring, simply because they do not receive it in the wild. In the high places where these saxifrages grow nutrients are released by the action of the weather on the rocks and reach the plants in small but adequate amounts. A weak solution of balanced fertilizer should be applied at least once or twice in the spring and perhaps again in early autumn. It is best given in the evenings.

All these recommendations should be taken simply as guidelines, and the details may be disregarded where the situation of the garden allows. Dr Jri Josifko, an enthusiastic grower of 'Kabschia' saxifrages, emphasizes the differences between continental and oceanic climates. For example, at altitudes exceeding 500 metres and in Atlantic climates saxifrages will tolerate more sun than in continental climates.

Lastly, a few words on winter protection. Persistent winter rains are much more harmful than low temperatures. If there is any risk of damage from winter sunshine, the plants may be covered with conifer branches. In places not exposed to the sun this is unnecessary. It is essential to remove the covering promptly when the weather changes, so as to prevent the plants from becoming drawn. Mild or moderate frost is entirely harmless, but plantings in rock crevices should be checked in the autumn as there is some danger that frost may lift the plants out of the soil, especially if they are not firmly wedged with small stones.

Even when not in flower, the deep-green, grey-green, blue-green or silver-green cushions are a delight to the gardener. Buds begin to form about Christmas or sometimes even earlier. In favoured sites and mild winters the early varieties may start to flower at the end of January or the beginning of February, and will certainly do so in the alpine house. Under normal conditions most of them flower between the end of March and the end of April, but there are some which continue beyond this, in particular the 'Englerias'. Though their blooms are less striking, their beauty is enhanced by the reddish tinge of the flower stems and sepals, which persist for a considerable time. In spring and early summer the cushions grow and put out numerous new shoots. Then comes a resting period, after which the cycle is resumed by bud-formation.

## European species

### Saxifraga aretioides Lapeyr.

This small species is confined to the Pyrenees where it grows up to 2300 metres on limestone rocks, stabilized screes and starved, patchy grassland. The cushions are very small, flat and often uneven. The rosettes are closely packed, and the leaflets 0.5–0.7 cm long and 0.15–0.2 cm wide. The scapes, 3–6 cm high, carry 3–5 small bright yellow flowers.

Its similarity to *S. ferdinandi-coburgii* has often led to confusion in gardens and it is not easy to obtain the true *S. aretioides.* Furthermore, it has interbred with *S. media*, which occurs in the same region of the Pyrenees.

*S. aretioides* is often difficult to grow, although it tolerates considerably more sun than other species. The flowers are small and not particularly showy. It is of some importance as the parent of various fine hybrids, to which it has transmitted its brilliant yellow flower colour. Older cushions often become bald in the middle; the only remedy is to divide them and replant in fresh soil.

### Saxifraga burserana L.

Named after the physician and botanist Joachim Burser (1585–1649), who discovered it in the Radstätter Tauern, it is often spelt *S. burseriana*. It is endemic to the eastern Alps, where it occurs in two separate areas, one in the north-eastern and one in the south-eastern limestone Alps; common in the Dolomites, the Tridentine mountains, the Veronese limestone Alps and the Julian Alps; also found east of the Traun in the Kaisergebirge and Karawanken, and in the Carniolican Alps; in the Bavarian Alps only to the east of the River Inn. Growing as it does in widely separated localities, it has produced local forms which differ especially in flower size. This characteristic is also influenced by the conditions in which the plant grows, in particular soil moisture. In nature it is always found in lime-rich soils or dolomite, usually on rock ledges, in fissures or on rocky pastures, within the montane and alpine zones, generally in shady spots. It is sometimes encountered on river gravels or alluvial soils, having been carried there by the waters from the melting snows.

S. *burserana* forms hard hemispherical cushions grey-green in colour and has stiff narrow spiny leaves arranged in an imbricate pattern, with 5–7 lime-secreting pits on the upper surface near the margin. Each of the reddish-brown scapes carries one flower, or very occasionally two. The flower size varies considerably, and the five obovate petals are 0.5–1.5 cm long. The flowers are white with reddish veins. Valued for its early flowering, in gardens it prefers a somewhat shady position and looks best in crevices between stones of dark colour. Mature cushions may be up to 15 cm in diameter. Depending on origin and form, the scapes are 3–8 cm high. Suitable neighbours include *Thlaspi stylosum*, yellow species of *Draba*, *Erica carnea*, *Hutchinsia alpina* and related saxifrage species and hybrids. The following subspecies, local varieties and selected forms are in cultivation:

**S. burserana** var. *burserana* (*S. burserana* 'Minor', *S. burserana* var. *minor*). This high-altitude plant has considerably smaller rosettes and smaller flowers on 2.5 cm scapes. It is usually regarded as the typical *S. burserana*. In his book *Saxifrages*, Winton Harding writes that he found the type species near Tarvisio in Italy. It is closer to *S. burserana* var. *burserana* than to *S. burserana* var. *tridentina*. There seemed to be slight morphological differences.

**S. burserana** var. *tridentata* (syn. *S. burserana* var. *tridentina*) is a variety which occurs in the mountains surrounding the town of Trento. It appears to be identical with *S. burserana* var. *major* (syn. *S. burserana* 'Major' E. H. Jenkins), a form commonly seen in gardens and nurseries, and the latter is indistinguishable from *S. burserana* 'Magna'. It is an attractive plant, often flowering in the garden in February and certainly in March–April. It has one or two white flowers on salmon pink scapes 8 cm high.

**S. burserana** var. *major*. See *S. burserana* var. *tridentata*.

**S. burserana** 'Seissera' (also listed in catalogues as *S.b.* 'Seisserach') is a recent introduction collected near the Seiseralm in the Dolomites, forming beautiful rounded cushions with fine needle-shaped leaves, and white flowers on red scapes 5–6 cm high.

**S. burserana** 'Brookside' probably has larger flowers than any other white 'Kabschia'. Red scapes, 5–8 cm high, with one or occasionally two flowers. In favourable conditions they can reach 2.5 cm in diameter. Mature cushions up to 15 cm across.

***S. burserana*** 'Crenata' (*S.b. gloriana*). Scapes 5–6 cm high seldom carrying more than one flower. Small white slightly notched petals. Early-flowering. The cushions particularly compact.

***S. burserana*** 'Gloria'. Another selected form with large flowers, similar to *S.b.* 'Brookside'. 'Gloria' is distinguished by its blackish brown scapes, 10–12 cm high, and its late flowering season.

***S. burserana*** 'Cordata', 'Crenulata', 'Grandiflora', 'Ornata' are further forms not greatly different from those listed above.

## *Saxifraga diapensioides* Bell.

A very small western alpine species extending from the Pennines (Walliser) to the Maritime Alps, chiefly on the central mountain ranges, it is usually on limestone rocks or stabilized scree at altitudes of 1800–2300 metres, though in the Maritime Alps it descends to lower levels. It forms hard compact cushions made up of small tight rosettes. The club-shaped stems are 0.5–1.0 cm in diameter and grow in length after flowering. The scapes vary in height from 2–8 cm depending on the situation in which the plant is growing. The leaves are often coated with lime. The scapes are almost entirely covered with glandular hairs. The inflorescence is a short cluster or corymb usually containing 3–6 flowers, but sometimes 2–9. The five white or yellowish-white

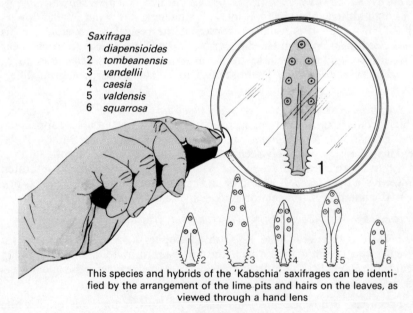

Saxifraga
1  diapensioides
2  tombeanensis
3  vandellii
4  caesia
5  valdensis
6  squarrosa

This species and hybrids of the 'Kabschia' saxifrages can be identified by the arrangement of the lime pits and hairs on the leaves, as
viewed through a hand lens

*Fig. 29*

petals are narrowly obovate and 0.6–0.8 cm long. It usually flowers in April. In the garden it grows very slowly and is usually shy-flowering. In general it is difficult in cultivation and susceptible to any form of stagnant moisture. In England good results and more generous flowering have been obtained by growing it in double pots, watering during the winter being confined to the material in the outer pot.

## Saxifraga ferdinandi-coburgi Kell. et Sünd.

This species, named after King Ferdinand of Bulgaria, grows in its typical form on limestone rocks and scree in the Pirin mountains. It forms firm blue-green cushions consisting of small close-set rosettes with very short pointed leaves. The branching scapes, about 5 cm high, carry numerous flowers, usually 7–12, occasionally more. The colour is bright golden-yellow and the buds are reddish.

Besides the type, there is *S. ferdinandi-coburgii* var. *pravislavii* (otherwise var. *radoslavovii*). It comes from Ali Botusch in Macedonia and is even finer than the type. It grows more luxuriantly, flowers more willingly and abundantly and has larger blooms of deeper yellow. The scapes and sepals are reddish brown. Flowering time is March–April. The grey-green cushions are of great beauty even out of flower. *S. ferdinandi-coburgii* var. *rhodopea* (syn. *S. rhodopea*) is another beautiful and easily grown plant, having somewhat darker leaves. It is of importance as a parent of numerous hybrids.

## Saxifraga grisebachii Deg. and Dörfl. (syn. *S. porophylla* var. *montenegrina* (Hal. and Bald., Eng. and Irmsch.)

Found in Albania and the adjacent parts of Greece and Yugoslavia, and also in southern Bulgaria, this is one of the finest rock garden plants. The rosettes grow in loose clumps without forming mats and are flat and silvery with upward-pointing leaves. In diameter they are 3.5–5 cm, or occasionally even 7–8 cm. The rosette leaves are spathulate and grey-green. In March they throw up scapes up to 15 cm high, covered with silky hairs and glands. The recurved stem leaves are reddish with green tips. The inflorescence is a nodding cluster, reddish purple in colour.

All forms of *S. grisebachii* like plenty of humus and limestone chips in the compost. They have a long flowering season (3–4 weeks).

There is also the selected form *S. grisebachii* 'Wisley' which is more vigorous and even brighter in colour. It flowers in March–April and is said to have come from the mountain of Tsukala in Albania.

*S. grisebachii* 'Feuerkopf' has narrower and more pointed rosette leaves than the type. The inflorescence is narrower and brighter carmine red in colour, and up to 17 cm in height.

*S. grisebachii* ssp. *montenegrina* has considerably smaller but no less beautiful rosettes. The inflorescence is darker reddish purple and only 8 cm high.

### Saxifraga × luteopurpurea Lap.

This natural hybrid from the Pyrenees (*S. media × aretioides*) is somewhat closer to *S. aretioides*. It is highly variable, 11 forms having been named by Sündermann and other authors. Only one of these is at all common in cultivation:

*Saxifraga × luteopurpurea* n.m. 'Aurantiaca' (syn. *S. benthamii* 'Aurantiaca', *S. aurantiaca*). Dwarf grey cushions. Several orange yellow flowers on 6 cm scapes in April.

*S. luteopurpurea* 'Erubescens' is occasionally seen. Grey-green cushions, pinkish purple buds and pale yellow flowers. Larger and more vigorous than the other form and flowers later.

### Saxifraga luteoviridis Schott et Kotschy (syn. *S. corymbosa* Boiss. non Luce)

From the Carpathians and Bulgarian mountains and also from Turkey, this is a small plant which grows well though comparatively slowly, with large silvery flat rosettes made up of spathulate leaves, scapes 7–8 cm (occasionally up to 10 cm) high, inflorescence corymbose or paniculate, normally with 4–5 greenish-yellow flowers, occasionally up to 15. Not a spectacular plant, but recommended for enthusiasts, it is somewhat susceptible to winter wet. In summer it likes somewhat more shade than other 'Englerias'.

### Saxifraga marginata Sternb.

A southern European plant with a wide distribution in the Apennines, Abruzzi, Albania, Greece and the Carpathians, always on limestone. There are many varieties and forms. Flat bluish-green cushions are made up of lime-encrusted rosettes. In the wild cushions exceeding 50 cm in diameter have been found. Dense corymbs of pure white flowers occur on 8 cm scapes. All the forms of *S. marginata* prefer somewhat more sun than most of the species of this section. They must have plenty of limestone chippings in the compost and the roots must be given enough room to spread out. The following forms and varieties are of horticultural importance:

*S. marginata* var. *coriophylla* (Griseb.) Engl. f. *coriophylla* (syn. *S.m.* var. *coriophylla* f. *eucoriophylla*). From Montenegro. Dense cushions. Small rosette leaves (0.4–0.6 cm long) with scaly deposits of lime. Flowers white, sometimes with a tinge of pink, on 2–5 cm scapes.

*S. marginata* var. *marginata* (syn. *S. marginata* var. *eumarginata* Engl. et Irmsch., *S. boryi* Boiss. et Heldr.). Looser in growth and less free-flowering than the above form. The cushions grow vigorously. Leaves 0.5–1.2 cm long and 0.3–0.5 cm wide.

*S. marginata* 'Purpur' (syn. *S. rocheliana purpurea*). White flowers and reddish buds.

*S. marginata* var. *karadzicensis* (syn. *S.m. karadzicensis*). Low flat cushions (about 3 cm high). Probably the smallest type. The small rosettes thickly lime-encrusted.

*S. marginata* var. *rocheliana* (Sternb.) Engl. et Irmsch. The type from Italy. Luxuriant grey-green hard cushions. Flat rosettes with fairly long leaves. Distinguished from var. *coriophylla* by its rosettes, which are twice as large. Leaves blunt spathulate with densely encrusted margins. White flowers in dense corymbs on 10 cm scapes in May.

*S. marginata* 'Major' (syn. *S. rocheliana major*). Tall scapes (about 10 cm). Luxuriant olive-green cushions. Leaf margins outlined by lime encrustation.

*S. marginata* 'Minor' (syn. *S. coriophylla* 'Minor'). Small flat cushions, flowers considerably earlier than the other forms. Beautifully encrusted.

*S. marginata* 'Intermedia' (syn. *rocheliana* var. *intermedia*). Origin unknown. Small cushions, white flowers.

## Saxifraga media Gouan (syn. *S. calcyflora* Lap.)

An 'Engleria' from the Pyrenees, it grows on limestone rocks at altitudes up to 2500 metres, easily distinguished from related species by the rosette leaves which do not lie flat, but project at an angle of 45°, and then curve downwards near their tips. The leaves are spathulate, leathery, silver-grey and 0.7–2.0 cm long, rosettes 1.5–3.5 cm in diameter. The inflorescence is covered with glandular hairs, unbranched and more compact than in the other species. Sepals are dull red, flowers pale pink; scapes 7–8 cm high; cushions up to 15 cm in diameter. It hybridizes in the wild with *S. aretioides*.

## Saxifraga porophylla Bertol.

This is not identical with the plant sometimes sold under the name *S. thessalica* or *S. porophylla* var. *thessalica*. *S. porophylla* var. *montenegrina* is truly *S. grisebachii*, and *S. porophylla* var. *sibthorpiana* is *S. sempervivum*. *S. porophylla*'s home is in the mountains of Italy (Apennines, Abruzzi). It grows on rocks and limestone scree and is widely distributed, especially in the Abruzzi, where it lives in association with *S. callosa, S. paniculata* and *S. moschata*, distinguished from *S. media* by the shorter leaves and scapes. Close-set flat rosettes have spathulate leaves tapering to a point. The unbranched, reddish purple inflorescences, 7–8 cm high, droop, especially when young. Stems are slightly hairy.

## Saxifraga sancta Griseb.

A native of Greece, growing on marble on Mount Athos and also in western Asia Minor, often cited in the literature as *S. juniperifolia* ssp. *sancta*. I cannot accept the views put forward in *Flora Europaea* or in 'Zander', and prefer the classification advanced by Drs Horny, Sojak and Webr, who regard the Caucasian *S. juniperifolia* as a separate species. The subclassification is as follows:

*S. sancta* Griseb.
    ssp. *sancta*
    ssp. *pseudosancta* (Janka) Kuzm.
        var. *pseudosancta*
        var. *macedonica* (Deg.) Kuzm.

It forms firm flat bright green cushions which look like a moss. The small leaves are very short and pointed. Under ordinary garden conditions it does not flower freely but this can be overcome by starving it. The 5 cm scapes carry 3–5 deep yellow flowers, stiffly erect in a dense umbel. The stamens project far beyond the small yellow petals, and the stigmas have reddish tips. Flowering time is March–April. In the rock garden the plant needs plenty of lime chippings in the compost. Old plants tend to turn yellow or brown in the middle, but if not too far gone this can be dealt with by sprinkling compost mixed with fine chippings between the shoots. Otherwise it is better to divide the plant immediately after flowering, replant the pieces and shade them carefully. Division is also feasible in early spring or early autumn. The following subspecies and varieties are offered in the trade: *S.s.* ssp. *sancta* with large tight prickly cushions. *S.s.* var. *macedonica* (syn. *S. juniperifolia* var. *madeconica*) also has firm prickly cushions but the scapes are somewhat higher (7–8 cm) and the flowering time somewhat later. The petals are wider and more decorative. On the whole, *S. sancta* var. *macedonica* is the better plant.

## Saxifraga scardica Griseb. (syn. *S. sartorii* Heldr.)

Widely distributed in the mountains of Greece, Albania and Yugoslavia, it has relatively large, lime-encrusted rosettes. Leaves are narrowly obovate, tapering to a point. It forms beautiful firm grey-green cushions up to 15 cm in diameter. The scapes are hairy and 8–12 cm high (in cultivation). The inflorescence is a corymbose panicle carrying 2–6 or occasionally up to 11 white flowers, sometimes with a pink tinge. Flowering time is March–April. The species is susceptible to excessive winter wet, will not tolerate too much sun and is not easy to cultivate in the open. There are several varieties.

    *S. scardica* var. *scardica* (syn. *S. scardica vera, S. scardica* var. *euscardica*) is probably the type species. Much better known is *S. scardica* var. *obtusa* (syn. *S. scardica* var. *dalmatica*) which differs considerably from the type. It has narrow, bright green non-spiny leaves and 7 cm scapes carrying 3–6 white flowers. There is some doubt whether it is a hybrid, but probably it is in fact a variety. In cultivation it is much easier than the type and tolerates much more sun. Unfortunately the petals lack the substance and solidity of other 'Kabschias' and often look untidy. It flowers earlier than the type.

    *S. scardica* f. *erythrantha* Hal. has pink-tinged flowers and comes from Mount Olympus in Thessaly. It is also found on Mount Kyllene in the Peloponese. It is also known as *S. scardica* var. *rosea*. The pink tinge is more

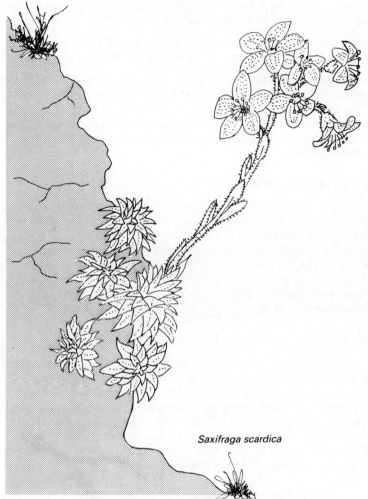

*Saxifraga scardica*

Section Porophyllum ('Kabschia' and 'Engleria')

*Fig. 30*

pronounced in the wild than in cultivation. *S. scardica* 'Vera' is a white form of unknown origin.

### *Saxifraga sempervivum* K. Koch (syn. *S. porophylla* Bertol. var. *sibthorpiana* (Griseb.) Engl. and Irmsch., *S. frederici-augustii* Bias.)

A variable species from the Balkans where it grows on limestone rocks and in scree. Several varieties and forms are available in the trade:

*S. sempervivum* f. *alpina* (syn. *S. sempervivum sibthorpiana*) has particularly small narrow, pointed lime-encrusted leaves. Slender inflorescence only 3–5 cm high. Introduced by Sündermann in 1910.

*S. sempervivum* f. *sempervivum* (Pirin mountains, Bulgaria) is the darkest of all red saxifrages ('dark purple'). Flowers in narrow nodding umbels.

*S. sempervivum* f. *stenophylla* (syn. *S. thessalica, S. porophylla* var. *thessalica*). Introduced by Sündermann in 1891. The rosettes have close-set leaves tapering sharply to a point. Flower clusters blood red. A selected form grown in England under the name *S. sempervivum* 'Waterperry' has a mauve tinge. Sündermann also distributed a small form under the name *S. sempervivum* f. *stenophylla* 'Minor'.

### Saxifraga spruneri Boiss.

Found on a few mountains in Albania, northern Greece and southern Bulgaria, but not widespread, it is the only member of the section which has distinctly hairy foliage, a feature which points to its preference for hot dry places in the wild. For the same reason it is difficult in cultivation and is best grown in an alpine house. The small rounded cushions somewhat resemble those of *Androsace helvetica*. Leaves spathulate, with grey hairs. Flowers yellowish-white on thin 5 cm scapes. In the wild the cushions grow up to 20 cm in diameter. A plant for the enthusiast.

### Saxifraga stribrnyi (Velen.) Podp.

A native of northern Greece and Bulgaria (Rhodope mountains), it was discovered by Stribrny on rocks near Bachovo in Bulgaria in 1893. The rosettes are closely similar to those of *S. grisebachii*, but the plant is easily distinguished by its branching inflorescence and by the rosette leaves, which are more rounded at the apex. The scape is thickly covered with glandular hairs and is carmine pink above and whitish below. Its lateral branches and the flowers themselves are also hairy. Petals and sepals are of equal size, both carmine pink. Flowering time is March–April, the inflorescence up to 15 cm high.

There are two selected forms. *S. stribrnyi* 'Tristan' has firm lime-encrusted grey-white rosettes 1.5–2.5 cm in diameter and carmine pink flowers. *S. stribrnyi* 'Isolde' (syn. *S. montenegrina alba*) has almost white flowers. Also offered in the trade is *S. stribrnyi* 'Zollikoferi' with pink flowers. Older plants have rosettes up to 7–9 cm in diameter.

### Saxifraga tombeanensis Boiss. ex Engl. (syn. *S. diapensioides* Neilr.; not to be confused with *S. diapensoides* Bell.)

An endemic from the Judicarian Alps where it grows on limestone rocks from 1200 to 2300 metres. In favourable situations the cushions are up to 30 cm in diameter, in particular on Monte Baldo to the east of Lake Garda. It forms hard compact hummocks made up of small green rosettes with short leaves tightly pressed inwards. The 5 cm scapes carry two or three compara-

tively large white flowers. It flowers late in the season, about a fortnight after
*S. burserana*. In appearance it resembles *S. diapensioides* but has shorter
lanceolate leaves. Unfortunately it is shy-flowering though it does better
when planted in tufa. The cushions grow vigorously and it is easily
propagated by cuttings.

### *Saxifraga vandellii* Sternb.

An endemic of the southern Alps from Corni di Canzo eastwards over the
Bergamasque Alps to the Judicarians and the Ortler group, it grows on
limestone rocks at altitudes of 1000–2600 metres. It is not found in Germany,
Austria or Switzerland. It forms firm hemispherical green cushions with
prickly leaves. The stems with their imbricate leaf covering are 1–1.5 cm in
diameter and grow in length after flowering. The upright scapes are roughly
3–7 cm high, depending on the situation in which the plant is growing, and
are covered with glandular hairs along their entire length. The inflorescence
is a corymb with 3–5 flowers, or occasionally up to 7. The five white petals are
0.7–0.9 cm long, marked with fine reddish veins. It flowers freely in cultivation and grows well in the garden, especially in rock crevices or holes in tufa
though it may be somewhat difficult to establish. In nature it is associated
with *Saxifraga caesia*, *Primula auricula*, *Campanula raineri* and *Physoplexis
comosa* (syn. *Phyteuma comosum*). Mature cushions are about 8 cm in
diameter.

## Species from the Near East

### *Saxifraga caucasica* Somm. et Lev.

This species from the Caucasus is subdivided into *S.c.* var. *caucasica* (syn.
*S.c.* var. *levieri* Engl. and Irmsch.) and *S.c.* var. *desoulavyi* (Oett) Engl. and
Irmsch. (syn. *S. desoulavyi*). Only the latter is in cultivation.

A pretty plant with small deep yellow flowers on 3–5 cm scapes and neat
cushions of dark green rosettes, it is closely related to *S. juniperifolia* but
flowers somewhat earlier (in March). The leaves are narrower and the
rosettes smaller than those of *S. sancta* ssp. *sancta*. It likes good drainage, but
needs adequate moisture during the growing period.

### *Saxifrage juniperifolia* Adams

*S. juniperifolia* var. *juniperifolia* is widely distributed in the Caucasus and in
Bulgaria, a vigorous plant which forms large dark green prickly mats which
give the impression of being a moss. The hairy scapes are 5 cm high with
clusters of 4–8 flowers with small petals. Flowering time is March–April, but
in cultivation the flowers are sparse. Grown in a half-shaded spot with
somewhat more moisture than usual, it will develop into large cushions.
Despite its vigour, the plant does not like being divided and is better
propagated by summer cuttings. It is often confused with the closely similar
*S. sancta* ssp. *sancta*. There are several varieties and forms, but they are of no
horticultural importance.

## Saxifraga kotschyi Boiss.

A Turkish species from the Pontus district and the Taurus range, not all the plants offered under this name are the genuine article. *S. kotschyi* is not outstandingly attractive and is of interest mainly to the collector, a very small plant forming dense cushions of squat rosettes with short, grey-green, spathulate, lime-encrusted leaves. Scapes are 2.5–5 cm, with glandular hairs on stem leaves. The inflorescence is a short loose umbel with 7–13 small yellowish-green to yellow flowers. The flowers are held upright and the anthers project. Flowering time is March.

Much more important than the species is its hybrid with *S. marginata* var. *rocheliana*: this is known as *S. × pseudokotschyi* and produces light yellow flowers in large numbers.

## Saxifraga laevis Marsch. Bieb.

A peculiar species from the Caucasus, this is apparently related to *S. caucasica* var. *desoulavyi*, but its exact position is uncertain. It has small, somewhat lax cushions 10 cm in diameter, and scapes 3–5 cm carrying several pale yellow flowers late in the season. The form in circulation is *S. laevis* var. *pseudolaevis* (syn. *laeviformis, S. laevis* var. *eulaevis*). It requires lime-free soil and is rather difficult.

There are several other species which have not yet found a place in the garden.

  *S. artvinensis* Matthews (Turkey): 3–6 white flowers on each scape.
  *S. carinata* Oett. (Caucasus): single golden-yellow flowers.
  *S. colchica* Albow. (Caucasus): another yellow-flowered species.
  *S. columnaris* Schmalh. (Caucasus): single white flowers.
  *S. dinnikii* Schmalh. (Caucasus): single yellow flowers.
  *S. iranica* Bornm. (Iran): 3–4 white or pale violet flowers on each scape.
  *S. koelzii* Schöng.-Temessy (Iran): bright yellow single flowers.
  *S. scleropoda* Somm. et Lev. (Caucasus): multiple sulphur-yellow flowers.
  *S. subverticillata* Boiss (Caucasus): yellow flowers.
  *S. wendelboi* Schöng.-Temessy (Iran): 3–4 white flowers on each scape. Now available in the trade.

## Species from the Himalayas, Central Asia and China

## Saxifraga hypostoma H. Sm.

From the mountains of Central Nepal, it grows on stony slopes and rocks at altitudes of 4500–5500 metres, forming dense cushions or mats, bright green or with silvery hues due to lime deposits. The rosettes are 0.8 cm in diameter, the leaves fleshy, narrow ovate to broad elliptical, with rounded ends. The upper half of the leaf margin is whitish and transparent and has small hairs which give the entire rosette a bristly appearance. The relatively large single flowers are 1.0 cm in diameter. They sit in the middle of the rosette and are totally sessile.

This species produces little or no seed in cultivation, but can be propagated by rosette cuttings rooted in sharp sand. The cushions reach a diameter of 8–10 cm and flourish in the usual compost employed for 'Kabschia' saxifrages. Given good drainage and moderate moisture, it will even grow in sunny places.

## *Saxifraga lilacina* Duthie

This species from the western Himalayas grows on acid sandy peaty soils, forming flat mats of tiny grey-green rosettes. The flowers often sit directly on the mats, but sometimes they have scapes up to 2.5 cm high, each scape carrying one relatively large lilac pink flower with a deeper colour in the centre. Flowering time is March–April, but the species is very shy flowering. It will grow in a shady position, but the soil must be acid and must contain grit to provide drainage. Adequate moisture is essential and it is advisable to add some sphagnum to the compost. Though of little importance as a garden plant, it is the parent of several beautiful garden hybrids, e.g. *S.* × *irvingii* 'Jenkinsae', *S.* × *anglica* 'Myra' and *S.* × *anglica* 'Cranbourne', most of which have been raised in England. There is a selected colour form, *S. lilacina* var. *purpurea*, which originated from Sündermann. Older plants may be up to 10–12 cm in diameter.

## *Saxifraga stolitzkae* Duthie

From the Kali Gandaki region in Nepal, *S. stolitzkae* forms handsome cushions which reach a diameter of up to 15 cm in 5 years. It will grow on the compost generally used for 'Kabschia' saxifrages. Winter protection is not necessary. Rosettes are about 1.5 cm in diameter. New rosettes develop from the axils of the basal leaves of old rosettes. Leaves are fleshy, spathulate to narrow ovate, 0.6 cm long and 0.25 cm wide, widest near the apex. The blunt point is curved outwards. The upper half is dark green with a pale stripe running towards the centre, and the lower half is pale green. The inflorescence is 1.5–2 cm high, pedicels up to 1 cm long. Each pedicel carries 4–6 pure white, faintly scented flowers. The green parts of the inflorescence have short glandular hairs. The plant is usually propagated by cuttings, which grow rapidly, and is closely related to *S. andersonii* Engler, which is distinguished by having larger leaves bearing more numerous lime pits.

## *Further species*

Besides the three species just mentioned there are more than 50 others, chiefly from the mountains of western China. Very few of them are in cultivation and it is uncertain whether they would be hardy. There are difficulties in accommodating them in the classification of Engler and Irmscher.

*S. andersonii* from Nepal is grown by a few enthusiasts in Great Britain. It forms cushions of lime-encrusted rosettes up to 1.5 cm in diameter. The scapes carry 5–7 white or pale pink flowers, but it does not flower freely in cultivation.

*S. lowndesii* with mauve pink flowers is also in cultivation. In his book *Saxifrages*, Winton Harding lists: *S. afghanica, S. chianophila, S. georgei, S. kumuanensis, S. likiangensis, S. meeboldtii, S. pulchra, S. pulvinaria* (syn. *S. imbricata*) and *S. rupicola*. It remains to be seen whether they have a future in cultivation or in the raising of new hybrids.

Drs Horny, Sojak and Webr list 58 central Asiatic species but there is little likelihood of their becoming available at present.


## 'Kabschia' and 'Engleria' hybrids

No attempt has been made to subdivide these hybrids according to their ancestry; they are simply listed in alphabetical order. Where possible the new names have been given, these being based on the nomenclature of Drs Horny, Sojak and Webr, and they are listed in the order published in the Czech periodical *Salnicky* No. 1, 1974. This is a useful method of bringing some order into the amazing multitude of hybrids which have arisen from the relatively small number of species.

These three Czech botanists have divided all hybrids of known parentage into groups each containing hybrids from the same pair of parents. This may mean species × species or species × filial generation. The cross first filial generation × first filial generation is conceivable but has not yet emerged. Without wishing to belittle the labours of these botanists, it must be said that if hybridization continues and the ancestry of hybrids comes to involve more and more species, the system will break down. The only practicable course will then be to accept such hybrids without attempting to unravel their ancestry. There are already some hybrids which cannot be fitted into this classification and are simply listed under their varietal names.

The names of the hybrids are as follows:

> *S. × anglica = S. lilacina × S. × luteopurpurea*
> *S. × anormalis = S. laevis × S. stribrnyi*
> *S. × apiculata = S. marginata × S. sancta*
> *S. × arco-valleyi = S. lilacina × S. marginata*
> *S. × bertolonii = S. sempervivum × S. stribrnyi*
> *S. × biasolettii = S. grisebachii × S. sempervivum*
> *S. × bilekii = S. ferdinandi-coburgii × S. tombeanensis*
> *S. × boeckeleri = S. ferdinandi-coburgii × S. stribrnyi*
> *S. × borisii = S. ferdinandi-coburgii × S. marginata*
> *S. × boydii = S. aretioides × S. burserana*
> *S. × bursiculata = S. × apiculata × S. burserana*
> *S. × clarkei = S. media × S. vandellii*
> *S. × doerfleri = S. grisebachii × S. stribrnyi*
> *S. × edithae = S. marginata × S. stribrnyi*
> *S. × elisabethae = S. burserana × S. sancta*

*S.* × *eudoxiana* = *S. ferdinandi-coburgii* × *S. sancta*
*S.* × *finnisae* = *S. aizoides* × *S. anglica*
*S.* × *fleischeri* = *S. grisebachii* × *S. luteoviridis*
*S.* × *fontanae* = *S. diapensioides* × *S. ferdinandi-coburgii*
*S.* × *geuderi* = *S.* × *boydii* × *S. ferdinandi-coburgii*
*S.* × *gloriana* = *S. lilacina* × *S. scardica*
*S.* × *grata* = *S. aretioides* × *S. ferdinandi-coburgii*
*S.* × *gusmusii* = *S. luteoviridis* × *S. sempervivum*
*S.* × *hardingii* = *S. burserana* × *?S.* × *luteopurpurea*
*S.* × *heinrichii* = *S. aretioides* × *S. stribrnyi*
*S.* × *hoerhammeri* = *S. grisebachii* × *S. marginata*
*S.* × *hofmannii* = *S. burserana* × *S. sempervivum*
*S.* × *hornibrookii* = *S. lilacina* × *S. tombeanensis*
*S.* × *ingwersenii* = *S. lilacina* × *S. tombeanensis*
*S.* × *irvingii* = *S. burserana* × *S. lilacina*
*S.* × *kayei* = *S.* × *boydii* × *S.* × *eudoxiana*
*S.* × *kellereri* = *S. burserana* × *S. stribrnyi*
*S.* × *kewensis* = *S. burserana* × *S. porophylla*
*S.* × *leyboldii* = *S. marginata* × *S. vandellii*
*S.* × *malbyana* = *?S. aretioides* × *S. diapensioides*
*S.* × *mariae-theresiae* = *S. burserana* × *S. grisebachii*
*S.* × *megaseaeflora* = *S. burserana* × *?S.* × *anglica*
*S.* × *paulinae* = *S. burserana* × *S. ferdinandi-coburgii*
*S.* × *petraschii* = *S. burserana* × *S. tombeanensis*
*S.* × *pragensis* = *S.* × *edithae* × *?S. ferdinandi-coburgii*
*S.* × *prossenii* = *S. sancta* × *S. stribrnyi*
*S.* × *pseudokotschyi* = *S. kotschyi* × *S. marginata*
*S.* × *rosinae* = *S. diapensioides* × *S. marginata*
*S.* × *salmonica* = *S. burserana* × *S. marginata*
*S.* × *schottii* = *S. luteoviridis* × *S. stribrnyi*
*S.* × *semmleri* = *S.* × *eudoxiana* × *S. laevis*
*S.* × *smithii* = *S. marginata* × *S. tombeanensis*
*S.* × *steinii* = *S. aretioides* × *S. tombeanensis*
*S.* × *stormonthii* = *?S. caucasica* × *S. sancta*
*S.* × *stuartii* = *S.* × *luteopurpurea* × *S. stribrnyi*
*S.* × *thomasiana* = *S. stribrnyii* × *S. tombeanensis*
*S.* × *urumovii* = *S. ferdinandi-coburgii* × *S. luteoviridis*
*S.* × *wehrhahnii* = *S. marginata* × *S. scardica*

**S.** × **anglica** 'Beatrix Stanley' (*S.* 'Lady Beatrix Stanley'). The cushions have small dark green lime encrusted rosettes. The flowers appear in March–April, 1–2 in number on 3–5 cm scapes, and are a rich red in colour. It resembles 'Iris Prichard', and is rather slow to grow into a good-sized cushion.

**S.** × **anglica** 'Cerise Queen' (*S.* 'Christine', *S.* 'Cerise Gem'). This English hybrid forms straggly dark green cushions seldom reaching 10 cm in diameter. Leaves acute, silvery. The 3–6 cm scapes carry 1–3 small flowers, light cherry red to salmon pink in colour. Flowering time March–May.

**S.** × *anglica* 'Cranbourne' (*S.* 'Cranbourne'). Medium-sized, dark grey-green mats of flat compact close-set rosettes. Fairly large bright reddish pink or lilac flowers, 1–3 in number, on 3–5 cm scapes in March–April. The flowers fade to a somewhat paler pink after a week. One of the best of the 'Kabschias', a reliable grower which should be in every collection.

**S.** × *anglica* 'Grace Farwell' (*S.* 'Grace Farwell'). Broad medium-sized firm grey-green cushions. Two or more flowers on each scape, appearing somewhat later in April–May. They have an unusual wine red or carmine red colour but are rather closed in form. Height only 3 cm.

**S.** × *anglica* 'Myra' (*S.* 'Myra'). An old hybrid raised by Farrer, one of the first to involve *S. lilacina*. Resembles *S.* × *anglica* 'Cranbourne', but is deeper in colour and not so vigorous. The grey-green mats reach an ultimate diameter of 10–12 cm. Silver-grey rosettes with fine lime deposits. Bright salmon pink flowers, later becoming cherry red, on 5 cm scapes. Flowering time usually April. A fine variety, strongly recommended.

**S.** × *anglica* 'Priory Jewel'. Compact silvery grey cushions 8 cm in diameter with pink flowers on 3 cm scapes.

**S.** × *anglica* 'Valerie Keevil'. A pretty variety with deep pink flowers.

**S.** × *anglica* 'Winifred' (*S.* 'Winifred'). An outstanding English hybrid of recent origin. *S. lilacina* is one of the parents. Small cushions made up of grey-green rosettes. Relatively large dark carmine pink flowers in March or April. Height 3 cm, the flowers often sitting only just above the rosettes. Deeper coloration towards the base of the petals.

There are several other forms of *S.* × *anglica*, mostly of English or American origin. Among them are 'Arthur', with single dark purple flowers; 'Aubrey Prichard', dark purple; 'Beryl', deep pink, mostly single flowers; 'Brenda Prichard', clear pink; 'Clare', pale lilac pink, single flowers; 'Delight', clear pink; 'Elysium', cushions 10 cm diameter, bright pink flowers on 2.5 cm scapes; 'Felicity', carmine pink; 'Glorious' ('Gloriosa'), red flowers on 2.5 cm scapes, cushions 10–12 cm; 'Sparkling', pure pink.

**S.** × *anormalis* 'Gustav Hegi' (*S.* × *anormalis*). *S. laevis* × *S. stribrnyi*. Multiple orange-yellow flowers, 8 cm high, March–April.

**S.** × *apiculata* 'Alba'. A sport from *Saxifraga* × *apiculata* 'Gregor Mendel' (*S.* × *apiculata*), identical with the original except in having pure white flowers.

**S.** × *apiculata* 'Gregor Mendel' (*S.* × *apiculata*). *S. marginata* var. *rocheliana* × *S. sancta*. Karl Foerster's ivory saxifrage, originated in 1894. An old but valuable hybrid which forms magnificent green mats often exceeding 40 cm. Flowering time March–April, usually early April. Pale yellow flowers, often 10–12 in number, on 6 cm scapes. Grows well, recommended for beginners. Likes somewhat more humus than other kinds.

**S.** × *apiculata* 'Primrose Bee' (*S.* 'Primrose Bee'). Vigorous dark green cushions; rosettes encrusted at edges. Flowering time March–April. Scapes 5–7 cm high carrying several primrose-yellow flowers.

**S.** × *apiculata* 'Pseudopungens' (*S.* × *pseudopungens*). An old hybrid which forms large firm mats. Flowering time March–April. Scapes 5 cm high carrying several primrose yellow flowers.

**S.** × *apiculata* 'Pungens' (*S.* × *pungens*). Large firm dark green rosettes. Flowering time March–April. Several light yellow flowers on each 6–8 cm scape. An old hybrid, introduced by Sündermann in 1907.

**S.** × *arco-valleyi* 'Arco' (*S.* × *arco-valleyi*). An old but still valuable plant raised by Sündermann in 1919. Dwarf cushions, most suitable for tufa. Relatively large, pale lilac-pink flowers on short scapes (3 cm) in March–April. Petals of good substance and longer than those of most other hybrids. A meritorious and free-flowering dwarf form.

**S.** × *arco-valleyi* 'Dainty Dame' (*S.* 'Dainty Dame'). A charming plant of English origin with fairly large pale salmon-pink flowers borne individually on thin scapes 3–5 cm high. Flowering time March–April.

**S.** × *arco-valleyi* 'Hocker Edge' (*S.* 'Hocker Edge Seedling'). Raised in England, this plant has relatively large grey-green rosettes. Scapes 3–4 cm each carrying 1–2 salmon-pink to pale lilac-pink flowers in March–April. This hybrid has the largest flowers of all the pink 'Kabschias'.

**S.** × *arco-valleyi* 'Ophelia' (*S.* × *arco-valleyi* 'Alba'). Decorative cushions with single creamy white flowers.

**S.** × *bertolonii* 'Amabilis'. A little known variety with several carmine flowers on each scape.

**S.** × *bertolonii* 'Antonio' (*S. bertolonii*). *S. stribrnyi* × *S. sempervivum*. An old 'Engleria' hybrid raised by Sündermann in 1907. Small cushions, about 10 cm in diameter in old plants, made up of fairly large rosettes about 1.3 cm in diameter. Conspicuous lime deposits on the long pointed leaves. Carmine purple flowers in March-April on 8 cm scapes. Likes limestone chippings in the compost.

**S.** × *biasolettii* 'Crystalie'. A hybrid of *S. grisebachii* × *S. sempervivum*, in appearance intermediate between its parents. Fine carmine-red flowers.

**S.** × *biasolettii* 'Lohmuelleri' (*S.* × *lohmuelleri*). An 'Engleria' hybrid with red flowers on 8 cm scapes.

**S.** × *biasolettii* 'Phoenix' (*S. biasolettii*). *S. grisebachii* × *S. sempervivum*. Raised by Sündermann in 1912. Perhaps the best of this group, outstandingly beautiful rosettes. Older cushions up to 15 cm in diameter. Bright carmine purple flowers, slightly drooping, 10–15 cm high, in April.

**S.** × *bilekii* 'Castor' (*S.* × *bilekii*). There seem to be two different plants in circulation under this name. In Great Britain the name is applied to a hybrid of *S. aretioides* × *S. tombeanensis*. It is intermediate between the parents, having small firm grey-green cushions 10–12 cm in diameter. The large pale yellow flowers on 3 cm scapes appear in April. The hybrid offered under the same name in German nurseries is probably a cross between *S. aretioides* × *S. ferdinandi-coburgii* and has deep yellow flowers, 3–5 in number, on 8 cm scapes. Its parentage is alternatively stated as *S. ferdinandi-coburgii* × *S. tombeanensis*.

**S. × boeckeleri** 'Armida' (*S. × boeckeleri*). *S. ferdinandi-coburgii* × *S. stribrnyi*. Small cushions of silver-grey rosettes. Branched inflorescences 6–8 cm high. Small drooping orange-ochre flowers in March–April.

**S. × borisii** 'Aemula' (*S. × aemula*). 5 cm high, yellow flowers.

**S. × borisii** 'Faustus'. *S. ferdinandi-coburgii* × *S. marginata*. Previously known as *S. rocheliana* 'Lutea' or *S. marginata* 'Rocheliana Major Lutea'. Firm flat cushions with splendid pale yellow flowers, appearing somewhat later than most of the other 'Kabschia' saxifrages. Height 8 cm.

**S. × borisii** 'Josef Manes'. Vigorous grey-green cushions with intense lime encrustation on the leaves. Primrose yellow flowers on 6 cm scapes in March–April.

**S. × borisii** 'Karlstejn'. A beautiful hybrid from Czechoslovakia with relatively large rosettes. Brilliant yellow flowers in umbels on hairy, reddish-brown scapes 6–7 cm high. Flowering time March–April.

**S. × borisii** 'Kyrillii' (*S. × kyrillii*). *S. marginata* × *S. ferdinandi-coburgii*. More similar to *S. marginata*, except that the leaflets are longer and narrower. Small cushions with up to 9 pale yellow flowers on brown glandular scapes 5–8 cm high.

**S. × borisii** 'Margarette' (*S. × coriophylla lutea*). Vigorous cushions with multiple pale yellow flowers on 8 cm scapes in March–April.

**S. × borisii** 'Marianna'. Neat grey-green cushions with bright yellow flowers on 4–6 cm scapes in March–April.

**S. × borisii** 'Pseudoborisii' (*S. × pseudoborisii*). Very beautiful and free-flowering. Firm grey rosettes with narrow pointed lanceolate leaves. The interior of the cushion is darker green. Primrose-yellow flowers on 6–8 cm scapes in March–April.

**S. × borisii** 'Pseudokyrillii'. An old hybrid, now seldom seem. Multiple yellow flowers.

**S. × borisii** 'Sofia' (*S. × borisii*). An old hybrid which originated in the Botanic Garden, Sofia, from a cross between *S. ferdinandi-coburgii* × *S. marginata*, and was introduced by Sündermann in 1909, at the same time as *S. × kyrillii*, which was derived from the same cross. Both of them were named after Bulgarian kings. *S. × borisii* 'Sofia' is clearly distinct from other 'Kabschia' saxifrages; in appearance it resembles *S. ferdinandi-coburgii*, though in size it approaches *S. marginata*. The leaflets are somewhat longer and wider than those of *S. ferdinandi-coburgii*. The flowers are yellow or pale yellow and are carried in heads of 7–12 on brown scapes 6–8 cm high, having glandular hairs which give them a reddish tinge. The individual flowers are comparatively large and appear in March–April. The blue-green cushions may ultimately reach a diameter of 16 cm.

**S. × borisii** 'Vesna'. 6 cm scapes carrying reddish-brown buds which unfold into umbels of pale yellow flowers.

**S. × borisii** 'Vincent van Gogh'. Firm grey-green rosettes forming a rather lax cushion. The rosette leaves are widely expanded and encrusted with lime on their margins. Early flowering, generally in March. Buds purple, opening to primrose-yellow flowers on 6–7 cm scapes.

Among new crosses from Czechoslovakia are *S. × borisii* 'Marie Stivinova' with multiple yellow flowers and *S. × borisii* 'Mona Lisa' with multiple pale yellow flowers. Neither has yet been distributed.

**S. × boydii** 'Aretiastrum' (*S.* 'Valerie Finnis', *S. × aretiastrum*). One of the best of the yellow-flowered 'Kabschia' hybrids. Small tight cushions made up of spiny grey-green rosettes, resembling those of *S. burserana*. Numerous large pale yellow flowers carried singly on short reddish scapes. Petals fairly wide. A reliable grower with a good constitution.

**S. × boydii** 'Cherry Trees' (*S.* 'Cherry Trees'). Also described as *S. × elisabethae* 'Cherry Trees'. Cushions 10–12 cm in diameter. Several lemon-yellow flowers on scapes 5–8 cm tall in March–April.

**S. × boydii** 'Faldonside' (*S. × faldonside*). Hard blue-green hummocks up to 16 cm. Lemon yellow flowers, 1–2 in number, on 5–6 cm carmine red scapes in March–April. The colour becomes paler towards the end of the flowering season. The flowers are somewhat better in form than those of *S. × boydii* 'William Boyd'. Also raised by Dr Boyd. Will stand more sun than most forms.

**S. × boydii** 'Hindhead Seedling' (*S.* 'Hindhead Seedling'). Pale yellow flowers, 2–3 on each scape, in March–April.

**S. × boydii** 'Luteola' (*S. burserana* 'Luteola'). Another similar yellow hybrid.

**S. × boydii** 'Mondscheinsonate' (*S. × boydii alba*). A dwarf plant with small tight cushions. One or occasionally 2 white flowers on each scape.

**S. × boydii** 'Pilatus'. Recently raised by J. Eschmann, Emmen. Vigorous, attractive cushions. Large sulphur-yellow flowers on carmine scapes 8 cm high. Flowers March–April.

**S. × boydii** 'Sulphurea' (*S. burserana* 'Sulphurea', *S.* 'Moonlight'). The solitary, pale sulphur-yellow flowers have a greenish-yellow centre. Scapes 5 cm;

flowering time March–April, but tends to flower early. The grey-green cushions grow readily.

**S. × boydii** 'William Boyd' (*S. × boydii*). A hybrid between *S. burserana* × *S. aretioides*. Named after the British plant-breeder Dr James Boyd of Melrose (1890). It is often more difficult to manage than other 'Kabschia' hybrids, but it is a handsome plant with blue-green rosettes and needle-shaped leaves. Cushions up to 13 cm in diameter. Lemon yellow flowers, 1–2 or occasionally 3 on each scape. Early flowering. There is a very rare white form.

Under the heading *S. × boydii* there are two other hybrids: *S. × boydii* 'Old Britain' with 1–3 yellow flowers and *S. × boydii* 'Pollux' with 1–2 pale yellow flowers.

**S. × bursiculata** 'King Lear' (*S. × bursiculata*). A hybrid from *S. burserana* × *S. × apiculata* (*S. × apiculata* = *S. marginata* × *S. sancta*). An old hybrid raised by Mr Jenkins of Hampton Hill, it was winning prizes in England as long ago as 1912. It grows readily, forming greyish cushions. Scape 5–8 cm, usually carrying 4 relatively large white flowers, sometimes with a faint ivory tinge. Flowers in March.

*Saxifraga* 'Cambridge Seedling'. Parents unknown. An English hybrid, not yet widely distributed, forming medium-sized cushions. White to pale pink flowers, several on each scape, in March–April.

*Saxifraga* 'Camyra'. Parents unknown. Elegant cushions with 1–3 pastel yellow flowers on each scape in March–April.

*Saxifraga* 'Chumbey'. Parents unknown. White flowers on 5 cm scapes. Not widely distributed.

*Saxifraga × clarkei* 'Sidonia' (*S. × clarkei*). Pink flowers on 5 cm scapes in March–April. Introduced by Sündermann in 1908.

*Saxifraga* 'Columbeana'. Parents unknown. An unclassifiable hybrid which occasionally begins to flower in autumn. Yellow flowers on 3–4 cm scapes.

*Saxifraga* 'Delia'. *S. lilacina* is one parent. Seagreen cushions with blunt-leaved rosettes and large lilac-pink flowers on 3–5 cm scapes in March or more usually April. Old cushions up to 15 cm in diameter.

*Saxifraga* 'Doldensis'. Parents unknown. Medium-sized, low rounded light grey-green hummocks. Fairly large rosettes, 0.9–1 cm in diameter. Leaves acute, recurved inwards, with lime deposits. Late flowering, April–May. Brilliant yellow flowers on 6 cm scapes.

**S. × doerfleri** 'Ignaz Dörfler' (*S. × doerfleri*). *S. grisebachii* × *stribrnyi*. One of the older 'Engleria' hybrids, flowering in March–April. Dark carmine-red flowers on branching 12 cm scapes, densely covered with glandular grey hairs.

**S. × edithae** 'Bridget' (*S.* 'Bridget'). A hybrid between *S. marginata* var.

*coriophylla* × *stribryni*. Handsome silvery cushions, often exceeding 20 cm in diameter. Each of the 6 cm scapes carries several pale salmon-pink flowers with a lilac tinge. An outstanding cross of British origin. Flowers in April.

*S.* × *edithae* 'Edith' (*S.* × *edithae*). *S. marginata var. rocheliana* × *stribrnyi*. Low growing sea-green or grey-green cushions. Each scape carries 6–10 somewhat bell-shaped pale pink flowers. Late flowering (April) and floriferous.

*S.* × *edithae* 'Pseudoedithae'. Several pink or whitish flowers on each scape. Not widely distributed.

*S.* × *elisabethae* 'Boston Spa' (*S.* 'Boston Spa') *S. burserana* × *S. sancta*. Fine vigorous dark-green cushions with pointed rosette leaves. Early-flowering (March–April). Reddish scapes, 7 cm high, each carrying 3–4 medium-sized yellow flowers. A robust and satisfactory plant.

*S.* × *elisabethae* 'Carmen' (*S.* × *elisabethae*). *S. sancta* × *S. burserana*. One of the best growers among the 'Kabschia' hybrids, forming large vigorous grey-green cushions. Partial shade is not absolutely essential; it will even tolerate full sun. Splendid pale-yellow flowers, 3–4 on each scape. This is a very old hybrid which has inherited the best qualities from each parent and which should be in every collection. Free-flowering in some places, but shy-flowering in others.

*S.* × *elisabethae* 'L. C. Godseff' (*S.* 'Godseff'). Rounded blue-green hummocks. Pale yellow flowers on 5 cm scapes in March–April.

*S.* × *elisabethae* 'Mrs Leng' (*S.* 'Mrs Leng', sometimes spelt *S.* 'Mrs Lang'). A vigorous hybrid with yellow flowers on 5 cm scapes.

*S.* × *elisabethae* 'Ochroleuca' (*S.* × *ochroleuca*). Introduced by Sündermann in 1906. Handsome blue-green or seagreen cushions up to 20 cm in diameter. Reddish scapes 4–5 cm high carrying 1–3 yellow flowers in March or more commonly April. Easily grown.

There are several less well known cultivars of *S.* × *elizabethae* including 'Elisabeth Sinclair' with yellow flowers; 'Icicle' with 1–2 whitish flowers on each scape; 'Jason' with 3 or occasionally up to 5 pale yellow flowers; 'Midas' with yellow flowers; 'Millstream Cream' with 1–2 creamy yellow or yellowish flowers and 'Lorelei' with 1–5 yellow flowers.

*S.* × *eudoxiana* 'Eudoxia' (*S.* × *eudociae*). Low-growing cushions averaging 15 cm in diameter. Leaves narrow and elongated, sharply pointed. Scapes 5–7 cm carrying 6–8 pale yellow flowers. Closer to *S. ferdinandi-coburgii* than its other parent. Its ancestry is not entirely certain, as there is a manuscript correction by F. Sündermann stating that the parents were *S. ferdinandi-coburgii* × *S. burserana* 'Parviflora'.

*S.* × *eudoxiana* 'Haagii' (S. 'Haagii'). *S. ferdinandi-coburgii* × *S. sancta*. A very old hybrid introduced by Sündermann in 1908, it is a plant with a strong constitution, suitable for beginners, robust, rapid-growing and free-flowering. It quickly forms firm green cushions which in suitable rock crevices may reach a diameter of 40 cm. Each scape (6–8 cm high) carries 4–5 narrow-petalled flowers of deep golden yellow hue, resembling that of *S. ferdinandi-coburgii*. It flowers at the beginning of April and harmonizes nicely with Hepaticas.

*S. × finnisae* 'Parcevalis'. A little known cultivar with several orange flowers on each scape.

*S. × fleischeri* 'Buchholzii' (*S. × buchholzii*). A yellow-flowered 'Engleria' hybrid which blooms in March–April and has a pale yellow shade unusual among 'Englerias'. Height 6 cm.

*S. × fleischeri* 'Mephisto' (*S. × fleischeri*). An 'Engleria' hybrid raised by Sündermann with brilliant red flowers on 6 cm scapes.

*S. × fontanae* 'Amalie' (*S. × fontanae*). Three yellow flowers on each scape, not widely distributed.

*Saxifraga* 'Frederici-Augustii'. Probably a natural hybrid of *S. porophylla*. Tight grey cushions. Small narrow leaves, tipped with lime. Late-flowering (April–May). Scapes 8–10 cm, drooping, with small pink flowers in large furry wine-red sepals. The overall impression is purple.

*Saxifraga* 'Gelber Findling'. Parents unknown. A seedling which originated by chance at the nursery of J. Eschmann, Emmen. Its appearance gives no clue to its parentage. Blue-green lime encrusted rosettes. Buds purple, inflorescence 4 cm, corymbose. Flowers 5–7, pale yellow to primrose yellow. Early flowering, February–April.

*S. × geuderi* 'Eulenspiegel' (*S. × geuderi*). *S. × boydii × S. ferdinandi-coburgii*. Handsome dwarf cushions. Large single brilliant yellow flowers on 3 cm scapes in March–April.

*S. × gloriana* 'Amitie' (*S. × amitie*). *S. lilacina × S. scardica*. Other sources suggest *S. lilacina × S. marginata*-form as the parents. Grey-green cushions with small leaves. Single flowers, buds deep lilac, petals pale violet pink, later fading to white. Height 5 cm. Flowers March–April.

*Saxifraga* 'Gold Dust'. Parents unknown. Compact cushions made up of dainty tightly packed rosettes. Inflorescences of up to 9 golden-yellow flowers on 10 cm scapes in March–April.

*S. × grata* 'Annemarie' (*S. × grata*). Handsome cushions with 3 cm scapes carrying several flowers in March–April.

*S. × grata* 'Gratioides' (*S. × gratioides*). Yellow flowers on 3 cm scapes in March–April.

*S. × grata* 'Loeflingii' (*S. × loeflingii*). Deep yellow flowers on 5 cm scapes.

*S. × gusmusii* 'Perluteiviridis'. Grows slowly to an ultimate size of 15 cm. Silvery rosettes with 10 cm scapes carrying several greenish-yellow flowers.

**S. × gusmusii** 'Subluteiviridis'. Like the above but has blackish-red flowers.

**S. × hardingi** 'Iris Prichard' (*S.* 'Iris Prichard'). Distinguished by its unusual flower colour which ranges from pale pink to buff-apricot. Flowers extremely early, from the end of January in sheltered spots. Scapes 5–6 cm, most of them carrying 3 flowers. Attractive lime encrusted rosettes.

**S. × heinrichii** 'E. Heinrich' (*S. × heinrichii*). *S. aretioides × S. stribrnyi*. Reddish-grey rosettes about 2.5 cm in diameter. The yellowish petals and reddish sepals give a bicolor effect. Scapes 5–6 cm, branching. Profuse flowers in March–April.

**S. × hoerhammeri** 'Lohengrin' (*S. × hoerhammeri*). *S. grisebachii × S. marginata* var. *coriophylla*. Beautiful rosettes, particularly attractive when in bud. Pink flowers on 8 cm scapes in March–April.

**S. × hofmannii** 'Bodensee' (*S. × hofmannii*). Small cushions with dark rose-pink flowers on 5 cm scapes in March–April.

**S. × hofmannii** 'Ferdinand' (*S.* 'Ferdinand', *S. burserana* 'Ferdinand'). Pale pink flowers on 5 cm scapes.

**S. × hornibrookii** 'Riverslea' (*S.* 'Riverslea'). *S. lilacina × S. porophylla*. A pretty hybrid which should be in every collection. One of the best of its colour, free-flowering but slow-growing. The hard compact cushions of silver grey rosettes ultimately reach about 15 cm. Scapes 3.5–5 cm carrying 1–3 comparatively large bell-shaped flowers in April. The colour is variously described as carmine, wine-red or purple-salmon-pink.

**S. × hornibrookii** has a few less well known cultivars: 'April', numerous wine red flowers; 'Juliet', numerous dull red flowers; 'Romeo', numerous dark wine red flowers.

**S. × ingwersenii** 'Simplicity'. Seldom seen; 1–3 white flowers with a pink tinge.

**S. × irvingii** 'Gem' (*S.* 'Gem'). *S. burserana × S. lilacina*. Delightful dwarf cushions. Salmon pink flowers on 3 cm scapes in March–April (more often April). Cushions not more than 10 cm in diameter when mature.

**S. × irvingii** 'Harry Marshall' (*S.* 'Harry Marshall'). Medium-sized cushions about 16 cm in diameter. Flowering time March–April. Scapes 3–5 cm carrying a single pale salmon-pink flower which turns almost white as it fades.

**S. × irvingii** 'His Majesty' (*S. burserana* 'His Majesty'). Small cushions about 15 cm in diameter when mature, scapes 5 cm, each carrying 1–2 relatively large white flowers with a pink tinge. Very early flowering, usually in March.

**S. × irvingii** 'Jenkinsae' (*S. × jenkinsae*). Another hybrid from *S. burserana × S. lilacina*. A reliable plant which grows well and should be in every collection. Early flowering (March). Silvery grey-green cushions 15 cm diameter. Single flowers on 5 cm scapes, pale pink, deeper towards the middle. Likes plenty of fine grit in the compost. A good variety for the beginner.

**S. × irvingii** 'Mother of Pearl' (*S.* 'Mother of Pearl'). Silver grey cushions flowering in March–April. Large flowers of a beautiful pink borne singly on very short scapes.

**S. × irvingii** 'Rubella' (*S. × rubella*). Firm spiny mats. Though a dwarf, it grows vigorously, the cushions reaching 15 cm in diameter when mature. Flowers profusely, early to midseason, chiefly in March. Single flowers, pale pink or lilac, on 5 cm scapes. The colour darkens as the flowers fade. Thrives well in a moist, well-lit place.

**S. × irvingii** 'Walter Irving' (*S. × irvingii*). Dwarf cushions with tight grey-green rosettes, attractive even when not in flower. An old hybrid, raised by Mr W. Irving in Kew Gardens. Flowers early, usually in March. One or occasionally two flowers on 3–4 cm scapes. Flower colour pale pink to dull lilac, with a somewhat deeper eye. Buds red. A vigorous grower, but not quite as reliable as the similar *S. × irvingii* 'Jenkinsae'. Not to be confused with *S. × salmonica* 'Irvingiana' (*S. × irvingiana*).

There are several other forms of *S. × irvingii*, but they are not often grown: 'Eliot Ford', single pale pink flowers; 'Lusanna', mostly single pale pink flowers; 'Mother Queen', single deep-pink flowers; 'Russel Prichard', mostly single pale pink flowers; 'Timmy Foster', single pink flowers.

**Saxifraga** 'Jendinii'. Parents unknown. Small grey-green cushions made up of tight rosettes 0.6 cm in diameter. Free flowering, April–May. Pure yellow flowers on 5 cm scapes with a reddish tinge.

**S. × kayei** 'Buttercup'. 1–3 deep yellow flowers on each scape; beautiful dwarf cushions.

**S. × kellereri** 'Johann Kellerer' (*S. × kellereri*). *S. burserana × S. stribrnyi*. An old but excellent hybrid introduced by Sündermann in 1906. Flowers very early, in February–March, or even at the end of January in sheltered spots. Silvery rosettes about 2.5 cm in diameter. Several, usually 3, flowers of a delicate peach colour on 8–10 cm tall branching scapes. A vigorous grower.

**S. × kellereri** 'Landaueri' (*S. × landaueri*). Believed to be derived from a cross between *S. × kellereri × S. marginata* var. *rocheliana*. Vigorous cushions made up of large rosettes thickly encrusted with lime. Easily grown, but likes lime chippings in the compost. Mature cushions up to 15 cm in diameter. Flowers white with a tinge of pink on 6 cm scapes in March–April.

**S. × kellereri** 'Pseudosuendermannii' (*S. × acutifolia*). An easily grown plant, introduced by Sündermann in 1915. Cushions reach about 15 cm when mature. Red scapes each carrying up to 3 deep pink flowers in March.

**S. × kellereri** 'Schleicheri' (*S. × schleicheri*). Cushions up to 13 cm in diameter, rosettes grey-white. White flowers with a pink tinge on 5 cm reddish or brown scapes in April–May. Resembles *S.* × *kellereri*, but smaller in all its parts.

*S.* × *kellereri* 'Suendermannii' (*S.* × *suendermannii* 'Purpurea'). Firm tight grey-green cushions. Flowers purplish, scapes at first very short, ultimately 6–7 cm high. Flowers profusely.

*S.* × *kellereri* 'Suendermannii Major' (*S.* × *suendermannii* 'Major'). Medium-sized grey rosettes, salmon-pink flowers fading to pale pink, on 6–7 cm scapes in March–April. Introduced by Sündermann in 1920.

*Saxifraga* 'Kenneth Rogers'. A new hybrid with 2–3 pink flowers on each scape. Not yet widely distributed.

*S.* × *kewensis* 'Big Ben' (*S.* × *kewensis*). *S. burserana* × *S. porophylla*. Compact grey-green cushions up to 15 cm across, made up of large star-shaped rosettes. 1–2 flowers on 5–8 cm reddish scapes in March–April. The flowers are pale pink, often almost white, but they do not always open fully.

*Saxifraga* 'Laeviformis'. Parents unknown. Yellow flowers on 5 cm scapes.

*S.* × *leyboldii* 'August Heyek' (*S.* × *leyboldii*). A slow-growing dwarf, ideal for holes in tufa. Multiple white flowers.

*Saxifraga* 'Lomieri'. Parents unknown. An uncommon 'Kabschia' hybrid with red flowers.

*S.* × *malbyana* 'Primulina' (*S. diapensioides* 'Lutea', *S. aretioides* var. *primulina*). Small cushions not exceeding 10 cm in diameter with 4 cm scapes each carrying 3–5 light yellow flowers in April.

*S.* × *mariae-theresiae* 'Gaertneri'. A beautiful hybrid with multiple pink flowers.

*S.* × *mariae-theresiae* 'Theresia' (*S.* × *mariae-theresiae*). An attractive plant with vigorous grey-green rosettes. Fiery red buds and small pink flowers on reddish scapes 5–7 cm high. Cushions about 10 cm in diameter.

*Saxifraga* 'Mrs G. Prichard' (*S.* 'G. M. Prichard'). Parents unknown. Ashen-grey cushions with large pink flowers.

*S.* × *megaseaeflora* 'Robin Hood'. (*S.* × *megaseaeflora*). Firm grey cushions reaching 10 cm in diameter when mature. The rosettes resemble those of *S. burserana*. Scapes 3–5 cm, usually carrying one flower, less often 2 or 3, in March–April. The flowers are relatively large and have an unusual rose-pink colour. This is a beautiful cultivar which always attracts admiration.

*Saxifraga* 'Monika'. A new hybrid from Sündermann. Parents unknown. Handsome yellow flowers.

*S.* × *paulinae* 'Franzii' (*S.* × *franzii*). *S. burserana* × *S. ferdinandi-coburgii*. Leaflets somewhat more obtuse than those of *S. burserana*. This plant flowers profusely in March–April, with up to 6 pale yellow flowers on each 5 cm scape.

**S.** × *paulinae* 'Kolbiana' (*S.* × *kolbiana*). Tight spiny cushions. It flowers very early, often starting during mild periods in winter. Beautiful yellow flowers on 4–6 cm scapes.

**S.** × *paulinae* 'Paula' (*S.* × *paulinae*). *S. burserana* 'Minor' × *S. ferdinandi-coburgii*. Another valuable hybrid introduced by Sündermann in 1905, in appearance it is closer to its second parent but has larger rosettes with narrow prickly leaves and a lighter grey tinge. The compact cushions reach 16 cm in diameter when mature, and flower early and abundantly, usually in March. Scapes 5 cm, reddish, carrying 1–3 pale yellow flowers 0.6–0.7 cm in diameter.

**S.** × *paulinae* 'Pseudopaulinae' (*S.* × *pseudopaulinae*). Another yellow-flow-ered hybrid with several flowers on each scape in March–April.

*Saxifraga* 'Perle Rose'. Parents unknown. Low, rounded cushions, some-what lax. Large bright-pink flowers and 3 cm scapes in March–April.

*Saxifraga* 'Petra'. Parents unknown. Beautiful iron-hard cushions. There is striking contrast between the purple buds and the white flowers, 1–3 in number on 3–5 cm scapes in March–April.

*Saxifraga* 'Pink Pearl'. Parents unknown. Small cushions with magnificent pink flowers in March–April, one flower on each scape.

**S.** × *petraschii* 'Ada' (*S.* 'Ada'). A hybrid derived from *S. burserana* and *S. tombeanensis*. Tight, compact cushions reaching a diameter of 13 cm when mature. White flowers on 5 cm scapes in March–April. The flowering time is unusually prolonged. Another plant with pale pink flowers is in circulation under the same name.

**S.** × *petraschii* 'Affinis' (*S.* × *affinis*). Dwarf cushions about 3 cm in diameter. 1–2 white flowers on 7 cm scapes in April.

**S.** × *petraschii* 'Dulcimer'. A little-known variety with 1–2 white flowers on each scape.

**S.** × *petraschii* 'Hansi' (*S.* 'Hansii', *S.* × *hansii*). Lime-encrusted rosettes. 1–2 white flowers on 5 cm scapes in March–April.

**S.** × *petraschii* 'Kaspar Maria Sternberg' (*S. petraschii*). More or less inter-mediate between its two very different parents, this is one of the finest white hybrids, with small compact grey-green cushions, reaching a diameter of about 15 cm when mature. Scapes 3–5 cm carrying usually three deep red buds which open into large well-formed white flowers with slightly frilled petals. The contrast between the red buds and white flowers is extremely striking. Late flowering April. An old hybrid introduced by Sündermann in 1907.

**S.** × *pragensis* 'Golden Prague' (*S.* 'Zlata Praha'). *S.* × *edithae* × ?*S. ferdi-nandi-coburgii*. Beautiful blue-green cushions made up of fairly large lime-encrusted rosettes, each about 2 cm in diameter. Several flowers on each 5 cm scape over a long period in March–April. Sepals purple, petals orange yellow. Highly recommended.

*S.* × *prossenii* 'Regina' (*S.* × *prossenii*). *S. sancta* × *S. stribrnyi*. Firm cushions up to 15 cm in diameter made up of small rosettes having a deeper greenish tinge than most others of this group. Several flowers on 5–7 cm scapes over a long period in April–May. Sepals coppery, petals ochre-yellow to orange-yellow.

*S.* × *prossenii* 'Regina Orange' (*S.* × *prossenii* 'orange'). A colour form with beautiful orange flowers.

*S.* × *pseudokotschyi* 'Denisa' (*S.* × *pseudokotschyi*). An old variety, seldom seen, with multiple pale-yellow flowers. It is closely similar to *S. kotschyi*. Sterile.

*Saxifraga* 'Rosemarie'. Parents unknown. Magnificent cushions with 1–2 large rose-pink flowers on each scape in March–April.

*S.* × *rosinae* 'Rosina Sündermann' (*S.* × *rosinae*). An old hybrid with small rounded cushions reaching a diameter of 15 cm when mature. Multiple whitish flowers on short scapes in March–April.

*S.* × *salmonica* 'Assimilis' (*S.* × *assimilis*). Small grey-green cushions, not exceeding 10 cm in diameter. Large white flowers with a darker spot on 3–5 cm scapes in March–April.

*S.* × *salmonica* 'Grosser Prinz'. A new cross introduced by J. Eschmann, Emmen, it flowers later than most other varieties, not until April–May. Loose grey-green cushions with large white bell-shaped flowers on 7 cm scapes.

*S.* × *salmonica* 'Jenkinsii' (*S.* 'Jenkinsii', *S.* × *jenkinsii*). Not to be confused with *S.* × *irvingii* 'Jenkinsae' (*S.* × *jenkinsae*). Rather coarse grey-green rosettes. Several white flowers on 4–6 cm scapes in March–April.

*S.* × *salmonica* 'Irvingiana' (*S.* × *irvingiana*). *S. burserana* × *S. marginata*. Not to be confused with *S.* × *irvingii* 'Walter Irving'. 1–3 white flowers on 5–6 cm scapes in March–April.

*S.* × *salmonica* 'Marie Louisa' (*S.* Marie Louisa). Flowers very early, in February–March. Striking contrast between the reddish 5 cm scapes and the large white flowers.

*S.* × *salmonica* 'Obristii' (*S.* × *obristii*). Also derived from a cross between *S. marginata* × *S. burserana*, it has larger rosettes than the latter. Leaves are pointed, resembling those of *S. marginata*, but with numerous white lime dots on the margins. The grey cushions remain rather lax and reach a diameter of 16–18 cm. The 5 cm scapes carry 3–4 reddish buds which open into large flowers resembling those of *S. marginata*.

*S.* × *salmonica* 'Pichleri' (*S.* × *pichleri*). Small grey cushions with pointed leaves and 1–2 white flowers on each scape.

**S.** × *salmonica* 'Prospero' (*S.* 'Prospero'). Medium-sized cushions with 1–2 white flowers on each scape in March–April.

**S.** × *salmonica* 'Pseudosalomonii' (*S.* × *pseudosalomonii*). Another hybrid with several white flowers on each scape in March–April.

**S.** × *salmonica* 'Salomonii' (*S.* × *salomonii*). One of the oldest 'Kabschia' hybrids, introduced by Sündermann in 1894. Its parents are *S. burserana* × *S. marginata*, and in appearance it is closer to the former but grows more vigorously. The leaves are somewhat broader than those of *S. burserana* but resemble them in having sharp points. Small tight rounded cushions are made up of ashen grey starry rosettes. There is a pleasing contrast between the reddish scapes and buds and the large white flowers, 1-3 on each scape.

**S.** × *salmonica* 'Schreineri' (*S.* × *schreineri*). Beautiful though lax cushions reaching 15 cm in diameter when mature. White flowers on 5 cm scapes in March–April.

**S.** × *salmonica* 'White Star'. Large white flowers on 6–8 cm scapes in March–April.

There are several less well known varieties of *S.* × *salmonica*: 'Boyd's Variety', with multiple white flowers; 'Kestoniensis', with multiple white flowers; 'Melrose', with 2–3 white flowers on each scape; 'Rosaleen', with multiple white flowers.

**Saxifraga** 'Schelleri' (*S.* × *schelleri*). Dwarf cushions 10–12 cm in diameter with white flowers on 2.5 cm scapes.

**Saxifraga** 'Schmulleri'. A beautiful variety with red flowers, not yet classified.

**S.** × *schottii* 'Perstribrnyi' (*S.* × *schottii*). An attractive hybrid with branched inflorescences covered with reddish glandular hairs. It has flat silvery rosettes. Each scape carries several small flowers with a cinnabar-red tinge.

**S.** × *schottii* 'Substribrnyi'. Like the preceding, but has pale ochre-yellow petals and copper-red sepals.

**S.** × *semmleri* 'Martha' (*S.* × *semmleri*). *S.* × *eudoxiana* 'Haagi' × *S. laevis*. Medium-sized cushions with a profusion of yellow flowers. Relatively undemanding.

**S.** × *smithii* 'Vahlii' (*S. vahlii*). A true dwarf from the cross between *S. marginata* var. *coriophylla* × *S. tombeanensis*. Up to 5 white flowers on each scape in March–April. This is a free-flowering plant which looks well in rock crevices.

**Saxifraga** 'Sonja Prichard'. Parents unknown. Single pale yellow flowers.

**S.** × *steinii* 'Agnes' (*S.* × *steinii*). Tough cushions made up of small silvery rosettes. Up to 6 creamy white or light yellow flowers on each short scape. A generous and late-flowering hybrid.

*S.* × *stormonthii* 'Stella' (*S.* × *stormonthii*). An old hybrid with tight prickly cushions. Free-flowering (yellow) and a rapid grower, soon forming cushions 20 cm or even more in diameter.

*S.* × *stuartii* 'Lutea' (*S.* 'Stuartii'). Well-shaped rosettes of great beauty. A good grower which produces numerous side rosettes. Late flowering, not until April–May. Scapes 6–8 cm. Sepals reddish, petals yellow, giving an overall yellow-pink impression.

*S.* × *stuartii* 'Rosea'. Several flowers on each scape, dull purple or brownish.

*S.* × *thomasiana* 'Magdalena' (*S.* × *thomasiana*). Small cushions with pink flowers on 5–7 cm scapes.

*S.* × *urumovii* 'Ivan Urumov' (*S.* × *urumovii*). Slow-growing grey-green dwarf cushions with yellow flowers on 5 cm scapes in March–April.

*S.* × *wehrhahnii* 'Hannelore' (*S.* 'Hannelore'). Vigorously growing cushions with several white flowers on each scape in March–April.

*Saxifraga* 'Wheatley Rose'. Parents unknown. A new hybrid with 1–2 pale pink flowers on each scape in March–April.

## Other hybrids of obscure origin

Besides the crosses of unknown parentage included in the list above, there is a considerable number of other hybrids of obscure origin. Most of these are better known in Great Britain than in Germany. Some of them are listed below. Some of these are very old hybrids and now almost unobtainable, but the list also includes some new hybrids and some older plants which have recently been renamed, together with varieties from Czechoslovakia.

*White flowers*: 'Banshee', 'Biegleri', 'Comet', 'Fanfare', 'Friesei', 'Laura Sinclair', 'Mrs Helen Terry', 'Pseudoscardica', 'Sabrina'.

*Yellow or cream-coloured flowers*: 'Allenii', 'Bayswater', 'C. M. Prichard', 'E. D. Doncaster' (bronze-yellow), 'Forsters Gold', 'Galahad', 'Helios', 'Icombe Hybrid', 'Pseudofranzii', 'Sartorii', 'Sigston Thompson', 'Trimmersfield', 'W. S. Rogers'.

*Pink, red, carmine or violet-red flowers*: 'Amenity', 'Appleblossom', 'Bellisant', 'Bornmuelleri', 'Coningsby Queen', 'Duke', 'Etheline', 'Gabrielle', 'Goeblii', 'Grey's Seedling', 'Joachim Burser', 'Laurent Ward', 'Ludmila Subrova', 'Miranda', 'Mrs G. Welch', 'Myra Cambria', 'Peach Blossom', 'Pseudokellereri', 'Rosamunda', 'Roxanne', 'Unique', 'Volgeri', 'Walpolei', 'Westmooriensis'.

## SECTION DACTYLOIDES (MOSSY SAXIFRAGES)

From the gardener's standpoint this section differs from the other horticulturally important sections of the genus in that the wild species are of much less importance in the garden. The main emphasis lies on the hybrids.

Nevertheless, there are a few valuable species such as *S. hypnoides, S. trifurcata* and *S. moschata* which should be grown in every rock garden. Furthermore, the section is so extensive that it makes a happy hunting ground for the specialist collector. There are many enthusiasts who take delight in growing some of these difficult species, even though they are not as showy as the hybrids.

The species and cultivars of Section Dactyloides (mossy saxifrages) form small green rosettes and most of them have divided leaves. The rosettes do not die after flowering. By putting out runners and shoots they weave dense low-growing cushions. Some of the hybrids are extremely vigorous and soon cover large areas. If they become too large the cushions can be reduced in size without difficulty, a task which can be done without tools.

The hybrids are valuable because they grow into good cushions even in semishaded places and flower profusely. This is one way of bringing colour into a shady garden otherwise dominated by green. They are decorative throughout the year, even in autumn and winter, and when the rosettes are coated with hoarfrost they look enchanting. Some of them assume a beautiful reddish coloration in autumn, in particular certain forms of *S. hypnoides*, notably *S. hypnoides* 'Kingii'.

Mossy saxifrages are not plants for dry, sunbaked places. The ideal spot is in partial shade with moist soil. Their flowering season begins at the end of April and extends into June.

As the cushions age, many mossy saxifrages tend to die out in the middle and must then be divided and replanted. They soon recover from this operation. As nearly all the hybrids are vigorous growers they must be given plenty of space at planting time. They should never be placed close to delicate slow-growing plants. If they are to be used to carpet large areas, divisions or pot-grown plants should be planted at intervals of about 30 cm. The intervening spaces will soon be covered.

The hybrids are not fussy about soil provided they are given a reasonable amount of moisture. A moist sandy loam is the ideal and for large plantings efforts should be made to approximate to it. Peaty sandy soils are also suitable, though they often fail to retain enough water. The requisite soil composition depends on the situation. The sunnier the site, the more water-retentive must be the soil. If the soil contains too little loam its water-holding powers can be enhanced by adding peat, leaf mould, Bentonite meal, expanded polystyrene chips, bark compost and similar materials.

Fertilizers must be used with care. An excess will make the cushions too soft and luxuriant so that they lose their firm compact appearance. The best fertilizer is dried pulverized cow dung, strewn on the cushions in early spring. In my garden there are some cushions which have received no manuring for ten years and still look healthy and flower profusely.

Normally the flowering stems should be cut off as the flowers fade. This is an easy task. Grasp a handful of stems and cut them off just above the cushion with a sharp saw-edged knife. If this operation is left too late the plants will produce self-sown seedlings, among which may be some passable new cultivars.

Though the hybrids flourish in moist soil, among the species there are some difficult customers which are by no means easy to grow. Some of these come from the Alps and others from the mountain ranges of Spain. When mixing compost for them every effort should be made to imitate the conditions existing in nature. Admixture of fine chippings – of igneous rock or limestone depending on the species – is often of great assistance. Chopped sphagnum moss often gives good results.

Certain species from Spain are not entirely winter-hardy. In the wild, some of them survive the summer drought by rolling their rosettes into little balls which remain green in the interior. As more northerly locations do not experience a dry period of this kind the annual rhythm of these saxifrages is easily deranged. Some of them can only be grown in an alpine house. When growing an unfamiliar species for the first time the gardener should keep a few rosettes in pots in a frame to provide a reserve if the plants in the open garden die.

Whereas the hybrids and a few of the species such as *S. hypnoides* and *S. trifurcata* are suitable for most rock gardens and semi-shaded areas, and even for carpet bedding, the difficult species should be reserved for the collector or the advanced alpine enthusiast who possesses an alpine house or who can grow these rarities in a trough in a semi-shaded spot.

## Species

### Saxifraga androsacea L. (syn. *S. pyrenaica* Scop., *S. multinervis* Dulac)

It occurs in the Pyrenees, the Auvergne (occasionally), the Alps, the Carpathians and the Rhodope mountains; and far removed from its European sites in the eastern Altai and the east Siberian Sajan ranges. It grows in moist grassland and scree, in snow-filled hollows and wet rock ledges, both on igneous rocks and alkaline subsoils, usually at altitudes of 1700–3000 metres.

Small mats, sometimes lax, sometimes compact. Rosette leaves narrow, obovate and wedge-shaped, narrowing at the base into an indistinct stem. Length 1–2 cm, width up to 0.5 cm. Three or occasionally 5 short teeth at the end of the leaf. Scapes 4–8 cm high or rarely higher, with 1–2 creamy white flowers. Sometimes 3–5 flowers forming an umbel. Flowering time May–June,

This is a pretty little plant, well worth growing in the garden; it requires moist soil and half-shade, and cannot withstand prolonged dryness.

In nature it is associated with *Ranunculus alpestris* (and its forms), *Viola calcarata, Soldanella alpina, Primula integrifolia, Gentiana bavarica* and *Veronica alpina*.

There are several varieties (var. *integrifolia* Ser., var. *tridentata* Gaud., var. *uniflora* Wulf., var. *pygmaea* Horn.) but the differences between them are not great. Plants from high altitudes are more compact and have shorter scapes than those from lower levels.

## Saxifraga aphylla Sternb. (syn. S. stenopetala Gaud.)

This species is of no horticultural importance other than for collectors and botanic gardens. It occurs only in the eastern Alps where it grows in limestone scree. Loose mats with lax scapes carrying inconspicuous flowers. Narrow pale-yellow petals, scarcely longer than the blunt sepals.

## Saxifraga sedoides L. (syn. S. trichodes Scop.)

A widely distributed plant, it is found in the eastern Alps, northern Apennines and Abruzzi, and Dinarian Alps; and in Bosnia, Herzegovina and Montenegro. In the eastern Pyrenees it is very rare. It grows only on limestone or dolomite, preferring northern aspects where the snow lies late, in scree and rock crevices.

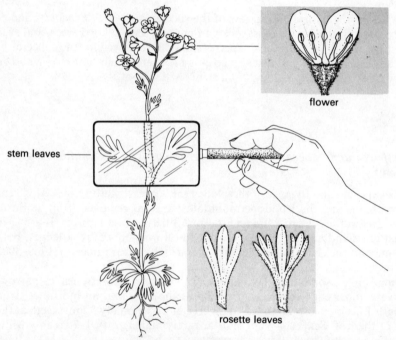

flower

stem leaves

rosette leaves

Important morphological features for distinguishing similar species

*Fig. 31*

The loose mats are made up of branching stems with numerous leaves above but fewer below. Flexible scapes 1.5–5 cm high, glabrous or with short glandular hairs. Flowers singly or 2–4 on each scape, pale greenish-yellow, lemon-yellow or reddish. This plant loves moist limestone scree and is not easy in cultivation. At low altitudes it soon becomes lax and untidy in appearance. There are two subspecies: ssp. *sedoides* L. and ssp. *prenja* Huber; the latter has 3-toothed leaves.

In nature it is associated with *Saxifraga androsacea, Hutchinsia alpina, Salix retusa, Ranunculus alpestris* ssp. *traunfellneri, Viola biflora, V. zoysii, Papaver burseri* (syn. *P. alpinum*), *Arabis pumila* and *Saxifraga squarrosa*.

### Saxifraga aquatica Lap. (syn. *S. adscendens* auct. non L.)

A handsome plant from the eastern and central Pyrenees, it occurs along streams from 1500 metres upwards, strong-growing, and forming large lax cushions. Leaves fleshy, shining, about 4 cm wide, with well-defined stems 5 cm long. Leaf blades resemble those of Ranunculus, being deeply cut into numerous triangular segments. Flowering stems tall (25–60 cm), upright and robust with numerous white flowers at the top. Petals 0.6–0.9 cm long.

The plant is not difficult to grow provided it can be given a site at the edge of a stream or pond where its roots can reach down to the water.

### Saxifraga cespitosa L.

Most of the plants offered under this name are hybrids of *S. cespitosa* with other species. It is widely distributed in arctic and subarctic regions, extending southwards to Wales, Scotland, the Faroe islands, Iceland, Greenland, the Urals and North America. Being so widely distributed, it is extremely variable and there are numerous local forms.

The leaf-bearing shoots are short and more or less upright, forming compact mats. The leaves are mostly 3-lobed, though occasionally 5-lobed, and recall those of the familiar *Saxifraga* Arendsii hybrids. The flowers, a somewhat dirty white in colour, are carried in groups of 1–3, or occasionally 5, on scapes ranging from 2.5 to 8 cm in height depending on the situation and the form. It is not a particularly attractive garden plant; the Arendsii hybrids are better.

### Saxifraga camposii Boiss. et Reuter (syn. *S. wallacei*)

From the limestone mountains of south-eastern Spain, chiefly between the vicinity of Ronda and the Sierra de Alcaraz, where it grows on limestone rocks, it forms neat compact cushions of slightly sticky, much divided leaves. Scapes 6–15 cm. Petals 0.8–1.1 cm long, narrowly obovate, white. It flowers in May. There are two subspecies (ssp. *camposii* and ssp. *leptophylla*), but as the plant is almost unobtainable they are of no importance to gardeners. It is a sun-lover, not absolutely hardy in severe winters, and best grown in the alpine house.

### Saxifraga canaliculata Boiss. et Reuter ex Engler.

From the Cordillera Cantabrica in northern Spain where it grows on limestone rocks and bare slopes, it forms broad cushions and the narrowly divided leaves give it the appearance of a moss. Leaf breadth 0.8–1.5 cm;

leaves are diamond shaped or semicircular in outline. Scapes 8–15 cm, petals 0.9 cm long, obovate, white. This one is not often seen in cultivation, but worth trying in the alpine house or in a sheltered spot.

### Saxifraga cebennensis Rouy et Camus

Confined to the Cevennes in southern France, it is tight, dome-shaped, up to fist-size, forming grey-green cushions on shady limestone rocks. Leaves up to 1 cm long, indistinctly 3-lobed, covered with fine glandular hairs. Scape 3–5 cm with 3–6 flowers in May. Flowers pure white, very attractive. This is a pretty species for a shady spot in the rock garden or a trough, ideal for holes in tufa.

### Saxifraga coarctata W. W. Smith

A Himalayan species doubtfully in cultivation.

### Saxifraga conifera Coss. et Durieu

A dwarf saxifrage from northern Spain (Pyrenees, Cordillera Cantabrica), it grows on limestone rocks. Leaf shoots 1–3 cm long forming a close mat. Leaves entire, linear lanceolate, like an ear of corn, pale silvery-green and 0.3–0.7 cm long. During summer the rosettes close up into pointed egg-shaped grey-green dormant buds which resemble *Sedum tenuifolium*. The slender scapes are 6–10 cm high and carry 3–5 white flowers. Petals 0.3–0.4 cm long. Occasionally offered by alpine plant nurseries, it is an interesting plant for the enthusiast, though not outstandingly attractive: not easy to manage and best grown in the alpine house or a trough.

### Saxifraga continentalis (Engl. et Irmsch.) D. A. Webb (syn. *S. hypnoides* ssp. *continentalis* Engl. et Irmsch.)

Very similar to *S. hypnoides*, it has now been given specific rank. Its area of distribution, southern France, northern Spain and northern Portugal, lies much further southwards than that of *S. hypnoides*. It is a lime-loving plant. The feature which distinguishes it from *S. hypnoides* is the stalked summer buds present in many of the leaf axils. They are covered by dry silvery leaf scales. *S. continentalis* is of much less horticultural importance than *S. hypnoides* and more difficult to grow.

### Saxifraga corbariensis Timb.-Lagr.

From the Corbières near the eastern end of the Pyrenees and from eastern Spain, it grows on limestone rocks and scree at altitudes of around 1500 metres, closely resembling *S. geranioides*. There are two subspecies: *S.c.* ssp. *corbariensis* from southern France has leaves 1.8 cm wide with 7–11 segments; *S.c.* ssp. *valentina* has leaves with 5 segments. The former has scapes 25 cm high carrying handsome, large white flowers. The broad firm mats flower in June. *S. corbariensis* should be grown in a sunny place or in the alpine house.

Saxifraga continentalis

Section Dactyloides

*Fig. 32*

## *Saxifraga cuneata* Willd.

A saxifrage from the western Pyrenees and the limestone mountains of Castille, it grows in shady places on limestone rocks, scree slopes and in walls. In appearance it resembles the *S. pentadactylis* group, but is clearly distinguishable by the characteristic shape of its leaves. These are thick, wedge-shaped, sticky and glandular, and in the autumn they are covered by grey deposits of lime. Leaves 1.5–3 cm long and wide. At the apex of the leaf stem the leaves tend to form a rosette. The flowering stems are 10–15 cm high and the white petals 0.6–0.7 cm wide. Flowers are fairly large, pure white.

The plant forms large domed cushions, dusted with white, which may be lax or dense depending on the situation. Flowering time June. A valuable species, it grows well in sunny places. The cushions are decorative even when out of flower.

### Saxifraga demnatensis Coss. ex Battand

A rare species from the Atlas mountains. Recently reintroduced into cultivation in England. Beautiful pale green mats. Leaves slightly sticky, aromatic, covered with glandular hairs. Rootstock thick. Flowering stems short, about 5–8 cm, with a compact inflorescence of up to 10 large white flowers with green veins. Alpine house cultivation is feasible, but its fate in the open garden is uncertain.

### Saxifraga depressa Sternb.

Found in the southern Alps, chiefly on igneous rock, at altitudes of 2000–2850 metres, it prefers moist scree and partial shade. Resembling *S. androsacea* var. *tridentata*, it has longer shoots, roughly 6–8 cm. Leaves 0.8–2.0 cm long and 0.7–1.0 cm wide, densely covered with short hairs, with 3 (sometimes 5) well defined lobes. There are 3–8 not very attractive flowers on each scape. *S. depressa* is of little importance to gardeners.

### Saxifraga erioblasta Boiss. et Reuter

Once classified as a variety of *S. globifera, S. erioblasta* is now recognized as a species in its own right, from the Sierra Nevada in southern Spain, where it grows on limestone soils. It is a neat plant which forms tight cushions. Leaves 0.5–0.7 cm long, wedge-shaped, 3-lobed. During hot weather the rosettes close up into tight, grey-brown buds with shaggy white hairs, in some respects resembling a dwarf cobweb houseleek (*Sempervivum arachnoideum*). Scapes 4–7 cm, slender, with 3–5 pale pink flowers resembling those of *S. globulifera*. A sun-loving plant for a favoured spot, it is safer in the alpine house.

### Saxifraga exarata Vill. (syn. *S. moschata* var. *exarata* Burnat).

Widely distributed in the high mountains of southern Europe (Pyrenees, Jura, Alps, Apennines, Balkans, Turkey, Caucasus), it grows in rock crevices and stabilized scree. Numerous upright shoots form a soft low mat. Leaves vary from 0.4–1.5 cm in size and also in shape (3–7 lobes). The leaves on the shoots overlap to form small rosettes. No resting buds. Easily confused with the closely similar *S. moschata, S. exarata* is distinguished by the rosette leaves which are more wedge-shaped, broader at the ends, more or less deeply 3–7 cleft and densely glandular-hairy. Scapes 3–7 cm high, inflorescences lax, corymbose or umbellate, usually with 3–8 flowers, occasionally up to 12, colour white to creamy yellow. The botanists distinguish *S.e.* ssp. *exarata* and *S.e.* ssp. *leucantha*, but these are of no importance to gardeners.

A useful plant for the rock garden, in nature it is associated with *Draba dubia, Saxifraga bryoides, S. paniculata, S. oppositifolia, Androsace multiflora, Primula hirsuta, P. latifolia* (syn. *P. viscosa*) and *Eritrichium nanum.* In cultivation it should be divided every 2–3 years.

### Saxifraga facchinii Koch. (syn. *S. planifolia* var. *atropurpurea* Koch, *S. muscoides* var. *facchinii*)

An endemic species from the Dolomites, it grows in stabilized scree and rock fissures. Closely related to *S. muscoides* but smaller. The stems are short and the leaf arrangement almost rosette-like. Flowering scapes upright, only 1–3 cm high, with several stem leaves. Inflorescence of 1–4 flowers, dull yellow tinged with purple. Despite its small range there are several varieties, including *S. facchinii* var. *leypoldii* Engl. et Irmsch., with 3-cleft leaves.

Seldom grown, though apparently a pretty plant. The flowers are even less impressive than those of *S. muscoides*.

### Saxifraga geranioides L.

A species from the eastern Pyrenees and north-eastern Spain, it grows on rocks and scree slopes. In appearance it resembles *S. corbariensis*. Leaves 1.5–3 cm wide, deeply divided into 9–27 acute, triangular-lanceolate segments. Scape up to 20 cm high, carrying at its top a compact inflorescence of 6–9 pure white, bell-shaped flowers with a faint scent. In the garden it prefers semi-shade and moist but not wet soil. In cultivation since 1770, it deserves to be more widely grown.

### Saxifraga glabella Bertol.

On calcareous rocks in the Apennines, eastern Alps and Balkans. Lax cushions made up of short shoots. Spathulate hairless leaves 0.8–1.0 cm long and 0.1–0.2 cm wide. Scapes 3–10 cm high with several small white flowers. Petals 0.3 cm long. Not of great garden value.

### Saxifraga globulifera Desf.

Comprises the formerly separate species *S. granatensis* Boiss. et Reuter and *S. gibraltarica* Boiss. et Reuter. *S. globulifera* is found in southern Spain and North Africa (Algeria), where it grows on limestone rocks and cliffs. Small lax mats. Leaf shoots spreading or upright, often only 1–2 cm long. Leaves ovate or kidney-shaped, with 3–7 lobes and glandular hairs. One distinctive feature is the long stalks of the lower leaves. The scapes carry 3–7 small white flowers. A likeable plant, if not particularly striking, it grows well in the alpine house.

The plant offered under the name *S. globulifera* var. *erioblasta* is in fact *S. erioblasta* (q.v.).

### Saxifraga hariotii Luizet et Soulie

From the western Pyrenees, where it grows on limestone rocks, it resembles

*S. moschata*, especially in the shape and colour of the flowers. *S. hariotii* is distinguished by its leaves, which are forked. Scapes 2–6 cm high carrying 1–4 creamy white or dull yellow flowers. It is probably not of much garden interest.

### Saxifraga hartii D. A. Webb

Found in only one isolated locality on the grassy cliffs of the Irish coast (Arranmore Island), it is intermediate in appearance between *S. cespitosa* and *S. rosacea*, distinguished from the latter by its short close-set glandular hairs and from *S. cespitosa* by its flatter rosettes. Compact inflorescence of fairly large white flowers on a robust scape 4–5 cm high. The red coloration of the upper half of the sepals gives it a characteristic appearance.

### Saxifraga humilis Engl. et Irmsch.

A Himalayan species doubtfully in cultivation.

### Saxifraga hypnoides L. (Dovedale Moss)

Widely distributed throughout north-western and central Europe – Iceland, British Isles, Faroe Islands and small localities on the west coast of Norway and in the Vosges above Géradmer – it forms large pale green mats varying in density according to the situation. Thin straggling shoots with rather sparse leaves and dormant buds in some of the leaf axils. Leaves long-stalked, deeply divided usually into 3 but sometimes up to 9 lobes, usually wedge-shaped or like an ear of corn in outline. The inflorescence is a loose corymb or umbel of 3–7 white flowers in May–June.

S. *hypnoides* var. *egemmulosa* Engl. et Irmsch. is a fine variety, grown under the names *S. gemmifera* hort. and *S. kingii* hort. It forms compact bright green carpets which assume a bronzy red tone in autumn, and it is sometimes described in the older books as *S. hypnoides* 'Purpurea'. In the wild it grows on mountains which enjoy abundant rainfall, and in the garden it likes a cool shady place. Though very pretty when in flower, its main value lies in the beautiful mossy cushions.

There is another garden form known as 'Whitlavei', often grown in Great Britain. It is more floriferous and has more flowers on each scape. Closely related is *S. continentalis* D. A. Webb, found in southern France and northern Spain and Portugal, previously known as *S. hypnoides* L. ssp. *continentalis* Engl. et Irmsch.

A similar species offered in the trade is *S. pulchella* Don, which forms large cushions with white flowers.

### Saxifraga italica Webb. (syn. S. tridens Jan.)

Found in the Abruzzi at altitudes of 2000–2500 metres, it resembles *S. androsacea* var. *tridentata* but has tighter and more compact cushions, closely pressed to the ground. Leaves hairy, scapes 2–4 cm high with milky white flowers, quite large in relation to the plant as a whole. Petals 0.2–0.7 cm long. *S. italica* is seldom available.

## Saxifraga maderensis D. Don

From Madeira, where it grows at altitudes of about 1000 metres, it is even more tender than *S. portosanctana*. A rare plant, it is hardly ever seen in cultivation, and quite different in appearance from the other species of this section. Leaves kidney-shaped, divided into 5 lobes each having 3–5 notches. Scapes 10–15 cm long carrying 5–7 handsome white flowers. It needs a frostproof alpine house.

## Saxifraga maweana Baker

From the mountains of Morocco. Leaves fleshy, 3-lobed, each lobe being divided into 2–3 segements. New shoots purple in their lower halves. Flowering shoots carry 4–9 white flowers in May–June. Although introduced in the 19th century, it is not easy to obtain, and requires an alpine house or cold frame.

## Saxifraga moncayensis D. A. Webb

From north-eastern Spain, where it grows in the Sierra del Moncayo, it was only recently given specific rank. It is intermediate between *S. pentadactylis* and *S. vayredana*, distinguished from *S. pentadactylis* by its larger cushions of soft, lighter coloured foliage, its covering of numerous very short glandular hairs and by its slightly larger petals; from *S. vayredana* it is distinguished by its larger leaf segments (up to 1 cm long), and its much fainter scent. Seldom seen in cultivation, it would be worth trying.

## Saxifraga moschata Wulf.

This one grows in southern and central Europe – Pyrenees, Auvergne, Alps and Carpathians, Sudeten mountains, northern Apennines, Balkans, Caucasus and Altai – on limestone and calcareous slate, in stabilized scree and thin stony grassland.

Because of its wide distribution, *S. moschata* is an unusually variable species. Mats moderately to very tight. Leaf shoots without resting buds. Basal leaves linear and usually undivided, or wedge-shaped, then having 3 teeth or clefts. Overall leaf length 0.3–1.5 cm. Inflorescences with few flowers, usually 2–5, occasionally up to 9, corymbose or umbellate. Scapes 1–10 cm in height, with 2–5 stem leaves. Flowers creamy white to dull yellow.

The botanists distinguish several varieties: *S.m.* var. *lineata* with undivided leaves, *S.m.* var. *moschata*, *S.m.* var. *carniolica*, *S.m.* var. *basaltica*. For the gardener these distinctions are of little interest. Wocke described a considerable number of different forms, most of which have disappeared from cultivation, including the delicate dwarf saffron-yellow *S.m.* var. *crocea* Gaud. from Monte Rosa; *S.m.* 'Pygmaea', with linear undivided leaves and only a single flower; *S.m.* 'Laxa', a shade-loving form; *S.m.* 'Allionii', up to 15 cm high; *S.m.* 'Acaulis' from Zermatt with only 1–2 flowers; *S.m.* var. *rhei* Schott from the Carpathians and *S.m.f. hemisphaerica* from the Himalayas, which reaches altitudes of up to 6000 metres on Mount Everest.

*S. moschata* is a good garden plant. Leaving aside all its doubtful garden names, there is a selected form known as 'Cloth of Gold' which has golden-yellow leaves all the year round. It deserves a carefully chosen place, such as a trough in semi-shade. Under the name *S. moschata* 'Compacta' there is a very low-growing form with white flowers, and there is also *S. moschata* 'Variegata'.

In the wild it is associated with *Festuca pumila, Dryas octopetala, Androsace chamaejasme, Aster alpinus, Silene acaulis, Draba aizoides, Petrocallis pyrenaica, Saxifraga squarrosa, Androsace villosa, Eritrichium nanum, Veronica aphylla, Gentiana terglouensis, Gentiana froelichii, Valeriana supina, Campanula zoysii, Carex firma* and *Festuca alpina*.

### Saxifraga muscoides All. (syn. *S. tenera, S. planifolia* Sternb.)

The range extends from the Cottian Alps as far as the Hohe Tauern; it grows in fine scree and high altitude grasslands up to 4200 metres. Although a native of the central Alps, it prefers calcareous schist and is seldom found on siliceous rocks. It forms dense firm low cushions with a resinous odour. Shoots are covered with overlapping leaves; flowering stems 2–5 cm high with pale yellow or whitish flowers in June–August.

Nearly all the plants grown in gardens under this name are not the true species but belong to the *S. cespitosa* group (this includes the widely grown *S. muscoides* 'Findling'), or are forms of *S. moschata*. The true species is difficult to keep in lowland gardens and is of little garden value, being of interest only to collectors and botanists. The mats often disintegrate from the middle outwards and must then be divided and replanted.

Among the plants associated with it in the wild are *Androsace helvetica, S. paniculata, S. moschata, S. oppositifolia* and *Draba aizoides*.

### Saxifraga nervosa Lapeyr.

In the central Pyrenees it grows on siliceous rocks. Semi-erect shoots form loose cushions of dark green hairy aromatic leaves with 3–5 segments. Scapes 4–10 cm high carrying 3–12 rounded white flowers. Rather difficult in cultivation.

### Saxifraga nevadensis Boiss. (syn. *S. pubescens* ssp. *nevadensis* Engl. et Irmsch.)

Grows in the Sierra Nevada in southern Spain at altitudes of 2600 metres and above. Creamy white flowers on 5–7 cm scapes in May–June. Resembling *S. pubescens*, it is available in the trade.

### Saxifraga oranensis Minby

Found in the mountains near Oran in Algeria, it resembles *S. globulifera* and is sometimes regarded as a subspecies. The main differences are that the leaves turn reddish in summer after flowering and that its white flowers are finer and more impressive. A beautiful plant for the alpine house, in mild districts it should also do well in the open if protected from winter wet. It is not difficult in cultivation.

### *Saxifraga pedemontana* All. (syn. *S. allionii* Terr.)

A plant with a wide distribution extending from the Pyrenees to the Carpathians and the Balkans, it has more or less upright leafy shoots forming low cushions. Leaf outline is wedge-shaped or semicircular, but deeply divided into 5–10 segments. Lower part of shoot covered with dead leaves. Fairly large white flowers form dense inflorescences, with narrow petals varying in length from 0.4 to 1.4 cm, depending on the origin of the plant. There are four subspecies. All the subspecies prefer siliceous rock in the wild. In the garden they are not difficult, especially if grown in moist shady places, but do not like stagnant moisture in the winter and are perhaps best grown in the alpine house.

*S. pedemontana* ssp. *pedemontana* from the south-western and central Alps. Leaves fleshy, but not so deeply divided, with short hairs. Scapes 6–15 cm high, petals 1.1–1.4 cm long.

*S. pedemontana* ssp. *cymosa* from the eastern Carpathians and the Balkan mountains. Leaves thin and delicate, with broad segments. Scapes rarely higher than 8 cm.

*S. pedemontana* ssp. *cervicornis* from Corsica and Sardinia. Clearly distinguished by the rosette leaves, which curve inwards as if in bud, and by the spreading segments. This dwarf Corsican plant was introduced by Sündermann in 1912.

*S. pedemontana* ssp. *prostii* from southern France and the Pyrenees. Leaves large, deeply divided into segments, fleshy and wedge-shaped; usually hairy. Scapes 3–7 cm high with 1–3 flowers in June–August. Forms handsome cushions.

### *Saxifraga pentadactylis* Lapeyr.

On the eastern Pyrenees and the mountains of central Spain it grows on rocks and scree, avoiding limestone. Loose cushions are made up of leafy shoots and woody stems. Leaves hairless, deeply divided into 3–5 grooved lobes, aromatic. Scapes 6–20 cm high, branching, with few leaves, and 3–30 small creamy-white flowers on each scape. *S. pentadactylis* is difficult to keep for long in the rock garden; the variety *S.p.* var. *willkommiana* is more robust.

### *Saxifraga portosanctana* Boiss.

Restricted to the island of Porto Santa in the Madeira group, it grows at about 500 metres on north-facing mountain spurs. Leaves thick, fleshy, light green. Scapes 10–12 cm, not straight but zigzag, with 2–3 large white flowers with conspicuous veining. It flowers in June, and is for the alpine house only.

## *Saxifraga praetermissa* D. A. Webb (syn. *S. ajugifolia* auct. non L.)

From the Pyrenees and Cantabrian mountains at altitudes of 1500 metres upwards, it is usually found on the stony shores of mountain lakes and in depressions where the snow lies late, always in moist or at least shaded spots. The spreading cushions are made up of leafy shoots 3–6 cm long with withered leaves at the base. Leave 1 cm long and 1.5 cm wide, sparsely hairy, deeply divided into 3–5 segments. Scapes upright, 6–12 cm, with 1–3 white flowers. It is worth growing if a suitable place is available.

## *Saxifraga presolanensis* Engl.

A rare endemic from the Bergamasque Alps, it grows in caves, recesses and chimneys on overhanging rock faces, usually north-facing, at altitudes of around 1800 metres, usually on limestone, but occasionally on other rock. The tight hemispherical yellow-green cushions are the size of a man's fist or somewhat larger. When growing in level scree the plant loses its characteristic shape. Scapes 6–12 cm, slender, with 2–4 greenish yellow flowers in August. Seldom offered, it would be worth introducing into cultivation. It would need conditions in the rock garden approximating to those in which it grows in the wild.

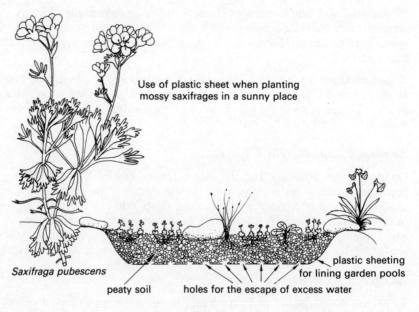

Use of plastic sheet when planting mossy saxifrages in a sunny place

*Saxifraga pubescens*

peaty soil          holes for the escape of excess water

plastic sheeting for lining garden pools

*Fig. 33*

## Saxifraga pubescens Pourret

A species from the Pyrenees, closely related to *S. exarata* and *S. moschata*, it is somewhat variable in appearance. Tight compact cushions. Rosette leaves deep green, usually 5-lobed, occasionally 3-lobed, covered with long glandular hairs.

*S. pubescens* ssp. *iratiana* occurs mainly in the central Pyrenees. Leaves 0.4–1.0 cm long, with segments twice as long as wide. Scapes 2–6 cm high, flowers white with red veins. More compact than the next subspecies, it is suitable for the alpine house or a sheltered spot in the open garden.

*S. pubescens* ssp. *pubescens*, found chiefly in the eastern Pyrenees, has leaves 1.0–2.0 cm long. Scapes 3–10 cm high with pure white flowers.

Also offered in the trade is *S. pubescens* ssp. *delphinensis* with white flowers on 5–8 cm scapes in May–June.

## Saxifraga rigoi Porta

This is found on limestone rocks in the mountains of south-eastern Spain (Granada). In the hot summer months the plant dries up and forms large red clumps which make a striking contrast against the white limestone. Leaves semcircular in outline, divided into 3–7 lobes, with glandular hairs. Scape 6–12 cm high carrying 2–3 large white flowers. Petals 1.2–1.5 cm long and 0.5 cm wide.

## Saxifraga reuterana Boiss.

Another species from southern Spain, notably the Granada region, it closely resembles *S. globulifera* but has shorter scapes (4–6 cm) carrying 1–2, or often 4–5, fairly large white flowers. Petals pure white, 0.6–0.7 cm long and 0.4 cm wide. It grows on vertical limestone cliffs and would be worth cultivating.

## Saxifraga rosacea Moench (syn. *S. decipiens* Ehrh., *S. cespitosa* ssp. *decipiens* (Ehrh.) Engl. et Irmsch.)

In north-western and central Europe it ranges from Poland to Iceland, through Germany, France and Great Britain, growing in rock crevices and scree on limestone and non-calcareous rocks. There are several local forms, some making dense compact cushions while others form spreading mats. Leaves hairy, usually 5-lobed. Scapes slender, without stem leaves, carrying 2–5 pure white or pale pink flowers. The parent of many mossy saxifrage hybrids.

There are two subspecies: *S. rosacea* ssp. *rosacea*, found in southern and central Germany, eastern France, Ireland, Iceland and the Faroe islands; and *S. rosacea* ssp. *sponhemica*, found in eastern France, western Germany, Czechoslovakia and south-western Poland. The botanical differences are of no horticultural importance.

In nature *S. rosacea* is associated with *Festuca cinerea*, small species of *Asplenium*, *Dianthus gratianopolitanus* and *Campanula rotundifolia*.

### Saxifraga seguieri Sprengel (syn. *S. planifolia* var. *seguieri* Sternb.)

From the central and eastern Alps, it is stated to be a lime-hater, but often found on calcareous schist. It grows in moist screes and wet crevices, and on old moraine rubble in north-facing sites which are covered with snow in winter.

S. *seguieri* resembles *S. androsacea*, and in the non-flowering state can be confused with it, but it is smaller and more compact. In *S. seguieri* the glandular hairs are short and more or less closely set, while *S. androsacea* has long ribbon-like hairs.

Leaves entire. Scapes 2–7 cm high, usually carrying 1 or occasionally 2–3 flowers. Buds reddish brown, opening into dull, creamy-yellow flowers in July–August. A charming plant for the enthusiast, it is often difficult in cultivation. In the wild it is associated with *Minuartia sedoides*, *Gentiana bavarica* var. *subacaulis*, *Veronica alpina*, *Eritrichium nanum*. *Saxifraga exarata*, *Luzula spicata* and *Ranunculus pygmaeus*.

### Saxifraga spathulata Desf.

From Algeria and other parts of North Africa. It is distinguished by its narrow undivided spathulate leaves, lax habit and absence of hairs. Scapes about 20 cm high and white flowers of no special beauty. It is an alpine house candidate.

### Saxifraga tenella Wulf. (syn. *S. arenarioides* Brignoli, *Chondrosea tenella* Haw.)

An endemic of the south-eastern Alps, it grows in mossy places on limestone or dolomite scree. It may be confused with *S. aspera*, but is distinguished by the almost superior ovary and the presence of several rows of hairs on the leaf margins.

S. *tenella* forms small long-lived cushions made up of creeping stems with close-set leaves having resting buds in the axils. Leaves 1 cm long, subulate or narrow lanceolate, entire and spreading, with a single row of bristly hairs at the base or round the margin. Scapes 5–10 cm high, thin and glabrous, with 2–8 yellowish white flowers in June. It grows well in the garden in half or full shade, and can even be used as a ground-coverer for small areas.

### Saxifraga trabutiana Engl. et Irmsch.

Another species from Algeria, closely related to *S. erioblasta* but not so compact. Scapes 5–6 cm high carrying 3–5 small white flowers. It requires alpine house cultivation.

### Saxifraga trifurcata Schrader. (syn. *S. ceratophylla*)

Growing in northern Spain from Asturia to Navarra and in the Pyrenees on limestone rocks and scree slopes, it forms large dull-green mats, sometimes rising into loose mounds. Shoots thin and brittle. Leaves leathery, on long petioles; outline kidney-shaped, 3-lobed. Scapes 15–20 cm high with corymbs of white flowers in May–June.

This is one of the best garden plants of its section. Its large cushions are extremely free-flowering and unlike many other species it will withstand full sun. Even when growing on rocks it will shoot up from below. Valuable for its late flowering season, it makes a good edging plant but needs plenty of space.

### *Saxifraga vayredana* Luizer

Found only in north-eastern Spain, near Montseny (north-east of Barcelona), it grows in shady places on siliceous rock and scree slopes. It forms rounded cushions which are almost completely hidden by the wealth of blossom at flowering time. Numerous thin semi-erect shoots. Leaves covered with very short glandular hairs which emit a powerful aromatic resinous odour. Leaf outline wedge-shaped or semicircular, deeply divided into 3–7 lanceolate segments. Overall appearance moss-like. Scapes very slender, 6–10 cm high, with a reddish tinge on the upper half. Each scape carries 3–10 white flowers with broad obovate petals. Not easy to obtain, it is well worth growing for its abundant and dependable flowering. Doubtfully winterhardy, it certainly needs alpine house cultivation.

### *Saxifraga wahlenbergii* Ball (syn. *S. perdurans* Kit.)

From the western Carpathians (Poland and Czechoslovakia), it resembles *S. praetermissa*, forming small mats and cushions. Leaves divided into 3–5 segments. Shoots short, prostrate, leafy. Scapes arise from the leaf axils on the lower part of the shoot. Scapes 4–7 cm high, shorter than those of *S. praetermissa*, carrying 1–3 white flowers. Petals 0.3–0.5 cm long. In the wild it grows on moist grassy slopes, and is well worth cultivating.

## Hybrids of Section Dactyloides

In this section the hybrids are of much greater horticultural importance than the species. Most of them are more beautiful and much easier to grow. In the early days only a few hybrids were available, but more and more have been added to their number and the range is now too large to list in detail. All the hybrids require fairly moist soil. Most of them flower in April–May, a few somewhat later. The stated heights are averages. Among the Arendsii hybrids, the height of the flower stem is strongly influenced by soil moisture, manuring and sunlight.

### 1. *Hybrids more commonly grown in Great Britain*

It is often uncertain whether an individual hybrid belongs to the *Saxifraga*

'Arendsii' complex and for this reason the English nomenclature has been given preference. A few English hybrids grown in Germany are mentioned in the following section.

*Saxifraga* 'Ballawley Guardsman'. A hybrid of recent date with velvety carmine scarlet flowers on 15 cm stems. Not too vigorous.

*Saxifraga* 'Bob Hawkins'. A new English hybrid. Compact cushions of deeply cut leaves with silvery variegation which contrasts with the reddish tinge of the older leaves. Flowers white, 15 cm.

*Saxifraga* 'Cambria Jewel'. A pretty hybrid with deep-pink flowers on 10 cm scapes.

*Saxifraga* 'Clare Island'. Fine cushions with pure white flowers.

*Saxifraga* 'Darlington Double'. A floriferous hybrid with deep pink double flowers. Grows very slowly and is hence suitable for troughs and favoured spots. About 5 cm high.

*Saxifraga* 'Diana'. Pale pink flowers on 15 cm scapes.

*Saxifraga* 'Edie Campbell'. An extremely floriferous hybrid with large pink flowers.

*Saxifraga* 'Elf'. A dwarf mossy hybrid with carmine-red flowers on very short stems. Late-flowering.

*Saxifraga* 'Fairy'. A white-flowered hybrid derived from *S. moschata*, but not closely resembling it. Similar in appearance to the other hybrids. Very low and compact. Late-flowering, white, scapes 7–8 cm.

*Saxifraga* 'Flowers of Sulphur'. Pale sulphur-yellow flowers, about 10 cm high, probably identical with *S.* × *arendsii* 'Schwefelblüte'.

*Saxifraga* 'Four Winds'. An outstanding hybrid with brilliant carmine-red flowers, borne in clusters of 5–9 on scapes 20 cm high.

*Saxifraga* 'Gaiety'. A valuable, very early-flowering hybrid with deep-pink flowers on short scapes.

*Saxifraga* 'Gnome'. A low-growing and late-flowering hybrid (height 5–8 cm). Flowers carmine-red.

*Saxifraga* 'Hartswood White'. White flowers with a tinge of pink. About 15 cm high.

*Saxifraga* 'James Bremner'. A robust hybrid with large white flowers about 2.5 cm in diameter growing to a height of about 25 cm. Origin obscure, but some authorities state that *S. granulata* was among its parents.

*Saxifraga* 'Kingscote White'. Handsome cushions with large white flowers on 10 cm scapes.

*Saxifraga* 'Knapton Pink'. Magnificent mossy cushions. Pink flowers 10 cm high.

*Saxifraga* 'Mrs Piper'. A low-growing hybrid with red flowers on 5–8 cm scapes.

*Saxifraga* 'Pearly King'. A dwarf mossy saxifrage with pure white flowers about 10 cm high.

*Saxifraga* 'Peter Pan'. A compact hybrid with carmine red flowers on 5–9 cm scapes.

*Saxifraga* 'Pixie'. A pretty saxifrage with rose-pink flowers on 5 cm scapes.

*Saxifraga* 'Red Admiral'. A good hybrid with splendid red flowers on 10 cm scapes.

*Saxifraga* 'Ruffles'. Resembles *S.* 'Darlington Double', but has double white flowers with a tinge of pink.

*Saxifraga* 'Sprite'. Carmine-pink flowers on 10 cm scapes.

*Saxifraga* 'White Pixie'. Resembles *S.* 'Pixie' in all respects except flower colour. Scapes 3–5 cm.

*Saxifraga* 'Winston Churchill'. Vigorous cushions with pure pink flowers.

## 2. Mossy hybrids grown in German-speaking countries

*Saxifraga × arendsii* 'Biedermeier'. A beautiful and distinctive white variety with frilled petals. 10–15 cm high, April–May.

*S. × arendsii* 'Blütenteppich' ('Flower Carpet'). Grown in a slightly moist spot, it forms luxuriant mossy cushions. Reliable and free-flowering. Height 10–15 cm, depending on situation. Flowers carmine pink.

*S. × arendsii* 'Carnival'. Brilliant rose-pink flowers on 15 cm scapes. The colour does not fade in the sun.

*S. × arendsii* 'Dornröschen' Benary ('Sleeping Beauty'). Large rosettes, rapid-growing, with pale-green hairless leaves and slightly tinted flowering stems 14–16 cm high. Height above cushion 10–12 cm. Flowers brilliant red with a salmon pink tinge, the colour remaining attractive even as they fade. Flowers about 2 cm in diameter and pleasing in shape. Long flowering period (introduced by Klose).

*S. × arendsii* 'Dubarry'. An English hybrid, but offered by nurseries in Germany. Of value for its late flowering. Comparatively large, deep carmine-red flowers. About 20 cm high.

*S. × arendsii* 'Farbenteppich' ('Colour Carpet'). A cheerful rose-pink shade.

*S. × arendsii* 'Feuerteppich' ('Fire Carpet'). Fine cushions with red flowers.

*S. × arendsii* 'Feuerwerk' ('Fireworks'). Firm mossy cushions, early flowering. Carmine rose-pink, 15–20 cm high.

*S. × arendsii* 'Grandiflora Alba'. One of the older hybrids, reliable and vigorous. White flowers about 20 cm high.

*S.* × *arendsii* 'R. W. Hosin'. An English cultivar, also grown in Germany. About 10 cm high with red flowers.

*S.* × *arendsii* 'Ingeborg' K. H. Marx. A recent introduction. Large dark red flowers on short compact foliage which does not split apart.

*S.* × *arendsii* 'Juwel' ('Jewel'). A low-growing form with red flowers.

*S.* × *arendsii* 'Leuchtkäfer' Benary ('Luminous Beetle'). Dense slow-growing cushions made up of small neat rosettes. Very hardy and does not tend to die out in the middle. Flowers slightly hairy, flower stems very dark. Overall height 15–17 cm; height above cushion 12–13 cm. Flowers deep red, sun resistant, relatively small (1.8–2 cm), circular. Very long flowering season and extremely floriferous. (Introduced by Klose.)

*S.* × *arendsii* 'Luschtinetz', also known as *S.* × *arendsii* 'Harder Zwerg'. An interesting cultivar which remains low (about 8 cm). Flowers blood-red, cushions fairly vigorous. Valuable for its good sun-resistance.

*S.* × *arendsii* 'Purpurmantel' ('Purple Cloak'). A vigorous plant with carmine-red flowers. Height 10–15 cm, depending on situation.

*S.* × *arendsii* 'Purpurteppich' ('Purple Carpet'). Vigorous cushions with pale carmine-red flowers on 15–20 cm scapes.

*S.* × *arendsii* 'Riedels Farbenkissen' ('Riedel's Colour Cushion'). A new German hybrid. Deep fire-red flowers fading to pink. About 20 cm high.

*S.* × *arendsii* 'Rosakönigin' ('Pink Queen'). Cushions somewhat lax, but valuable for its late flowering. Flowers pure pink, about 15 cm high.

*S.* × *arendsii* 'Rosenschaum' ('Rose Foam'). An uncommon variety with pink flowers on 15–20 cm scapes.

*S.* × *arendsii* 'Rosenzwerg' ('Rose Dwarf'). Very low-growing (about 3 cm). Flowers deep pink. Foliage unusually firm.

*S.* × *arendsii* 'Roseum Elegans'. An old cultivar but still useful. Flowers pink, about 8–10 cm high. Cushions very tight.

*S.* × *arendsii* 'Sanguinea Superba'. An old and reliable variety with blood-red flowers about 10 cm high.

*S.* × *arendsii* 'Schneeteppich' ('Snow Carpet'). A standard white variety. Masses of snow-white flowers 15–20 cm high. Individual flowers relatively large. Cushions firm.

*S.* × *arendsii* 'Schöne von Ronsdorf' ('Beauty of Ronsdorf'). Brilliant rose-pink flowers with less tendency to fade than most other varieties. About 10–12 cm high.

*S.* × *arendsii* 'Schwefelblüte' ('Flowers of Sulphur'). Firm tight cushions, very vigorous. Pale sulphur-yellow flowers about 10–15 cm high.

*S.* × *arendsii* 'Spätlese' (J.L.) ('Late Vintage'). Firm cushions with pale carmine-red flowers at the end of the season in May.

*S.* × *arendsii* 'Triumph'. One of the best hybrids. Widely grown in Great Britain. Flowers brilliant dark red, resistant to fading, 10–15 cm high. Flourishes in slightly moist soil. The cushions are decorative even when out of flower.

Other cultivars, not belonging to the *Saxifraga* Arendsii complex:

*S.* × *muscoides* 'Findling' ('Findel') ('Foundling'). Raised by Arends but derived from *S. cespitosa*, not *S. muscoides*. A valuable plant with tight dark-green cushions. Abundant white flowers in May.

*S.* × *muscoides* 'Purpurea'. Recently offered by nurseries, with red flowers.

*Saxifraga* 'Elegantissima'. Dense low-growing cushions, very long lived. Tolerates somewhat more sun than most others.

*Saxifraga* 'Gloriosa' and *Saxifraga* 'Amoena', with tiny cushions, are almost unobtainable.

# SECTION PORPHYRION

The species of this section form dense evergreen low-growing mats made up of slender shoots which root as they run along the soil. The leaves are mostly opposite, small, leathery and dark green. They are thickened towards the apex and sometimes scale-like. The flowers, almost stemless, are carmine-pink, red, pink, purple or occasionally white. The section is closely related to Section Porophyllum ('Kabschia').

The members of this group, and in particular *S. oppositifolia*, are among the finest alpines. Every gardener who has seen them in the wild will wish to grow them in his own garden. In nature they grow in the most inhospitable places, exposed to cold, snow, rain and wind, on soil consisting solely of rock débris, but in the garden they need care and attention. They are enthusiasts' plants, not to be mentioned in the same breath as *Aubrieta* and cushion phloxes. The site for their planting must be chosen with care. An east- or west-facing slope is suitable, but the plant must be shaded from the midday sun by a dwarf shrub or a rock. They will also grow on north-facing slopes or indeed in any place sheltered from direct sunlight, but they will not flourish in deep shade. The site must be cool and the soil must always be slightly damp and must never dry out; however, stagnant moisture must be avoided. The soil should contain a high proportion of rock chips or gravel together with some humus. In nature *S. oppositifolia* is found on calcareous and on igneous rocks. Most of the garden varieties are lime-loving and the compost should therefore contain plenty of limestone chippings. Granulated pumice is equally suitable, but if sintered clay is used the smooth round nodules should be broken or crushed. The plants should be given a periodic top dressing of sand mixed with peat. In my garden *S. oppositifolia* flourishes between tufa rocks.

Pot-grown plants can be planted at almost any time of year provided they are well rooted, but if this is not the case they should be planted in early spring. If planting is followed by dry sunny weather they should be shaded. Divisions taken from established plants should be potted up and grown for some time in a moist atmosphere before being planted out.

## Species

### *Saxifraga biflora* All.

Found only in the central and northern Alps in Germany, Austria, Switzerland and Italy, it grows in places where the snow lies late, chiefly in fine scree derived from limestone or calcareous schist, usually at altitudes of 2000–3000 metres, but sometimes up to 4200 metres. It is a member of the 'snowpatch flora' often associated with *Soldanella*. There are two subspecies, but the distinction is of no importance to gardeners.

It resembles *S. oppositifolia* and forms loose mats. Shoots creeping or upright, sparsely or sometimes thickly covered with leaves. Flower stems 1–5 cm high, depending on situation, covered with glandular hairs. Leaves opposite, obovate to circular, 0.5–0.9 cm long and 0.3–0.6 cm wide. Inflorescence a cyme or corymb with 2–9 flowers. Colour purple-pink to dull violet or occasionally dirty white.

Not easy in cultivation, it should be grown in humus-rich compost with limestone chippings: a plant for the enthusiast.

### *Saxifraga oppositifolia* L.

This species has an enormous range: Sierra Nevada, Pyrenees, Jura, Auvergne, Alps, Apennines, Sudeten mountains, Carpathians, Balkans. It is a circumpolar plant found in Iceland (and depicted on an Icelandic postage stamp), Scandinavia, Lapland, Siberia, Alaska, Northern Canada, Greenland, Spitzbergen, Franz-Josefs Land, Bear Island, and Novaya Zemlya. It also occurs in the mountains of Great Britain and Ireland, and on the Atlantic side of North America southwards to Vermont, on the Pacific side as far as the Yellowstone area. The deviant subspecies *S.o.* ssp. *asiatica* is found in the Altai, Dahuria, Alatau, Tien-Shan, western Tibet and Kashmir.

*S. oppositifolia* grows on rock ledges, scree, moraine slopes, gravel banks, cliffs and ridges, river gravels and patchy grassland at altitudes from 600 to 3800 metres. It occurs on igneous and calcareous rocks alike.

It forms flat cushions, loose or compact. The lax creeping stems have stiff opposite narrow obovate leaves, bent back at the tips. They are arranged in four rows and have 1–3 very small lime pits. Scapes upright, very short, often completely suppressed, with glandular hairs. The 5 petals are wine-red to purple-pink, obovate to elliptical, 0.5–2.0 cm long. Flowers turn pale violet to blue as they fade. There is a rare white form. As would be expected from its wide range, there are numerous natural forms, and in addition gardeners have selected outstanding clones. *S. oppositifolia* is among the hardiest of plants. In places not covered by snow it will stand temperatures as low as −40°C. When exposed to such extreme cold the green cushions assume a brownish-red or dark purple tinge. The buds are formed in autumn and unfold as soon as the snow melts. The upper leaves serve to protect them.

In the wild it is associated with *Ranunculus glacialis, Sedum alpestre, Saxifraga exarata, S. seguieri, Androsace alpina, Primula latifolia* (syn. *P.*

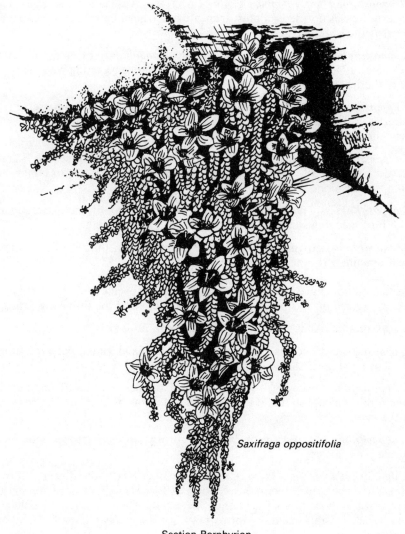

*Saxifraga oppositifolia*

Section Porphyrion

*Fig. 34*

*viscosa*), *Gentiana bavarica* var. *subacaulis*, *G. brachyphylla*, *Eritrichium nanum*, *Linaria alpina*, *Silene exscapa*, *Saxifraga bryoides*, *S. paniculata* and *Primula hirsuta*.

The following subspecies are distinguished:

**S. oppositifolia** ssp. *rudolphiana*. A form from the eastern Alps with very close firm cushions. Leaves 0.15–0.25 cm long, the outer third or quarter being devoid of marginal hairs.

**S. oppositifolia** ssp. *blepharophylla*. From the Austrian Alps, especially Tauern. Leaves obtuse or almost truncated; marginal hairs becoming longer towards the leaf apex.

**S. oppositifolia** ssp. *murithiana* (syn. *S.o.* ssp. *glandulifera*). From the Western Alps, Sierra Nevada, Pyrenees. The leaves have a lime-secreting water groove (hydathode).

**S. oppositifolia** ssp. *latina*. From the Apennines. Leaves with 3 lime-secreting water grooves. Especially early flowering. Flowers deep purple with very short stems. Grows well in the garden and flowers profusely.

**S. oppositifolia** ssp. *speciosa*. From the Apennines and Abruzzi. Large flowers. The apical part of the leaf has a broad cartilaginous margin. Compact cushions.

**S. oppositifolia** ssp. *amphibia*. From the Lake Constance district. Loose mats with long creeping stems. Water grooves not lime secreting.

**S. oppositifolia** ssp. *asiatica*. From Asia. Larger flowers than any other form. Leaf tips finely toothed, unlike all other forms.

Certain authors have elevated these subspecies to specific rank, but botanists are not agreed on this point. Gardeners have selected the following forms:

**S. oppositifolia** 'Allos'. Extra-large purple-pink flowers.

**S. oppositifolia** 'Coccinea'. Grown chiefly in England. Small deep-red flowers. Cushions up to 20 cm in diameter, about 2.5 cm high.

**S. oppositifolia** 'Splendens'. Low mats with stemless flowers of fine purple pink. Prefers a cool spot and a calcareous soil. Flowers freely and grows well in the garden.

**S. oppositifolia** var. *superba*. A beautiful form from the Pyrenees with deep purple pink flowers.

**S. oppositifolia** var. *alba* (syn. *S.o.* var. *albiflora*). The white-flowered form. Makes an ideal contrast with the red forms. Flowers medium-sized, but in the right spot it flowers so freely that the whole plant is often completely smothered. Possibly an albino form of *S.o.* ssp. *murithiana*. Usually found on lime-free soils.

**S. oppositifolia** 'W. A. Clark'. A very old form, grown chiefly in English gardens. Brilliant carmine-red flowers. A beautiful plant, but not as vigorous as *S.o.* 'Splendens' or *S.o.* ssp. *latina*.

**S. oppositifolia** 'Wetterhorn'. A wild form collected many years ago. It grows well and has rose-pink flowers. Perhaps not quite as fine as 'W. A. Clark'.

## Saxifraga retusa Gouan (syn. *S. purpurea* All.)

A handsome species, at first sight it resembles a small compact *S. oppositifolia*, but is distinguished from it by its upright flower stems 1.5–3 cm high and its corymbose inflorescences. There are two subspecies: *S. retusa* ssp. *retusa* (syn. *retusa* ssp. *baumgartenii*) from the Pyrenees, south-western Alps, Carpathians, Transylvania and the Rila and Panina ranges in Bulgaria. *S. retusa* ssp. *retusa* grows on siliceous rocks from 2000 metres upwards, usually on exposed north-facing sites, though at very high altitudes it may be found on south-facing slopes, in places which are often windswept and free from snow. It is never on calcareous rocks. *S. retusa* ssp. *augustana* is a lime-loving plant of the southern Pennine and south-western Alps.

*S. retusa* forms small dense cushions. The stems are columnar, leaves 0.3–0.5 cm wide, arranged in four rows. Flowers are reddish purple with orange anthers. *S. retusa* ssp. *retusa* has hairless sepals and 1–3 flowers on each scape. *S. retusa* ssp. *augustana* has fine hairs on the sepals and 2–5 flowers on each scape, larger than those of the other subspecies. Scapes often up to 10 cm high.

*S. retusa* ssp. *retusa* is not easy in cultivation. It must have chippings of granite or some other igneous rock with a little humus, and it needs good drainage with adequate moisture. A lime hater! *S. retusa* ssp. *augustana* is much more amenable. It likes a similar soil mixture, but with limestone chippings.

# SECTION ROBERTSONIANA

All the species and hybrids of this not very large section are useful plants for shade or semi-shade. The best-known representative of the section is the plant grown under the incorrect name *Saxifraga umbrosa*. There is a genuine *Saxifraga umbrosa*, but this is seldom seen. The plant usually offered by nurseries under this name is in fact *S.* × *urbium*, a hybrid of *S. spathularis* and *S. umbrosa*, London Pride. The other hybrids are difficult to tell apart, but the leaf shape is often helpful.

London Pride is a plant stocked by almost every nursery. In the right place it is one of the least demanding low-growing perennials and is easily propagated by tearing off rosettes. In half-shade or full shade these hybrids form handsome dense dark-green cushions. In the rock garden they are ideal in shaded or sunless positions provided they have a certain minimum of moisture. They will grow in acid or alkaline soil but flourish best in loamy sand with some peat. The evergreen rosettes are fully hardy. The plants will stand a modicum of sun provided they have sufficient soil moisture. 'London

Pride' has been used for edgings since the early nineteenth century, and because of the red spots on the flowers children are told that flies use them to learn their multiplication tables. The flowers are produced freely, even in shade. Unfortunately, because it is so undemanding and easily propagated, the plant is undervalued. All the garden plants of this section are suitable for adorning graves.

## Species

### Saxifraga cuneifolia L.

Found in the Sierra Meirama in north-western Spain, in the Pyrenees, Cevennes, Alps, and Apennines, in Croatia and Slovenia, and in the eastern Carpathians and Transylvania, it grows on stony slopes and moist shady rocks, not at great altitudes, but in mixed woodland, especially spruce and larch. In the Tessin and the Valais it is found at somewhat higher altitudes, up to 2200 metres. It usually grows on siliceous soils; where it is found on pure limestone there is an intervening layer of acid humus (in the Karawan-ken mountains).

It forms loose mats of evergreen rosettes, often superimposed one above the other, and spreads by overground runners. Leaves are wedge-shaped, glabrous, matt, thick and leathery, with cartilaginous margins, only faintly toothed. In winter the under surfaces often turn reddish violet. Flower stems upright, 8–25 cm high (usually 20 cm), leafless, with glandular hairs. Inflorescence a loose panicle with few branches, often corymbose. Flowers small, white, starry, with yellow spots at the base. Flowering time is June–July. The plant is suitable for dry walls and rock garden slopes in broken sunlight or shade.

Besides the true *S. cuneifolia* there is another form which is much neater, with smaller, usually entire leaves. It is found in the Maritime Alps and in Tuscany and goes under the name *S. cuneifolia* var. *capillipes* or *S. cuneifolia* f. *appennina*. The flowers are spotted with purple. Another form is *S. cuneifolia* var. *subintegra* with larger, bluntly toothed leaves, and a yellow spot at the base of the petals.

### Saxifraga hirsuta L.

Found in northern Spain, the western and central Pyrenees, in south-west Ireland and in the Vosges, it is not very different from the true *S. umbrosa*. Evergreen cushions with over-wintering rosettes. Spreads by overground runners. The basal leaves have long narrow stalks, 2 to 14 times as long as the blade and, like the latter, with hairs on both sides. The blade is circular or kidney-shaped; heart-shaped at the base and about 1.5 cm long. Scapes 12–30 cm high, with glandular hairs. The inflorescence is a panicle with many flowers. Petals 0.4–0.5 cm long, white, yellowish at the base. Not difficult to grow, it likes plenty of humus and somewhat more moisture than the other species.

## *Saxifraga spathularis* Brot.

Found in the mountains of northern Portugal and north-west Spain and also in Ireland, it forms mats of overwintering rosettes, and spreads by means of overground runners. Leaf stalks fairly wide (0.2–0.4 cm) and flat, distinctly longer than the blade and gradually broadening towards it. Hairs usually confined to the lower half or third. Blade ovate, spathulate or almost semicircular, 1–6 cm long, leathery, hairless, with a wide cartilaginous margin. There are 4–7 triangular teeth on each side. Scapes 10–40 cm high with glandular hairs. Petals 0.4–0.5 cm long, white with 1–3 yellow spots at the base, and fine carmine red stippling as well. Not often seen in gardens, *S. spathularis* is important as one of the parents of *S.* × *urbium*.

## *Saxifraga umbrosa* L.

The plant widely grown in gardens and nurseries under this name is not the true *S. umbrosa* L. but a hybrid, the correct name of which is *S.* × *urbium*. Its parents are *S. umbrosa* and *S. spathularis*. See page 144.

The true *S. umbrosa* L. grows in the western and central Pyrenees. It forms dense mats of flat rosettes. Leaves leathery, obovate to narrow ovate with broad indentations and a definite cartilaginous margin. Leaf stalks broad and flat, thickly covered with hairs. Petals white with numerous red dots.

## Hybrids

### *Saxifraga* × *geum (S. geum)*

This hybrid was long regarded as a species but it is undoubtedly a natural hybrid of *S. hirsuta* × *S. umbrosa*, intermediate in appearance between its parents. It is found in those parts of the Pyrenees where both parents are present and also as an escape in other districts. The plants vary considerably. The leaf blades tend to resemble those of *S. umbrosa* and the leaf stalks those of *S. hirsuta*. The rosettes are very lax, but form firm dark-green carpets. Leaves long-stalked, hairy, rounded or oval. Leaf margins slightly indented. Scapes 18–30 cm high, reddish, very brittle, hairy above. The inflorescence has relatively few branches and carries small white flowers with yellow and red spots in June and July. It prefers cool, half-shady places. Various forms are mentioned in the older books ('Crenata', 'Dentata', 'Hirsuta', 'Major', 'Minor'). Most of these are selected wild forms but they are now almost unobtainable.

### *Saxifraga* × *polita*

The parents are *S. hirsuta* and *S. spathularis*. It is less attractive and hence seldom seen in gardens. A natural hybrid, it is found in northern Spain and western Ireland where its two parents grow. Leaves usually semicircular to broad obovate, leaf stalks narrow and moderately hairy.

### *Saxifraga × urbium* 'London Pride'

This hybrid, produced by crossing *S. spathularis × S. umbrosa*, is an important garden plant. Though not a natural hybrid it has escaped and run wild in

Saxifraga × urbium
(*Saxifraga umbrosa* of gardens)
Section Robertsoniana

*Fig. 35*

some places. In appearance it is exactly intermediate between its two parents. It has loose rosettes which form dense dark-green carpets. Leaf blades are obovate to spathulate, reddish on the under surface, narrowing into a short, slightly winged stalk. Scapes about 30 cm high, sticky, carrying a loose panicle. Flowers small and starry, white with a reddish tinge in the middle. Stamens longer than the petals. There are sterile and fertile forms. Flowering time May–June.

There are numerous garden forms, often confused and difficult to distinguish, but all of them are handsome vigorous plants.

*S.* × *urbium* var. *primuloides* is a neat miniature form found wild in the Pyrenees, in contrast to the ordinary *S.* × *urbium* which occurs only as a garden plant or an escape. Leaves considerably smaller, flowers bright pink on scapes 15–28 cm high. *S. umbrosa* 'Minor' mentioned in the older literature is probably identical. There are two selected forms which are often confused. In Germany the best known of these cultivars is *S.* × *urbium* var. *primuloides* 'Elliott's Variety' (*S. umbrosa* 'Elliott's Variety' of gardens). It forms compact clumps and in late spring its pink flowers, carried on reddish scapes 20 cm high, make a striking picture. It is useful for edgings in semi-shade. The other selected form is *S.* × *urbium* var. *primuloides* 'Ingwersen's Variety', which is even smaller and has neat rosettes which often assume a coppery tinge. The scapes are reddish and the flowers are somewhat deeper pink than those of the previous type. Its origin is uncertain. A vigorous plant, it is ideal for shady places between ferns. A selection is offered under the name *S.* × *urbium* var. *serratifolia* 'Morrisonii'.

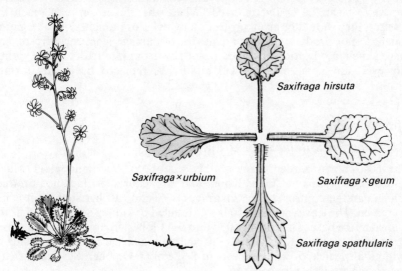

*Saxifraga hirsuta*

*Saxifraga* × *urbium*

*Saxifraga* × *geum*

*Saxifraga spathularis*

The members of Section Robertsoniana can be distinguished by their leaf shapes

*Fig. 36*

*S.* × *urbium* 'Aureopunctata' (*S. umbrosa* 'Aureopunctata', *S. umbrosa* 'Variegata Aurea'), with golden-variegated leaves, is widely grown and provides a splash of colour in a shady spot, though the contrast is most marked when it is grown in moist soil in full sun.

Another form, *S.* × *urbium* 'Variegata', has white-variegated leaves, often with a pink tinge at the margins. It is nowadays seldom seen. British nurseries offer *S.* × *urbium* 'Colvillei' with neat serrated leaves and white flowers.

## SECTION DIPTERA

If they are to thrive in the garden these woodland plants from eastern Asia need a carefully chosen place. Given such a position they are rewarding garden plants, in particular *S. cortusifolia* var. *fortunei* 'Rubrifolia' and *S. stolonifera* 'Cuscutiformis'. Their horticultural requirements are not the same. *S.c.* var. *fortunei* 'Rubrifolia', like the other forms of this species, is calcifuge and will tolerate only small amounts of lime. It must be grown in a shady or sunless place; one day's exposure to full sun will leave it lying flat on the ground. The compost must contain plenty of humus (peat or leaf mould) and must be moisture-retentive. *S. stolonifera* 'Cuscutiformis' and *S. veitchiana,* though by no means sun-loving plants, will tolerate somewhat more exposure and some degree of dryness. Moreover, they are both lime-tolerant and flourish on limy soils. In fact, they grow well in limestone or tufa crevices, provided they have a certain minimum of moisture. They increase rapidly by their long stolons, but never become troublesome. If a rosette is in the way, it can be easily removed. Where the winter sun can reach the rosettes, they should be given protection by twigs or branches. All the species which do not produce runners are at risk of damage from early frosts, and indeed their newly formed leaves are at risk from late frosts in the spring. However, any spoilt rosettes will rapidly be replaced by freshly formed leaves.

## Species

### *Saxifraga cortusifolia* Sieb. et Zucc.

The best-known garden plant of this section. A woodland plant widely distributed in Japan, China, Korea and Manchuria, it does not produce runners and in contrast to the saxifrages of Section Robertsoniana it is not evergreen. The leaves are long-stalked, rounded or kidney-shaped, and heart-shaped at the base. They are divided into 5–11 lobes, fleshy, brittle and glossy green. The flower stems are 25–30 cm high and carry an umbellate or pyramidal panicle of white flowers in September–October. Several varieties and forms are grown in gardens.

*S. cortusifolia* Sieb. et Zucc. var. *fortunei* (Hook) Maxim. It comes from Japan. In England it is usually known simply as *S. fortunei,* more often cultivated in gardens than the type. Leaves 7-lobed, brownish-green. It flowers somewhat later than the type. The flowers are often destroyed by the first frosts of autumn, and the fleshy leaves also suffer. In favourable situations the inflorescences are up to 40 cm high and carry large numbers of flowers. Petals 5, narrow, white, unspotted. One or sometimes two of the petals are toothed and are several times longer than the others. They project downwards, giving the flower an orchid-like appearance.

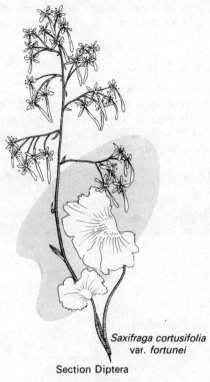

Saxifraga cortusifolia
var. fortunei

Section Diptera

*Fig. 37*

Botanically there are three local forms with differences in leaf shape (*crassifolia, incisolobata, obtusolobata*), but these are of no horticultural interest. However, there are some important garden forms.

**S. cortusifolia var. fortunei** 'Rubrifolia'. This has red flower stems and reddish-brown leaves which make a striking contrast with the snow-white flowers. It is of value because it blooms in September and is hence at less risk of frost. A form with fairly deep-purple leaf coloration is widely grown, especially in Great Britain, under the name 'Wada' or 'Wada's Form'. There is now a hybrid between 'Rubrifolia' and 'Wada'.

### *Saxifraga cuscutiformis* Lodd. Sometimes spelt *S. cuscutaeformis*.

This little plant grows only about 10 cm high and has small leaves with white veins and threadlike runners. It is not frost-hardy in cold areas. Plants offered under this name are not the true species but are really *S. stolonifera* 'Cuscutiformis'.

### *Saxifraga madida* Makino

Grown in Japan and closely resembles *S. cortusifolia*, to which some botanists assign it. It is somewhat larger than *S. cortusifolia*, and its leaves are longer, stouter and more uniformly covered with hairs. Seldom seen in gardens.

### *Saxifraga rufescens* I. B. Balf.

A Chinese version of the Japanese *S. cortusifolia*. Formerly known as *S. sinensis*. Flowers in July. Distinguished by its red flower stems, thickly covered with hairs. It is the only species of this section in which the reddish tinge extends into the flowers. Seldom if ever seen in cultivation, it would be of value because of its early flowering.

### *Saxifraga stolonifera* Meerb., Mother of Thousands (syn. *S. sarmentosa* L.)

From China and Japan, it was introduced into Europe in 1771. The lax rosettes emit numerous long branching runners. The leaves are rounded or

*Saxifraga cuscutiformis* with runners growing
in a dry wall in complete or partial shade

*Fig. 38*

kidney-shaped, domed, with shallow lobes. Upper surface olive-green with a network of silver-grey veins. Lower surface reddish. Leaf stalks covered with red hairs. Flower stems hairy, ending in a branched panicle. Flowers zygomorphic, white with red spots. A well-known and much-loved house-plant, it is often used for hanging baskets and for ground cover especially in pans and glass cases. It is on the borderline of frost-hardiness. Even in such a cold place as Upper Franconia it has survived for some years in a moist shady spot. Yet it is not an ideal indoor plant for centrally-heated houses, preferring temperatures between 0 and 10° C. At higher temperatures it is prone to attack by aphids. Anyone who has a plant can easily harden off a few offsets and try them in the open garden. Another form offered by nurseries is *S. stolonifera* 'Tricolor' with leaves of three colours. This prefers somewhat higher temperatures and is quite unsuitable for outdoors.

*S. stolonifera* 'Cuscutiformis' is an important form but there is some doubt regarding its identity. This outstanding hardy form of *S. stolonifera* must not be confused with *S. cuscutiformis* Lodd. (page 147) which is not frost-hardy. *S. stolonifera* 'Cuscutiformis' is a more robust plant which forms lax rosettes. It is a pity that it is not more widely grown. Personally, I regard it as the most valuable plant of its section, as it is fully hardy. The rosettes put out red thread-like runners. The leaves are rounded or kidney-shaped, 5–9 cm wide, with 7–10 lobes, somewhat domed, matt or glossy, brownish-green, with a network of pale grey veins. Upper surface hairy, lower surface glabrous and

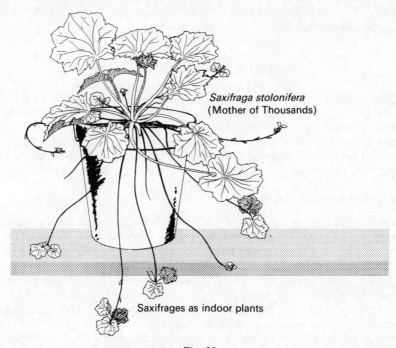

*Saxifraga stolonifera*
(Mother of Thousands)

Saxifrages as indoor plants

*Fig. 39*

reddish. Flowers white, comparatively large, the lower two petals being considerably longer than the others. Scapes 20–40 cm high, flowering season July–August. Once established in a shady crevice, or at least a spot where it is not exposed to full sun, the plant will readily spread by means of runners. It can also be used to plant level surfaces.

### *Saxifraga veitchiana* Balf.

Discovered in western Hupeh (China) in 1900, it closely resembles *S. stolonifera*, but is somewhat smaller and without veining. Forms lax rosettes with long reddish runners. Leaves rounded, slightly indented, with long stalks. Upper surfaces matt, dark green; lower surfaces covered with bristly hairs. Usually reluctant to flower. Scapes about 10 cm high, carrying panicles or corymbs of numerous white flowers with pink stippling on the upper part of the petals and a yellowish tinge below. The flowers have the 1 or 2 elongated petals typical of Section Diptera. *S. veitchiana* grows well in shady crevices or tufa. It can be planted on rock ledges or in walls. As it does not flower well, its decorative value lies in its rosettes. In shady spots it is hardy and flourishes even in the cold climate of Upper Franconia, but it is not nearly as attractive as *S. stolonifera* 'Cuscutiformis'.

Section Diptera contains several other species not yet in cultivation including: *S. aculeata* (Yunnan), *S. dumetorum* (Hupeh and Yunnan), *S. flabellifolia* (China), *S. geifolia* (Yunnan), *S. henryi* (Yunnan), *S. imparilis* (Yunnan), *S. nipponica* (Japan) and *S. sendaica* (Japan).

## SECTION NEPHROPHYLLUM

Section Nephrophyllum has not much to offer the gardener. The only plant of real garden value is *S. granulata*, especially in its double-flowered form. *S. irrigua* is also worth growing. However, there are certainly some species which would be worth a trial and others which have not yet been properly tested. The species differ in their requirements, some needing moist and others dry soil; some require lime while others prefer siliceous rock.

### *Saxifraga arachnoidea* Sternb.

From a small area of the southern Alps north-west of Lake Garda, where it grows in clefts in limestone rocks. Usually biennial. The whole plant is covered with long silvery sticky hairs. Leaves variable, usually rhomboidal or ovate, with 3–7 lobes. Flowers close together at end of scape. Petals greenish white or straw yellow. Mainly of botanical interest, not of much garden value. Very difficult to keep for long, it needs protection from rain, by overhanging rocks or otherwise, but must have atmospheric moisture. Requires perfect drainage; suitable compost consists of two-thirds old crumbly brick rubble and one-third peaty sandy loam with the addition of some shredded sphagnum.

## Saxifraga atlantica Boiss. et Reuter

From the western Mediterranean area. Together with *S. carpetana*, *S. dichotoma* and *S. graeca*, it forms a group having many features in common and all resembling *S. granulata*. However, it has more leaves on the flowering stems and its inflorescence is more compact. It has bulbils in the leaf axils instead of those at the base seen in *S. granulata*. Flowers large, white and scented. Scapes 15–25 cm high. It likes sandy loam with some humus, which should not be too coarse.

## Saxifrage biternata Boiss.

An interesting evergreen species from southern Spain, it resembles *S. gemmulosa* and *S. boissieri*, but is distinguished from them by its leaves, which are divided into 3 leaflets each made up of 3 segments. Flowers white, very handsome. The bulbils are formed in the leaf axils and after flowering they grow out as young plantlets still connected with the mother plant. Height 15–23 cm. *S. biternata* grows in moist limestone scree.

## Saxifraga boissieri Engl.

Growing in moist shady limestone rocks in the mountains of south-western Spain westwards of Ronda, it is closely related to *S. biternata* and *S. gemmulosa*. Forms lax cushions. Reddish bulbils at the base and in the axils of the lower leaves. Leaves deeply divided into three segments, with glandular hairs. Inflorescence much branched, with numerous small white flowers. The plant is of little or no garden value.

## Saxifraga bulbifera L.

Closely related to the well known *S. granulata*, it is widely distributed in southern Moravia, western Slovakia, Austria, Hungary, the northern Balkans, the western, central and southern Alps, and the Apennines. It grows on dry grassy slopes and in rocky places where there is fine soil, on limestone and siliceous rocks alike. In Hungary it is associated with *Adonis vernalis, Ornithogalum comosum, Iris variegata, Scabiosa ochroleuca* and *Chrysopogon gryllus*.

Considerably taller than *S. granulata*, it grows usually to between 25 and 50 cm. Bulbils develop in the axils of the stem leaves. The inflorescence is a compact umbel of 3–7 white or yellowish flowers. It is of no special garden value.

## Saxifraga carpathica Reichenb.

From the Carpathians and south-west Bulgaria. Leaves with 5–7 lobes, finely hairy. Bulbils in axils of basal leaves. 6–15 cm high. Flowers white, with pink veins. Grows in moist rocky places. Of little garden value.

## *Saxifraga carpetana* Boiss. et Reuter

A native of Spain. Closely allied to *S. atlantica, S. dichotoma* and *S. graeca*. It resembles *S. granulata*, but the flowering stems have more leaves and the inflorescence is more compact. Height 10–25 cm, flowers white. Doubtfully in cultivation.

## *Saxifraga cernua* L.

Occurring in Arctic and sub-Arctic Europe and North America, in Scotland, the Urals, the Alps, the Carpathians and the Altai, in Japan and the Rocky Mountains, it grows on moist rocks, in gorges kept wet by constant spray, and in open pioneer grasslands on both limestone and siliceous rocks. Flowering stems 15 cm or slightly taller, with drooping white flowers. Small bulbils in the axils of the stem leaves. Difficult to cultivate and not outstandingly attractive, it needs a shady spot with constant, but not stagnant moisture.

## *Saxifraga cintrana* Kuzinsky ex Willk.

Grows on limestone rocks and walls in the hills near Lisbon. Scapes 10–17 cm, flowers white. Resembles *S. granulata*, but because of its southern provenance it is of no value in our gardens.

## *Saxifraga corsica* (Duby) Gren. et Godron

Found in Corsica, Sardinia and eastern Spain, where it grows on shady rocks and walls and in scree. It closely resembles *S. granulata*, but is distinguished from it by its 3-lobed basal leaves and by the flower stems, which begin to divide quite low down forming a much branched inflorescence 20 cm high.

Botanists distinguish two subspecies, *S. corsica* ssp. *corsica* found in Sardinia, Corsica and the Balearic Islands, and *S. corsica* ssp. *cossoniana* found in Spain. It is worth growing for its beautiful white flowers but safe only in the alpine house.

## *Saxifraga debilis* Engelm.

Resembling *S. sibirica*, it grows in western North America (Rocky Mountains, Colorado, Utah, Arizona). Of little or no garden value.

## *Saxifraga dichotoma* Sternb.

From Spain and Portugal, it is grouped together with *S. graeca, S. carpetana* and *S. atlantica*. Basal leaves 1–3 cm wide, with glandular hairs. Scapes 10–13 cm high. Inflorescence less compact than *S. carpetana* or *S. graeca*. Petals 0.6–1 cm wide, white with pink veins or a pink tinge. Of doubtful garden value.

## *Saxifraga exilis* Stephan ex Sternb.

Resembling *S. sibirica*, it grows in Arctic regions (Arctic North America, south-western Kamtschatka, Kurile and Aleutian islands). Little or no garden value.

## *Saxifraga gemmulosa* Boiss. et Reuter

It grows on limestone rocks in southern Spain. Similar to *S. boissieri*, it has leaves divided into three segments, and a much branched inflorescence with numerous small flowers. No garden value.

## *Saxifraga graeca* Boiss.

From southern Italy, Sicily and the Balkans. It resembles *S. granulata*, and is often included under that species. Scapes 20–40 cm high, branching only near the top. Basal leaves kidney-shaped or heart-shaped, with glandular hairs. Leaf stalk usually longer than blade. Not of much garden value, and would probably need alpine house cultivation.

*Saxifraga granulata*
Section Nephrophyllum

*Fig. 40*

## Saxifraga granulata L.

Widely distributed from Scandinavia and the British Isles southwards to Spain, Portugal, Moroco and Sicily, and eastwards to Russia, Romania and Hungary, it usually grows in fairly moist meadows on neutral or slightly basic soils, but is also found in rather dry grassland and thin woodland. It also occurs on siliceous rocks.

Loose rosettes of long-stalked leaves with deeply indented kidney-shaped blades. Scapes 30–40 cm high, branching into a loose panicle at the top. Scape and inflorescence glandular and sticky. Milk white flowers in May–June. Small bulbils between the roots and in the leaf axils.

Although this native meadow plant looks very fine when planted in groups in the rock garden, the best garden plant is the double form *S. granulata* 'Plena'. The double white flowers somewhat resemble those of stock (gillieflower). The plant disappears soon after flowering. It is propagated by the resting buds, which resemble grains of corn and are produced in large numbers. *S. granulata* flourishes best in light soils but requires a certain amount of moisture – it is very pretty as a cut flower.

## Saxifraga haenseleri Boiss. et Reuter

On the mountains of southern Spain, it grows in dry rock crevices. Closely related to *S. granulata*, it is however only 7.5–12.5 cm high. The characteristic bulbils form at the base, but are below the ground surface. The wedge-shaped basal leaves are divided into three segments and the whole plant is covered with glandular hairs. The relatively large white flowers are carried on an inflorescence branching from the base. Seldom seen in cultivation, it is not easy to grow.

## Saxifraga hyperborea R. Br.

From Greenland and arctic North America. Related to *S. rivularis*, it is distinguished by a reddish tinge affecting the whole plant, including the petals, which are smaller, and by the absence of stolons. Of little or no garden value.

## Saxifraga irrigua Bieb.

In the Crimea, it grows in moist or shady places in the mountains, forming loose light-green rosettes; leaves kidney-shaped and divided into three. Scapes 10–30 cm high, usually branching in the upper half. The inflorescence is a corymbose cyme with many white flowers in June. The whole plant is covered with soft hairs, and usually dies after flowering, but is easily propagated by seed. It likes a shady place in the rock garden with plenty of humus in the soil. It does well in the alpine house.

## Saxifraga latepetiolata Willk.

Growing on limestone rocks in a small area of eastern Spain, it is a biennial.

In its first year it develops into a symmetrical hairy rosette of long-stalked kidney-shaped leaves. In the second year it puts out a hairy scape, 15–30 cm high, branching from the base and carrying numerous large milk-white flowers. The flowering season is May–June and often lasts up to 6 weeks. Despite being biennial it deserves to be more widely cultivated. In the wild it is not exposed to severe frost or much winter wet, and it will therefore need appropriate shelter; alternatively it could be grown in a frame or a cold house.

### Saxifraga rivularis L.

From the arctic and subarctic regions of Europe, it extends southwards to southern Norway and central Scotland. It closely resembles *S. carpathica*. Basal leaves 1–1.5 cm wide, with 3–5 lobes. The plant puts out short stolons on which bulbils form. Each scape carries several small white flowers. Not particularly attractive, it is of little garden value.

### Saxifraga sibirica L.

A rare and handsome species which grows in eastern Russia and the western Himalayas, and also in south-eastern Bulgaria and north-eastern Greece. Basal leaves ivy-shaped; scapes 15 cm high with large drooping white flowers. It forms elongated bulbils at the base. It might well be worth cultivating.


## SECTION HIRCULUS

This section contains more than 170 species, most of them from the Himalayas and neighbouring areas, though some come from the northern and subarctic regions of Europe, Asia and America. The species differ widely in appearance.

Most of them are not easy to grow and despite repeated introduction many of them have been lost. All of them like moist peaty lime-free soil. Old recipes recommend one-half granulated peat and moorland soil and one-half finely chopped sphagnum, but this mixture may be more suitable for the arctic group.

Among the numerous species of this section there are certainly some others which would be worth introducing. The range at present available is very meagre. Nurserymen's catalogues from Great Britain, Germany and Switzerland offer only *S. diversifolia, S. hookeri, S. flagellaris, S. brunoniana, S. strigosa* and *S. cardiophylla*. Seed of other species may be available from botanic gardens or the seed exchanges.

### Species

### Saxifraga aristulata Hook. f. et Thoms.

From alpine and subalpine levels in the Himalayas, it grows usually at altitudes of 4000–5000 metres, where it flowers in September. It is a small compact plant forming blue-green mats, the narrow undivided leaves grouped into small rosettes. Scape about 5 cm high carrying a single handsome yellow flower. Seldom seen in cultivation, it likes acid soil, partial shade and moderate moisture.

### Saxifraga brachypoda Don

From Nepal, Sikkim and western Yunnan, it grows at altitudes of about 4000 metres, flowering from July to September, depending on the altitude. Usually found in wet rocky places, it forms small tufts made up of narrow leaves, glossy above and ash-grey below. Scapes 7–12 cm high carrying single flowers of pale or golden yellow.

### Saxifraga brunoniana Wall.

From Sikkim, Yunnan and southern Tibet at altitudes of 3500–4500 metres, it flowers from July to September. A very delicate plant, it forms threadlike overground runners which carry the new rosettes. The latter are pale green in colour, making a beautiful contrast with the red runners. Scapes 10–15 cm high, relatively large, pale yellow. Despite its delicate appearance the plant is tolerably hardy. Though it often disappears in winter, new plants soon develop from the surviving rosettes. Its beauty lies not so much in the flowers as in the fine network of runners and leaves.

### Saxifraga candelabrum Franch.

From Yunnan, it grows in rock crevices and gorges, flowering in July. Monocarpic, it forms handsome rosettes, each with a scape 15–20 cm high carrying yellow flowers. The yellow petals are considerably narrower than the green sepals. It is of little garden value.

### Saxifraga cardiophylla Franch.

Found in Yunnan and Szechuan, it grows usually in open mountain meadows at about 3500 metres. It flowers in August–September, and is still in cultivation in Britain. Scapes about 20 cm high, each carrying 4–8 orange yellow flowers. It flourishes in moist soil with plenty of humus.

### Saxifraga chrysantha A. Gray

From Pacific North America, in particular the Rocky Mountains, it flowers in July–August. Tufts of small rosettes with thyme-like leaves. Brittle scapes 2–4 cm high carrying 1–2 golden yellow flowers. Difficult to cultivate, it likes wet places.

### Saxifraga diversifolia Wall.

From Sikkim, Yunnan, Szechuan and upper Burma, it grows on mountain peaks, and in shady places in pine woods, flowering from July to September, depending on altitude. There are several local varieties (var. *diversifolia*, var. *soulieana*, var. *parnassifolia*, var. *foliata*). Basal leaves long-stalked, heart-shaped. Scapes 15–20 cm high, with smaller heart-shaped leaves, but these

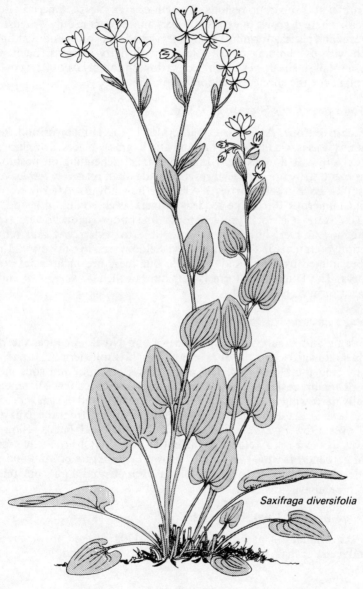

*Saxifraga diversifolia*

Section Hirculus

*Fig. 41*

have short stalks. Several golden yellow or ochre flowers. This is a handsome plant when grown in the right place.

### Saxifraga eschscholtzii Sternb.

From arctic and subarctic regions of north-eastern North America (Bering Sea area), where it grows in exposed places and flowers in July–August, this is a peculiar species, forming dense mats made up of cylindrical shoots covered with overlapping obovate leaves with hairy margins. Each shoot ends in a small sessile flower of white or yellowish colour. About 2.5 cm high, it is a plant for the specialist, seldom available.

### Saxifraga flagellaris Sternb. et Willd.

In northern Europe, Asia and Canada, also in the Himalayas and Rocky Mountains, this is usually found on sand and in grassy places near glaciers or perpetual snow. It flowers from June to August depending on position. A curious plant, there are masses of rosettes made up of relatively few leaves on short stalks. Each rosette carries 3–4 large yellow flowers. After flowering it puts out numerous threadlike reddish runners, each ending in a bud. Not easy to cultivate, it is worth growing for its fine butter-yellow flowers. It likes moisture in summer, but is very susceptible to winter wet and requires protection, preferably in the alpine house. Seldom seen in cultivation. Engler describes numerous forms and varieties, but these are of little interest to gardeners. The Himalayan form is sometimes called *S. komarovii* and the European form *S. platysepala*.

### Saxifraga hirculus L.

From arctic and subarctic Europe, Siberia and North America, the range extends southwards into the Jura mountains, the northern Alps and Carpathians, and the Himalayas. The plant grows on moorland soils in peat bogs, sphagnum cushions and stream beds. Basal leaves lanceolate, entire, gradually narrowing into the stalk, blade 1–3 cm long and 0.5 cm wide. Stalk twice as long as blade. Scapes about 30 cm high, arising from the axils of the basal leaves. Flowers terminal, single, or 2–5 in an umbel. Petals yellow with red spots at the base. A plant for the enthusiast, it is of little value for the general gardener. It would have to be grown in a mixture of sand and peat, and never allowed to dry out. There is a form 'Grandiflora', but this too seems to be unavailable.

### Saxifraga hookeri Engl. et Irmsch.

From the Himalayas at altitudes of 3600–4700 metres, it was recently reintroduced. It has interesting strap-shaped leaves and golden yellow flowers.

### Saxifraga jacquemontiana Decne.

From the Himalayas, especially Kashmir and Sikkim, at altitudes of

4500–6000 metres. Flowering time is July to September. This is a charming plant which grows in stony soil forming low cushions of glandular rosettes barely 1 cm in diameter. The rosettes are closely pressed together and from the centre of each develops an orange yellow flower with faint reddish spots at the base of the petals. Practically unobtainable, it would be well worth growing.

### Saxifraga palpebrata Hook. f. et Thoms.

From the Himalayas, notably Sikkim, at altitudes of 4000–4500 metres. It forms shoots 5–7.5 cm long covered with hairy leaves and carrying medium-sized golden yellow flowers. Practically unobtainable.

### Saxifraga pardanthina Hand.-Mazz.

From south-western China. Scapes about 30 cm high carrying deep orange flowers, marked inside with red. It grows well in acid soil with plenty of peat, and is available in England.

### Saxifraga pasumensis Marq. et Airy Shaw

Recently introduced from the eastern Himalaya and Tibet, at first it forms a single rosette about 7.5 cm in diameter, resembling a miniature *S. florulenta*. The rosette consists of numerous overlapping spathulate leaves, greyish-green in colour, edged with glandular hairs. From the centre of the rosette develops a branching scape with a few small leaves and numerous large yellow flowers. The rosette dies after flowering, but daughter rosettes form at its base and will flower in the following year. *S. pasumensis* has been in cultivation in Britain.

### Saxifraga strigosa Wall.

From the Himalayas (Nepal and Sikkim) at altitudes of 2900–4000 metres, it grows in moist rocky places and also in moist shady conifer woods. It flowers from July to October. This somewhat short-lived plant has deep yellow flowers, about 2 cm in diameter, with small red spots on the inside of the petals. It resists weather well and would be worth raising from seed.

### Saxifraga signata Engl. et Irmsch.

From western Szechuan and north-western Yunnan, where it flowers in September. Dense basal rosettes 3–5 cm in diameter consist of a number of fleshy spathulate leaves. From the centre arises a scape 8–18 cm high with stem leaves and a spreading panicle. The outer half of the petal is pale yellow while the inner half is greenish-yellow with red spots and markings. The species is monocarpic but would be worth trying if available.

### Saxifraga turfosa Engl. et Irmsch.

From Yunnan, where it grows in moist stony places and moist pastures from

2800–3500 metres, it flowers September–October. Scapes about 15 cm high with numerous yellow flowers. The plant puts out runners from the base. Doubtful availability.

### Saxifraga umbellulata Hook f. et Thom.

At altitudes of 4000–5000 metres in the Himalayas and southern Tibet, it is commonly found in meadows, where it flowers in August–September. Rosettes 5–7 cm in diameter. Scape branching in the upper half, flowers yellow. Similar to *S. pasumensis* and often confused with it.

## SECTION TRACHYPHYLLUM

These mat-forming plants from the mountains and northern regions of Europe, Asia and North America are not always easy to grow. Though they are not of great garden value there are some enthusiasts who cultivate them.

### Species

### Saxifraga aspera L.

From the eastern and central Pyrenees, the Alps, Apuan mountains and the Apennines, where it grows on rocks and scree, on stream banks and in low-lying mossy places in pinewoods, usually at altitudes between 1500 and 2200 metres. It is found only on lime-free soils, often associated with *Sempervivum arachnoideum*, *Astrantia minor* and *Silene rupestris*.

It is a mat-forming plant, and the non-flowering shoots tend to creep along the ground. The basal leaves are narrowly lanceolate with stiff bristles along their margins. The scapes are upright and 5–20 cm high. The inflorescence is a loose panicle or corymb of 2–5 flowers, occasionally more. The petals are yellowish, becoming darker, often orange, towards the base. An attractive plant for the rock garden or alpine house, it needs acid soil, constant moisture and plenty of grit.

### Saxifraga bronchialis L.

This is the North American counterpart of *S. aspera*, and is widely distributed throughout northern Asia, North America and the northern Urals. It forms dwarf mats made up of shoots covered with short tough leaves. Leaves bushy, undivided, linear, with an apical spine. Scapes 6–15 cm high carrying 3–5 white flowers. Petals marked with orange or purple spots in the apical half. Though not of outstanding beauty when in flower, the low mats make an attractive covering for rocks.

The best-known variety is *S. bronchialis* var. *austromontana* with scapes 6–15 cm high. There is also a Japanese variety, *S. bronchialis* var. *rebunshir-ensis*, with scapes only 4–6 cm high. According to *Flora Europaea* this species also comprises *S. spinulosa* Adams.

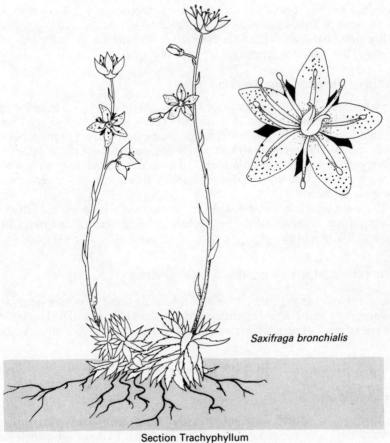

*Saxifraga bronchialis*

Section Trachyphyllum

*Fig. 42*

## *Saxifraga bryoides* L.

From the eastern and central Pyrenees, the Auvergne, Alps, Carpathians, and the mountains of Transylvania and Bulgaria, this species grows only on non-calcareous rocks, on screes and open grassland at altitudes of 2000–4000 metres. It is associated with *Ranunculus gracialis, Saxifraga exarata, S. seguieri, S. oppositifolia, Androsace alpina, Primula latifolia* (syn. *P. viscosa*), *Gentiana bavarica* var. *subacaulis, Eritrichium nanum, Veronica alpina* and *Linaria alpina*. It is sometimes regarded as a subspecies of *S. aspera*, but is clearly distinct from it. In certain features it approaches more closely to *S. bronchialis*. In the wild there is another species, *S. intermedia* Hegetschw., regarded as intermediate between *S. aspera* and *S. bryoides*.

*S. bryoides* forms large fairly firm mats. The non-flowering shoots are creeping, short and closely covered with leaves. Buds develop in the leaf axils. Basal leaves linear-lanceolate, with bristles at the margins. Near the apex there is a pit, but it does not secrete lime. Scapes upright, 2–6 cm high, with single flowers. Petals yellowish white, darker towards the base.

It is not too difficult to keep in the garden. The flowers are not particularly striking, but the light-green cushions are pleasing.

### *Saxifraga tricuspidata* Rottb.

A plant from the extreme north of Canada, Alaska and the ice-free coastal regions of Greenland, this is a dainty species with wedge-shaped leaves divided into 3 teeth at their extremities. Scape 5–6 (15) cm high, depending on situation. Petals yellowish white with fine purple spots in the upper half. The species flowers in early summer. Although not difficult to grow in a moist shady place, it is seldom seen. Nevertheless, the compact dark green cushions are quite attractive.

There are several other species from the far north, differing only in minor respects from *S. bronchialis*. They include *S. anadyrensis*, *S. cherleroides*, *S. firma* and *S. nischidae*.

## General comments on Section Trachyphyllum

These mat-forming plants from the mountains and northern regions of Europe, Asia and North America are not always easy to grow. Though they are not of great garden value there are some enthusiasts who cultivate them.

## SECTION XANTHIZOON

### *Saxifraga aizoides* L.

This species is widely distributed in the Alps, Apennines, Pyrenees, and Carpathians, and the mountains of the northern Balkans; also in Ireland, Great Britain, Scandinavia, Greenland, western Canada and the northern Rocky Mountains. It grows on moist scree, in stream beds and fens, usually at altitudes between 800 and 3000 metres, and also on river and stream banks at lower altitudes. It is associated with *Saxifraga stellaris, Tlaspis rotundifolium, Saxifraga oppositifolia, Linaria alpina* and *Doronicum grandiflorum*. It is found usually on calcareous subsoils.

*S. aizoides* forms loose mats of creeping and upright shoots, which branch freely. The non-flowering shoots have spreading leaves. Leaves linear, light green and fleshy, 1–2.5 cm long. Flowering stems upright, 5–30 cm high depending on situation. The inflorescence is a lax raceme or panicle with 2–10 flowers, the terminal flower being larger than the laterals. The 5 petals are yellow, orange or red, often marked with dark spots. There are several regional varieties.

Though the plant will grow in an ordinary garden, it will not display its full potential. However, where it can be given something approaching its natural environment it grows readily, and its deep coloration makes a pleasing picture. It requires abundant moisture in spring and early summer; at this season the roots like to be surrounded by water. The soil should be stony and a moist place in the rock garden, facing east or north-east, should be chosen.

Two colour forms are grown in gardens: *S.a.* var. *aurantiaca* and the deep red *S.a.* var. *atrorubens* from the Pustertal in Austria. Both have scapes only 8–10 cm high. They look well when grown side by side with *Campanula pulla*. *S. aizoon* can also be grown in an alpine house provided it can be given suitable conditions. Its hybrids with species of other sections (Section Robertsoniana, Euaizoonia and Porophyllum) are described under the heading Intersectional Hybrids, page 174.

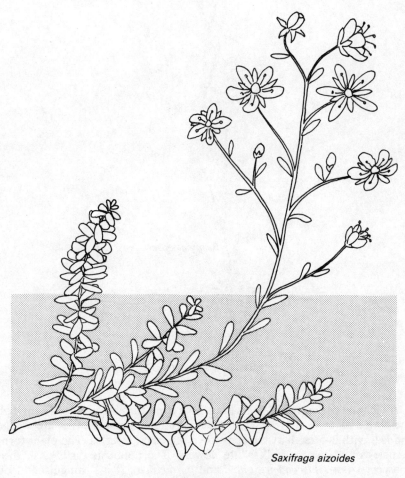

*Saxifraga aizoides*

Section Xanthizoon

*Fig. 43*

## SECTION TRIDACTYLITES

Section Tridactylites contains annual and biennial species and one perennial. They are of little garden value and are grown only by enthusiasts.

### *Saxifraga adscendens* L.

Widely distributed in the mountains of Europe and North America, ascending to over 4000 metres in the Rocky Mountains, it grows in stony and grassy places, usually on calcareous soils where there is plenty of moisture.

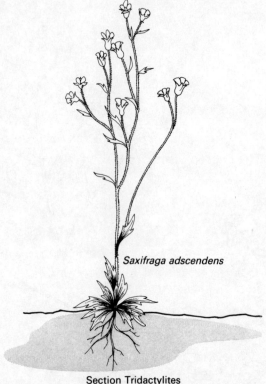

*Saxifraga adscendens*

Section Tridactylites

*Fig. 44*

A biennial with upright stems branching from the base and 10–20 cm high, the entire plant is covered with short glandular hairs. Leaves are wedge-shaped, with 2–5 teeth at the apex, forming basal rosettes. The plant forms panicles of numerous milk white flowers. The botanists distinguish three subspecies (ssp. *adscendens, blavii* and *parnassica*). It is distinguished from the closely related *S. tridactylites* by its biennial mode of growth and the deeper incisions in the leaves. An attractive plant for the enthusiast, it must be raised from seed every year. Good drainage is required.

## *Saxifraga berica* (Béguinot) D. A. Webb

Confined to a small area in northern Italy (Colli Berici near Vicenza), this is a perennial, closely resembling *S. petraea*. However, the hairs are shorter and the basal leaves are regularly toothed, or divided into 5–11 lobes, the incisions being less than half as deep as the distance from the stem. It requires calcareous soil and shade. *S. berica* is of little garden value.

## *Saxifraga nuttallii* Small

From western North America, chiefly Oregon and Washington, where it grows on wet rocks and flowers in June, this is a tall slender plant without basal leaves. Scapes covered with leaves from the base. Leaves 3-toothed. The flowers are small and the plant is of no garden value.

## *Saxifraga paradoxa* Sternb. (syn. *Zahlbrucknera paradoxa* (Sternb.) Riechenb.)

Found only in western Styria and eastern Carinthia and a few places in Slovenia, it grows in moist shady spots, chiefly under overhanging micaceous rocks. Uncommon, it does not extend to high altitudes. This is a perennial plant with brittle prostrate stems 5–20 cm long. Leaves long-stalked, kidney-shaped, 5–7 lobed, thin and almost translucent. Flowers solitary (occasionally two) arising from the leaf axils. Petals greenish.

This plant is an ancient relict of Tertiary times and is difficult to classify. It has been allotted by some to a section of its own (Discogyne) or even a separate genus (*Zahlbrucknera*). It is of no garden value, and not to be confused with the Euaizoonia hybrid *S.* × *paradoxa*.

## *Saxifraga petraea* L.

From Corni de Canzo on Lake Como through the south-eastern limestone Alps as far as Istria and Croatia, this is a lime-loving plant which grows on moist limestone and on projecting rocks in caves and other hollows. Biennial. Scape delicate, curving, 10–12 cm long, with a rosette of leaves at the base. Leaves palmate, 3-lobed; lobes coarsely 2–5 toothed. Middle lobe often entire and wedge-shaped. The entire plant is covered with soft glandular hairs, the inflorescence a loose panicle branching from the base, the flowers white. As the plant is extremely floriferous it is of greater value than the other species of this section, but new seedlings must be raised every year. It needs protection from winter rain, a shady position and plenty of limestone rubble.

## *Saxifraga tridactylites* L.

Occurring throughout Europe and in the Mediterranean region, eastwards to Iran, and northwards to Norway and Scotland, it grows on dry sunny slopes, in stony grassland, on vineyard terraces, rock outcrops and other warm dry places. It likes lime but can grow without it. An annual with an upright scape 2–18 cm high depending on situation, usually with a rosette of leaves at the base, the whole plant is covered with short glandular hairs. Basal leaves entire or divided into three shallow lobes, other leaves ternate. Very small white flowers. This one is of no garden value.

# SECTION MISCOPETALUM

The small Section Miscopetalum includes some useful garden plants of quiet beauty. *S. rotundifolia* is the only one generally available. This grows well in moist partially shaded spots, but will also flourish in the rock garden provided it is not exposed to full sun. These species cross with the closely related Section Robertsoniana and the hybrids are useful garden plants (see 'Intersectional Hybrids', page 174).

## *Saxifraga chrysosplenifolia* Boiss.

This species resembles *S. rotundifolia* and comes from the Balkans, especially southern Bulgaria, Greece and the Aegean islands. It is distinguished from *S. rotundifolia* by its leaf shape and the absence of the cartilaginous margin. Botanically there are two varieties, *S.c.* var. *fragilis* with an indented leaf margin and *S.c.* var. *rhodopea* with a serrated margin. The latter is somewhat larger. Both have branching inflorescences about 15 cm high carrying small white flowers with yellow or purple spots. In the garden it prefers a cool half-shady place and stony soil containing half-rotted twigs. Seed is available from botanic gardens. It would seem to have no advantages over the well-known *S. rotundifolia*.

## *Saxifraga rotundifolia* L.

From the mountains of central and southern Europe, it extends from France through the Apennines as far as Sicily and to Corsica and Sardinia. It is also found in the Carpathians, the Balkans, northern Turkey and the Caucasus. It grows in moist shady places at subalpine levels in corries, forest clearings and river gorges, found on calcareous and non-calcareous rocks. In the wild it is associated with *Aconitum paniculatum, Geum rivale* and *Doronicum austriacum.*

This is a small bushy perennial with a short root-stock. Leaves round or kidney-shaped, indented, pale green, long-stalked. Scapes 30–50 cm high with a loose panicle of numerous small white flowers with yellow and purple spots. Not spectacular, it is a useful garden plant which thrives in suitable places. It looks well in a moist spot in association with small and medium-sized ferns, primulas and the smaller species of *Hosta*. It can also be grown at the edges of small ponds; in favourable situations it sows itself freely without ever becoming a nuisance.

*S. heucherifolia* is closely related, but almost unobtainable.

## *Saxifraga taygetea* Boiss. et Heldr.

From Greece, Albania and small areas in southern Italy, *S. taygetea* grows

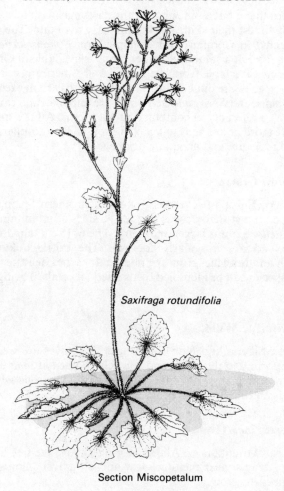

*Saxifraga rotundifolia*

Section Miscopetalum

*Fig. 45*

on mountain rocks. Similar to *S. rotundifolia* but smaller. Basal leaves kidney-shaped, leathery, bright green, with an indented margin. Scapes 10–20 cm, without stem leaves. Loose inflorescence of white flowers with pink spots, somewhat larger than the flowers of *S. rotundifolia*. It flowers in early summer. It is rarely offered but seed is sometimes available. It needs less moist soil than the other species of this section.

## SECTION MICRANTHES (FORMERLY BOROPHILA)

Section Micranthes contains a good many species besides those described below, but they are of even less garden interest. The ordinary gardener can safely disregard them, but alpine plant enthusiasts may wish to try one or two species, if only to test their skill. Stock is not easy to obtain. The only species at present offered in Germany, for example, are *S. manschuriensis* and *S. pennsylvanica*, though a somewhat wider range is available in Great Britain. Seed is sometimes available from the British and American seed exchanges.

Most of the species are difficult in cultivation, with certain exceptions such as *S. pennsylvanica* and *S. virginiensis*, which are fairly tall and can be planted in wild gardens, preferably in combination with ferns. All the species of this section require more or less acid soil, a cool spot, high atmospheric humidity, moderate soil moisture and adequate drainage.

## *Saxifraga clusii* Gouan

In south-western Europe (Cevennes, Pyrenees, northern Spain and Portugal), it grows on moist shady rocks and at the sides of mountain streams. It resembles *S. stellaris* but is larger and hairy. The 6–15 cm long leaves form a loose rosette and are irregularly toothed. The brittle-looking scape is 12–30 cm high and branches from the middle. It carries delicate white starry flowers. The species can be identified by its unequal petals, 3 being long and 2 short.

## *Saxifraga davurica* Willd.

From subarctic Siberia and North America. The leaves are wedge-shaped, narrowing uniformly to the stalks and coarsely toothed at their ends. Scapes 18–20 cm high, branching above the middle, with numerous white flowers. The plant is doubtfully in cultivation.

## *Saxifraga ferruginea* Grah.

From the Rocky Mountains to Alaska, it grows above the tree line on rocky slopes, along streams, near melting snow and on gravel. Almost unobtainable, it is difficult to grow.

## Saxifraga hicracifolia *Waldst. et Kit.*

One of the few species of this section which grow in central Europe, it is widely distributed throughout arctic and subartic Europe, northern Asia, North America (southwards as far as Yellowstone Park), eastern Greenland, Spitzbergen, the Auvergne, the eastern Alps and the Carpathians. Occurring on slopes, moraines, moist rocks and stream sides, it flowers from the end of June to July. Seeds mature in August. This is a lime-hating plant, local and scarce, with rosettes 6–8 cm in diameter. Rosette leaves ovate to narrowly obovate, thick and fleshy. Upper surfaces glabrous, lower surfaces and edges hairy. Inflorescence a narrow panicle, 10–50 cm high depending on situation. Flowers greenish or dirty yellow, with red margins. Of more interest to botanists than to gardeners.

### *Saxifraga integrifolia* Hook.

From Pacific North America, where it grows in colonies in moist places, it is closely related to *S. pennsylvanica*. Doubtfully in cultivation.

### *Saxifraga leucanthemifolia* Michx.

Found in an area from the Atlantic coast of North America to the Alleghany forests, especially on moist rocky mountain tops, it is of no special beauty and doubtfully in cultivation.

### *Saxifraga lyallii* Engl.

From the Rocky Mountains, where it grows in shady spots, it forms rosettes of long-stalked wedge-shaped leaves, serrated on their outer margins. Scapes 15–30 cm high, branching from the middle. Numerous small attractive white flowers. The leaves often have a reddish tinge. Not a striking plant, it is of interest to enthusiasts.

### *Saxifraga manschuriensis* Komarov

From northern China, Manchuria and Korea, it grows on the coasts and in the mountains on wet rocks and along streams. Leaves large, kidney-shaped, with indented margins. Scapes up to 40 cm high, hairy, with a compact panicle of white flowers, maturing in autumn into small reddish fruits. Though it is regarded as difficult, this plant flourishes in my own garden provided it has sufficient moisture and neutral or slightly acid soil. It is completely hardy and should be more widely grown by alpine plant enthusiasts.

### *Saxifraga merkii* Fisch.

From central and northern Japan and the Kurile islands, it occurs also in eastern China and eastern Siberia. The botanists divide it into var. *typica* and var. *idsuroei*. An attractive little plant, it is occasionally offered in the seed lists. Small lax rosettes. Leaves finely hairy, with one or two indentations. Scapes hairy, 6 cm high, with 1–4 relatively large white flowers. Well worth a trial.

### *Saxifraga mertensiana* Bong.

From the Pacific coast of North America to the Rocky Mountains, it grows on moist rocks. Leaves long-stalked, round, leathery, glossy, with toothed edges. Scapes 30–40 cm high, branching from the middle, carrying small white flowers with contrasting red anthers. It likes acid soil and a cool half-shady place in the garden, and should be more widely grown. There are two varieties, *S.m.* var. *eastwoodiana* and *S.m.* var. *bulbillifera*. The latter is taller (up to 50 cm) and has small reddish bulbils at the base of the scape.

## Saxifraga nivalis L.

Widely distributed throughout arctic and subarctic Europe, northern Asia, North America, Greenland, Spitzbergen, Ireland and the British Isles and the Sudetenland, it does not occur in the Alps. It grows on wet siliceous soils (snow patches), forming small rosettes made up of dark green leaves, reddish on the under side. Leaves rounded to narrowly ovate, with indented or toothed margins. Scapes 5–20 cm high carrying a short compact panicle of greenish-white flowers on short pedicels (var. *nivalis*). In var. *tenuis* the branches of the inflorescence are longer and the flowers have distinct pedicels. The bright-green rosettes pass the winter under a covering of snow. The flowers are formed in the previous autumn, so that flowering begins soon after the snow melts. Not a plant for every garden, it can be successfully grown by enthusiasts.

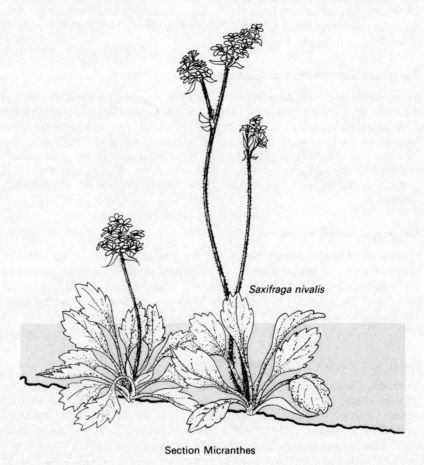

Saxifraga nivalis

Section Micranthes

*Fig. 46*

## Saxifraga pennsylvanica L.

In Atlantic North America it grows in moist boggy places. A large plant, up to 60 cm high, or in favourable circumstances even up to 1 metre, it is suitable for the wild garden, especially in shady spots between ferns. Large leathery leaves up to 30 cm long. The scape carries a wide pyramidal inflorescence of numerous small yellowish-white flowers. This species is not difficult in cultivation.

## Saxifraga punctata L.

Widely distributed in the arctic regions of Asia and America, it grows in moist gravel along streams, on moist rocks, in scree and near springs, forming rosettes of long-stalked kidney-shaped leaves with toothed margins. Scapes up to 50 cm high with a compact head of white flowers. *S.p.* ssp. *arguta* has longer stamens, almost as long as the petals. It is of no special beauty.

## Saxifraga reflexa Hook.

Occurring in arctic and subarctic North America, it grows on stony, rocky slopes. Rosettes of leaves 1–3 cm long and 0.6–1.5 cm wide with serrated edges. Scapes 10–16 cm high carrying a loose inflorescence of small white flowers. It is of little garden value.

## Saxifraga rufidula Macoun

From subarctic and Pacific North America, *S. rufidula* forms almost ever-green rosettes of leathery ovate leaves with indented margins and reddish hairs on their lower halves. Scapes short (6–8 cm), stiff, carrying white flowers with reddish stamens. It prefers a half shady spot and flowers in summer. This is an attractive plant, worth reintroducing.

## Saxifraga sachalinensis F. Schmidt

This plant grows on rocks in subarctic Asia, notably in central and northern Sakhalin. Not easy to grow, it is of little garden value. Scapes 30 cm high with a loose inflorescence of small flowers.

## Saxifraga stellaris L.

Widely distributed in the mountain ranges of Europe, from Scandinavia southwards to Portugal, Spain, Corsica, Macedonia and Bulgaria, it occurs also in the arctic areas of Russia, Siberia and North America. It grows near springs and streams, on wet rocks and on scree slopes among alder scrub at altitudes of 1200–3500 metres. It is also found at lower altitudes where it has been carried down by rivers. It forms loose rosettes of obovate leaves, light green, fleshy, glossy and toothed at the end. Scapes 5–15 cm high, carrying a much branched panicle of numerous small starry white flowers with yellow spots. Flowering time is early summer. In the garden it needs a cool moist spot and is difficult to please, though it is the most easily obtainable of its section.

### Saxifraga tenuis (Wahlenb.) H. Smith ex Lindman

Occurring in arctic and subarctic Europe (Scandinavia, Faroe islands, Iceland and Russia), it is very similar to *S. nivalis*, but the scape is more slender, the downy hairs are less dense and there are no long hairs. Of little garden value.

### Saxifraga tolmiei Torr. et A. Gray

From the Pacific coast of North America from southern Alaska to the Rocky Mountains. This species looks more like a *Sedum* than a saxifrage. It grows on gravel banks in streams fed by melting snow. It forms mats up to 50 cm in diameter with numerous thick succulent leaves about 1 cm long. Scapes 5–8 cm high. Flowers white or light yellow, over 1 cm in diameter, in a loose inflorescence. Seldom if ever in cultivation, it is likely to be difficult and would require moisture and very sharp drainage.

### Saxifraga virginiensis Michx.

On the Atlantic side of North America, it extends from the maritime provinces to the Mississippi woods. Leaves ovate, over 5 cm long, coarse and unattractive. Branched inflorescence up to 30 cm high carrying numerous small white florets in April–June. Much easier to cultivate than most of its section, it is not without some decorative value.

## SECTION CYMBALARIA

Section Cymbalaria comprises only four species, all of them annual or biennial. The only one commonly seen in gardens is *S. cymbalaria* ssp. *huetiana*. If it were not so difficult to obtain, *S. sibthorpii* might be interesting to grow. *S. cymbalaria* needs a damp shady spot on a wall or a piece of tufa and is not difficult to grow. It looks well among tufts of *Ramonda*. Although only biennial it persists by self-sown seedlings.

### Saxifrage cymbalaria L.

Occurring in Romania (eastern Carpathians), and Caucasus, the eastern Mediterranean area, Armenia and Iran, it grows near springs below the tree line, in the Caucasus often among rhododendrons. In gardens the type form is less commonly seen than the Romanian form: *S. cymbalaria* ssp. *huetiana* (Boiss.) Engl. et Irmsch. Annual or biennial. Leaves kidney-shaped, lobed, bright green and glossy. Scapes 3–10 cm high with yellow flowers from May to September. Easily grown in moist places in the garden, or in the alpine house, it will seed itself. It can also be grown in a trough, provided it has adequate moisture.

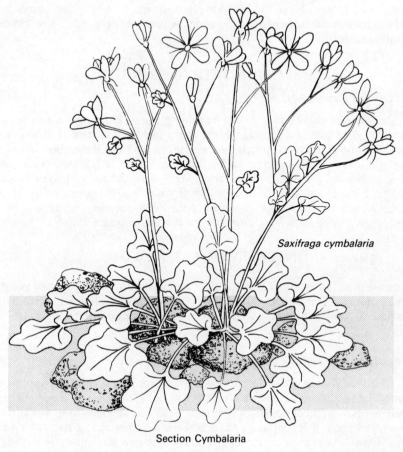

Saxifraga cymbalaria

Section Cymbalaria

*Fig. 47*

### Saxifraga hederacea L.

From the eastern Mediterranean region, extending westwards as far as Sicily, it grows on moist crumbling rocks, on shady walls and in wet fields. Annual or biennial. Sometimes on calcareous soils. Stems upright or sprawling. Leaves chiefly at the base, ovate or kidney-shaped, covered with glandular hairs. Flowers small, white (3 mm long). Of no garden value.

### Saxifraga hederifolia Hochst. ex A. Rich.

In Abyssinia it grows on wet rocks at altitudes of 3300 metres and above. Not in cultivation.

### Saxifraga sibthorpii Boiss.

A native of Greece, it resembles *S. cymbalaria*, but is distinguished by having somewhat larger, deep orange flowers and sepals which are somewhat deflexed when the flowers are fully open. A pretty little annual, now almost unobtainable.

## SECTION TETRAMERIDIUM

### Saxifraga nana Engl.

Engler created this section to accommodate this sole species, which comes from the province of Kansu in China. It has two peculiarities: the leaves are opposite and the flowers, which have no petals, have floral members in fours, not the usual fives. Apart from Section Diptera all other saxifrages have flowers which are divided into fives. The only other saxifrages having opposite leaves are those of Section Porphyrion (e.g. *S. oppositifolia*). More recently, however, several Himalayan species with opposite leaves have been discovered, some with floral members in fours and others in fives.

## INTERSECTIONAL HYBRIDS

Among the intersectional hybrids there are several first-rate garden plants. One point of interest is the part played by members of Section Robertsoniana as parent plants, though *S. aizoides* has also made an important contribution.

### Saxifraga × andrewsii Harvey

*S. hirsuta × S. paniculata*. In the older literature its parents are sometimes stated to have been *S. umbrosa × S. aizoon* or *S. × geum × S. aizoon*. These statements were occasioned by the confusion of nomenclature which then existed in Section Robertsoniana. *Saxifraga × andrewsii* is a natural hybrid which was discovered in Ireland. The seed parent *S. hirsuta* is a widely distributed native plant in western Ireland and the hybrid arose by chance pollination from *S. paniculata* growing in a garden. *S. andrewsii* is the best-known hybrid between species of different sections and is an ideal garden plant which will grow in sunny and shady spots alike, though it looks best in partial shade. It does not spread quite as vigorously as *S. × urbium*. It has loose rosettes of bright green, fleshy, narrow leaves with conspicuous teeth. The rosettes are tightly packed together to form a large mat. The scape, about 25 cm high, arises from the centre of the rosette. The inflorescence resembles that of *S. paniculata*, and the flowers, though not as numerous, are about twice as large. The scapes have a striking red tinge. The flowers are white, but because of the pink pistil and the red spots on the petals the overall impression is flesh-pink. This is a robust plant which should be grown in every rock garden.

### Saxifraga × arguta

A hybrid between *S. tenella* from Section Dactyloides and *S. tricuspidata* from Section Trachyphyllum, it forms handsome green mats of 3-lobed leaves, and snow-white flowers on branching stems about 15 cm high. It grows well in half shade, but may no longer be in cultivation.

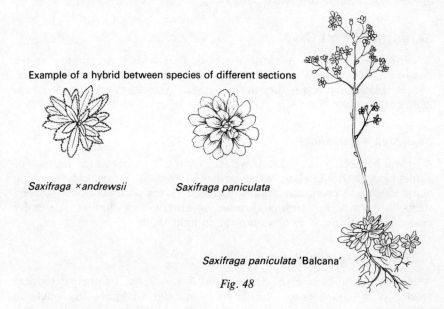

Example of a hybrid between species of different sections

Saxifraga ×andrewsii        Saxifraga paniculata

Saxifraga paniculata 'Balcana'

*Fig. 48*

## Saxifraga × forsteri Stein

*S. caesia × S. mutata.* An interesting plant, though not of great garden value, this rare natural hybrid was discovered in the Tyrol in 1877. It forms loose mats of small rosettes which resemble those of *S. caesia* but are green rather than grey. Scapes slender, brittle, with 1–3 brightly coloured flowers. It likes plenty of limestone grit and the soil should not be too dry. Protection from strong sun is necessary. It might do best in the alpine house.

## Saxifraga × hausknechtii Engl. et Irmsch.

*S. granulata × S. rosacea* (formerly *S. granulata × S. decipiens*). A natural hybrid found only in the Harz mountains near Treseburg, it forms profuse white flowers in May–June; about 25 cm high. Of more botanical than horticultural interest.

## Saxifraga × hausmannii

*S. mutata × S. aizoides.* A natural hybrid also known as *S. × girtanneri* Brueg., it is not uncommon in the northern limestone Alps and their foothills. In appearance it is closer to *S. mutata*, having coppery-orange flowers on short stiff scapes, 7.5–10 cm high. It flowers in early summer. Short-lived, it is interesting rather than beautiful, but worth cultivating.

### Saxifraga × guthrieana

A back-cross from *S.* × *andrewsii* and *S. paniculata*, it closely resembles *S.* × *andrewsii* but is somewhat smaller.

### Saxifraga × patens Gaud.

*S. aizoides* × *S. caesia*. A natural hybrid, it is widely distributed in the Bavarian Alps, Austria and Switzerland, but nowhere common. In appearance it is laxer and less silvery than *S. caesia*. The delicate scapes 5–7.5 cm high, carry yellow flowers in early summer.

### Saxifraga × primulaize

A hybrid between *S. aizoides* and a dwarf form of *S.* × *urbium* (*S. umbrosa* of gardens). A charming plant, widely grown in England, it forms low-growing mats of narrow evergreen slightly indented leaves with delicate branched stems, 5–8 cm high, carrying carmine or salmon-pink flowers. An easily grown plant, it flourishes on damp soil in light shade.

### Saxifraga × pseudo-forsteri

A curious hybrid between *S. crustata* and *S. cuneifolia*, it forms neat glossy rosettes of round leaves with cartilaginous margins. In April–May it puts up branching inflorescences 10–20 cm high, with white flowers.

### Saxifraga × regeli

A hybrid from the same parents as *S.* × *hausmannii*, namely *S. aizoides* × *S. mutata*, it is somewhat different in appearance. It tends more towards *S. aizoides*, but the influence of *S. mutata* is shown by the paucity of lime pits on the leaves. Of interest rather than beauty.

### Saxifraga × tazetta

*S. taygetea* × *S. cuneifolia*. A garden hybrid introduced in 1884, this is a pretty little plant with rosettes of leathery spoon-shaped leaves on long stalks. Scapes short, leafless. Flowers white, with red spots.

### Saxifraga × wildiana

*S. paniculata* × a form of *S.* × *geum*. An interesting and attractive hybrid with basal rosettes made up of ovate glossy leathery leaves with toothed margins. The flowers resemble those of *S.* × *andrewsii*. Scapes reddish, flowers white with red spots. Height 20–25 cm. Seldom seen in gardens, it has, however, been in cultivation since its original occurrence in the Dresden Botanic Garden in 1836.

## *Saxifraga* × *zimmetrii* **Kerner**

*S. paniculata* × *S. cuneifolia*. This very beautiful natural hybrid, occasionally found in eastern Tyrol, forms small tight mats made up of rosettes of glossy leathery leaves with a distinct grey edge. Scapes 10–15 cm high; flowers white with orange stamens. It prefers light shade. Of great garden value.

Besides the hybrids listed above there are numerous others which will not be described here, because they are of no horticultural importance or because they have been lost from cultivation. They include:

*Saxifraga* × *mattfeldii* Engl. = *S. cuneifolia* × *S. rotundifolia, Saxifraga* × *jaeggiana* Bruegger = *S. cotyledon* × *S. cuneifolia, Saxifraga* × *sotchensis* Engl. = *S. aizoides* × *S. squarrosa, Saxifraga* × *freibergeri* Ruppert = *S. granulata* × *S. rosacea* ssp. *sponhemica, Saxifraga* × *larsenii* = *S. paniculata* × *S. aizoides, Saxifraga* × *blytii* = *S. cotyledon* × *S. aizoides, Saxifraga* × *paxii* = *S. paniculata* × *luteoviridis.*

# NINE

# Other Saxifragaceae for rock gardens and half-shade

There are several other genera of Saxifragaceae which provide plants of value for rock gardens and shady places.

## ASTILBE

If we disregard the tall-growing Arendsii, Thunbergii and Simplicifolia hybrids, and the larger species, we need consider here only a comparatively small number of garden plants, but these include Astilbes for a wide range of different conditions, from cool moist corners to dry sunny spots.

### Astilbe chinensis var. pumila

A dwarf form of *Astilbe chinensis* (Maxim.) Franch. et Sav. selected by Arends in 1932, this is a treasure, but still not widely known. It is a low-growing plant which forms a close ground covering, and despite statements to the contrary will flourish in a sunny place provided the soil is not too light. It flowers at the end of August or beginning of September, at a time when other Astilbes are long over. By means of underground runners it soon covers a considerable area, but is not invasive. The narrow panicles, some 25 cm high, are lilac-pink, and some thought must therefore be given to their place in the colour scheme. It thrives in sun or shade. In time it may tend to grow out of the ground, but this can be corrected by a top dressing of peaty earth. In cold areas the young shoots are often affected by late frosts, but the damage is soon made good by new growth. This plant is ideal for the wild garden, placed in front of taller perennials, or for medium-sized areas in the rock garden.

### Astilbe crispa hybrid 'Perkeo'

A charming dwarf with wrinkled leaves, it grows only about 15 cm high. It was introduced by Arends in 1930. Stiff upright panicles of deep pink flowers occur in July. Unlike *Astilbe chinensis* var. *pumila*, it does not tend to spread sideways and is a slow-growing plant. It will tolerate more sun than the tall-growing Astilbes and is fitted for the choicest places in the rock garden or even in a trough.

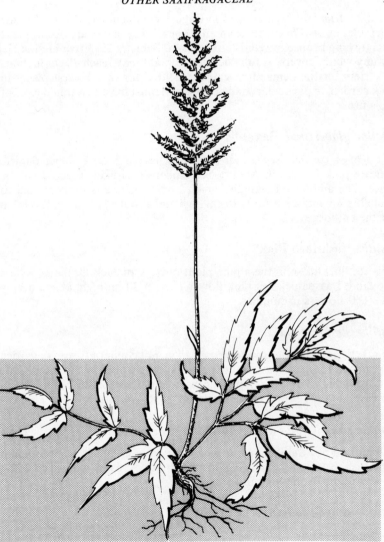

*Astilbe chinensis* var. *pumila*

*Fig. 49*

### *Astilbe crispa* hybrid 'Lilliput'

A counterpart of the foregoing variety, introduced in 1927. The flowers are salmon pink.

### *Astilbe* 'Dagalet'

The origin and status of this plant are uncertain. In German catalogues it is listed as *Aruncus* 'Dagalet', and in English catalogues as *Astilbe* 'Dagalet'; it resembles an *Astilbe* rather than an *Aruncus*. The leaves are deeply cut, fern-like, turning bronze or reddish in autumn. Panicles 25–30 cm high of elegant creamy white flowers. A fully developed plant may reach 40 cm in diameter. A variety for the demanding gardener, fitted for the choicest places in the rock garden, in particular shady crevices, it must have a certain degree of soil moisture.

### Astilbe glaberrima 'Saxatilis'

The leaves are handsomely divided and have a bronze tinge. Panicles of delicate pink flowers in August–September. This plant needs a cool moist place. The amount of sunlight which it will tolerate is proportional to the available soil moisture. Only 10 cm high and about 15 cm wide, this is a plant for the enthusiast.

### Astilbe 'Inshriach Pink'

This seedling arose in the alpine plant nursery of Jack Drake at Aviemore, Scotland. Lax panicles of pink flowers, about 30 cm high, above deeply cut leaves. It flowers in summer.

### Astilbe simplicifolia

This is the genuine wild species from Japan, not commonly seen in gardens. It has glossy toothed leaves and panicles of pure white flowers. Growing 15–20 cm high, it ultimately reaches a diameter of 25–30 cm. It is not invasive, and requires a certain amount of soil moisture.

### Astilbe simplicifolia × A. glaberrima var. saxatilis

Often listed in catalogues as *A. glaberrima saxosa*, this is a handsome plant for moist peaty soils, producing an abundance of foamy whitish or flesh pink flowers about 15 cm high in the summer.

### Astilbe simplicifolia hybrid 'Sprite'

A selected form of the wild species, it can be relied on not to grow too large. It has beautiful glossy bronze leaves and panicles of white flowers with a tinge of pink, and flowers from July to September. About 15–25 cm high and 30 cm wide, it is not too large for the rock garden. Very beautiful in a cool peaty place.

### Astilbe 'William Buchanan'

A novelty from Great Britain, it is low-growing (height about 25 cm, width about 30 cm). Glossy leaves with a carmine red tinge and creamy white flowers. There are various other selected forms which remain comparatively small, but most of them are too showy for the wild garden and look out of place. The following varieties do not exceed 40 cm in height: *Astilbe chinensis* 'Finale', *A. chinensis* 'Serenade', and the *A. simplicifolia* hybrids 'Aphrodite' and 'Altrosa'.

# *BERGENIA*

Low-growing perennials with large leaves, formerly included in the genus *Saxifraga*, there are about 10 species, all from eastern Asia, vigorous plants with a robust creeping root-stock. The leaves are large, evergreen, leathery, with multicellular sunken glands. The flowers, in panicles on stout stems, open very early in the year. In the bud there are 5 ovate overlapping sepals, and 5 petals, white, pink or deep purple in colour.

They will flourish in any part of the garden, but their place must be chosen with some care. They can be grown at the margins of large rock gardens, underplanted beneath trees or between rhododendrons or sited at the margins of ponds or streams, though they will not tolerate stagnant moisture. Even on dry-stone walls they grow vigorously. In cold areas the flowers are often destroyed by late frosts, and at this time of year suitable covering material should be kept at hand. In time the root-stocks tend to grow out of the soil; when this happens they must be divided or covered with loose earth.

## Species

### *Bergenia acanthifolia* hort. (?)

A somewhat tender species, not evergreen. Severe frost will destroy all the foliage except the leaf buds. Flowering begins early in March. Flower stems 20–30 cm high. Flowers pale pink, becoming darker as they fade. Leaves 13 × 7 cm, hairy, light green, with toothed edges. This species is suitable only for mild districts, and even there it should be given a sheltered place.

### *Bergenia ciliata* (Haw.) Sternb. (syn. *B. ligulata* var. *ciliata* (Haw.) Engl., *B. thysanodes* (Lindl.) Schneid., *Megasea ciliata* Haw.)

A native of the Himalayas (Nepal, Kumaon, Kashmir), it has leaves 22 × 28 cm, bright green, with hairs on both sides. Not evergreen. Flowering stems about 30 cm high, carrying large, clear pink flowers in early spring. A pretty plant, but very tender, it has been in cultivation since 1819.

### *Bergenia ciliata* f. *ligulata* (Wall.) Yeo (syn. *B. lingulata* (Wall.) Engl., *B. thysanodes* (Lindl.) Schneid., *Saxifraga thysanodes* Lindl.).

Sometimes listed as a separate species, it is found from eastern Afghanistan to Assam. The leaves are broad, rounded, with hairy margins; destroyed by severe frost. Flowers, in dense heads, open in early spring, petals almost white, making a pleasing contrast with the reddish sepals. About 23–25 cm high. This one is for sheltered places only. It has been in cultivation since 1820.

## *Bergenia cordifolia* (Haw.) Sternb. (syn. *Megasea cordifolia* (Haw.))

From the Altai mountains. It grows up to 40 cm high. The leaves are rounded or heart-shaped, hairless, leathery, green or brownish-green with indented margins. The flower stem branches at the apex; pedicels and sepals reddish. The panicle is at first spheroidal but later opens into an umbrella shape, so that the numerous flowers are ultimately held upright. The flowers are bell-shaped and vary in colour from rose pink to lilac. Flowering season is April–May. A valuable evergreen species, ultimately forming dense thickets, it has been in cultivation since 1779. There is a variety known as *B. cordifolia* 'Robusta'.

*Bergenia cordifolia*

*Fig. 50*

## *Bergenia crassifolia* (L.) Fritsch (syn. *B. bifolia* Moench, *Megasea crassifolia* (L.) Haw.)

From Korea, Mongolia and parts of Siberia. The large leaves are somewhat more elongated, though up to 20 cm wide. In shape they are obovate to broad ovate, somewhat wedge-shaped at the base, with margins indistinctly toothed; leaves hairless and evergreen. Flower-stem angled and reddish in colour. In sunny places the entire leaf assumes a reddish tinge. The inflorescence resembles that of *B. cordifolia*, but the flower-stalks are inclined to one side and not spread out in an umbrella shape. The flowers are bright purplish-pink, more or less drooping, appearing in March. They will stand slight frost. The plant was introduced in 1765.

### *Bergenia crassifolia* var. *pacifica* (Kom.) Nekr. (syn. *B. pacifica* (Kom.) Kom.).

From eastern Siberia as far as the Pacific coast, it is smaller in all its parts than the other species and less vigorous in growth, hence suitable for small rock gardens or even large troughs. The leaves are ovate, entire, glossy, turning reddish in winter. Flowers deep carmine-red.

### *Bergenia purpurascens* (Hook. f. et Thoms.) Engl. (syn. *Megasea purpurascens* Hook f. et Thoms., *B. delavayi* (Franch.) Engl., *B. yunnanensis* hort., *B. beesiana* hort.)

Occurring in the Himalayas, especially Sikkim, western Tibet and northern Burma, it grows on stony alpine meadows and under rhododendrons, up to 25–38 cm in height. The leaves are hairless or with a few marginal bristles; elliptical to ovate, usually somewhat domed above and with a reddish tinge below. Flower stem and branches brownish red or purple. Inflorescence compact, deflected to one side. Flowers dark purple-red, deeper in colour than those of the other species. Flowering time is April–May. It was introduced in 1850.

### *Bergenia stracheyi* (Hook. f. et Thoms.) Engl.

From the western Himalayas, this is a dwarf plant with small round leaves and short heads of white or pink flowers nestling between the leaves. In cultivation since 1851.

Also offered in the trade are *B. stracheyi* 'Afghanica', which is practically indistinguishable from the type, and *B. stracheyi* 'Alba', the pure-white form.

Other species, not available commercially, are *Bergenia ugamica* V. Pavlov and *Bergenia hissarica* Borris.

*Bergenia media, B.* var. *orbicularis* and other plants which masquerade in catalogues under botanical names belong in fact to the species listed above, or are subspecies, forms or hybrids. The nomenclature of *Bergenia* in plant collections and nursery gardens is extremely confused.

## Hybrids

### *Bergenia* × *schmidtii* (Regel) Silva-Tarouca

A hybrid between *B. ciliata* × *B. crassifolia*, better known as *B. stracheyi* var. *schmidtii* (Regel) hort. ex Werh. Other synonyms include *B. ligulata* 'Speciosa', *B. ornata*, and *B.* 'Ernst Schmidt'. The leaves are toothed, circular, deep-green, long-stalked. Flowers form short compact heads about 20 cm high. Petals pink with red sepals. A beautiful plant, it requires a carefully chosen, sheltered spot. In some places the first flowers often appear by the end of February. The long-stalked flowers are suitable for wreaths and bouquets.

### *Bergenia* × *smithii* **Engl. et Irmsch.**

Derived from the cross between *B. cordifolia* × *B. purpurascens*, it is also known as *B.* × *newryensis* Yeo. Certain English hybrids can be traced back to this cross.

### *Bergenia* 'Abendglocken'

Introduced by Georg Arends and Co. in 1971. The leaves are reddish green, about 10 cm wide and 20 cm long. Loose heads of bell-shaped carmine red flowers occur on stout stems about 40 cm high in April–May.

### *Bergenia* 'Abendglut'

Raised by Georg Arends in 1950, this is a plant with a complex pedigree. Broad ovate leaves have a reddish tinge turning bronze in autumn. Leaf margins are undulating or wrinkled, with short hairs. Dark red flowers are held upright on stout stems 20–30 cm high in April–May. The flowers are semi-double and the sepals also have a red tinge. The plant is seen at its best when grown among a carpet of sky blue forgetmenot (*Omphalodes verna*), which flowers at the same time.

### *Bergenia* 'Admiral'

A new variety with dark green leaves, 18–20 cm in diameter, turning reddish in winter. Bright red flowers on stout stems about 30 cm high in April–May.

### *Bergenia* 'Baby Doll'

Introduced in 1971, it has light-pink flowers, darkening as they age, on stems 30–40 cm high in April–May. Leaves are 15 × 16 cm, with short stalks, remaining green.

### *Bergenia* 'Ballawley'

A fine hybrid or variant from *B. purpurascens*, it was raised in Ballawley Park, Dublin, in 1950. The leaves are less coarse than those of certain other hybrids, glossy green, round, limp, 23 cm or more in diameter, turning brownish in winter. Stems are red with elegant spikes of bright rose-red flowers. The plant needs half-shade, shelter from cold winds and good soil. Ultimate dimensions 60 × 60 cm.

## Bergenia 'Bressingham Bountiful'

*B. ciliata* f. *lingulata* × *B. purpurascens*. Raised by Mr Pugsley at Bressingham Gardens in 1972, this compact hybrid with dark leaves, tinged with maroon in parts, has branching scapes with rose-pink flowers which darken as they age. Leaves somewhat tender.

## Bergenia 'Brilliant'

A new variety from England (*B. cordifolia* × *B. purpurascens*), it is not to be confused with the old variety 'Brilliant' raised by T. Smith in 1880. Leaves are small, circular, cordate at the base, margins reddish and indented. Flower stems, branches, ovaries and sepals are deep red, covered with short stalked glands. The flowers are drooping, bell-shaped; petals deep purple, becoming somewhat paler as they age. The plant flowers in April.

## Bergenia 'Distinction'

One of the older English hybrids, dating back to 1889 (*B. cordifolia* × *B. purpurascens*), it is derived from the old hybrids based on *Bergenia* × *smithii*, and resembles *B. cordifolia* in appearance. Leaves are 13 × 16 cm, short stalked, evergreen, forming distinct rosettes. The plant has pretty baby pink flowers, and is very late-flowering.

## Bergenia 'Glockenturm'

A new and outstandingly floriferous hybrid (Eskuche) with large heads of rose pink flowers, ultimate height is 50–60 cm, flowering time April–May. Leaves fresh green, 15 × 22 cm, finely toothed; undersides light green.

## Bergenia 'Margery Fish'

Raised by Mr H. C. Pugsley from a cross of *B*. 'Ballawley' × *B. ciliata*, this is very early-flowering. Leaves 20 × 24 cm. Branching heads of large reddish purple flowers. The outer leaves are often damaged by frost.

## Bergenia 'Morgenröte'

A hybrid of complex parentage raised by Georg Arends in 1950. Leaves somewhat smaller than in other similar hybrids, circular or obovate, margins undulating, with short hairs. Flower stems and sepals reddish. Flowers upright with 5–7 petals, purple when unfolding and bright carmine-pink when fully opened. It grows to 20–30 cm high, and flowers in April–May, sometimes again in September.

## Bergenia 'Oeschberg'

An unusually tall hybrid, the flower stems often reaching 50–60 cm or more. Leaves 19 × 23 cm, upright, long stalked, turning red in winter. Flowering stems much-branched, with numerous bell-shaped bright pink flowers, paler on the inside. Very late-flowering and hence suitable for districts prone to late frosts.

### Bergenia 'Perfect'

Leaves relatively small, with little tendency to change colour in winter. Flower stems 25–30 cm. Flowers drooping, carmine red.

### Bergenia 'Profusion'

An old hybrid or perhaps only a form of *B. cordifolia*, dating from 1880, it resembles *B. cordifolia*, with round green leaves with deep veins. Flowers pale pink to bright silvery pink. Late-flowering. In sunny positions the foliage turns reddish in autumn.

### Bergenia 'Progress'

An old hybrid raised by P. Smith in Britain in 1889. A *B. × smithii* type. Leaves 14 × 15 cm, remaining green in winter. The leaf-stalks are longer than those of 'Profusion', the flowers abundant, not drooping, carmine-red. Late-flowering.

### Bergenia 'Pugsley's Pink'

A new English hybrid. Leaves medium-sized, red beneath, long-stalked. The flower-stems are upright, 35–50 cm high, the flowers pink with brown sepals.

### Bergenia 'Pugsley's Purple'

Another new English hybrid which grows very vigorously, it has leaves 16 × 18 cm, dark-green with reddish borders. The flower-stems are robust, reddish, with a branched inflorescence of carmine-magenta flowers. Late-flowering, it's suitable for cold districts, but not very floriferous.

### Bergenia 'Purpurglocken'

A new hybrid from Georg Arends (1971), it flowers again in the autumn. Leaves 10 × 15 cm, green, slightly toothed. Flower-stems 40–60 cm high with numerous bell-shaped purple flowers in April–May.

### Bergenia 'Schneekissen'

A tall-growing variety from K. Foerster, it has leaves 16 × 19 cm, round, with wrinkled margins. Despite the name, the flowers are not pure white but pale pink, darkening as they age. They are relatively large and beautifully shaped. The plant is floriferous and suitable for cutting.

### Bergenia 'Silberlicht'

Raised by Georg Arends in 1950, it has a complex parentage. The leaves are large, faintly toothed, hairless apart from a few marginal bristles, reddish, obovate and long-stalked. Inflorescences and sepals are also reddish. The flower-stems divide from the middle upwards giving off short vertical-directed branches. The flowers are held upright, with 4–8 white petals which turn pink as they age. It flowers in April–May. A vigorous grower, it received an Award of Merit from the Royal Horticultural Society.

### Bergenia 'Sunningdale'

A new English hybrid (1964) selected from a large number of seedlings raised from the cross *B. cordifolia* × *B. purpurascens*, it has the pleasing winter coloration of *B. purpurascens* and is a much better ground-cover plant. It tolerates full sun and assumes its winter coloration only in sunny positions. The leaves are 10.5 × 13 cm with faintly toothed margins, flower-stems red with carmine-lilac flowers.

### Bergenia 'Sunshade'

*B. cordifolia* × *B. purpurascens* = *B.* × *smithii* type. Introduced by Barr and Sons in 1902, it has leaves 9 × 11 cm, with reddish, shallowly toothed margins. The leaf stalks are short and the leaves form close rosettes. The branching inflorescences have narrow drooping flowers, petals deep purple, sepals reddish. Flowering time is late April.

### Bergenia 'Walter Kienli'

A tall hybrid about 50 cm high, this is notable for the shape and arrangement of the beautiful leaves, which have undulating margins and measure 20 × 20 cm. It is late-flowering and not floriferous. The flowers, lilac-pink to carmine-red, form tightly compressed heads.

### Bergenia 'Wintermärchen'

The main asset of this hybrid is its foliage which will tolerate severe frost and displays a fine brownish-red coloration in winter. The leaves are smaller than those of most varieties (14 × 17 cm). The flower stems, 30–40 cm, carry numerous brilliant carmine-pink flowers. Late-flowering.

## CHRYSOSPLENIUM

*Chrysosplenium alternifolium* L. and *C. oppositifolium* L. are natives of Great Britain and Germany, where they grow inconspicuously on river banks, near springs and in bogs, though never where they are exposed to full sun. They have yellow-green flowers on stems about 10 cm high in early spring. They are of no horticultural importance, though grown by a few enthusiasts. The same is true of *C. americanum* and *C. glaciale*.

### *Chrysosplenium oppositifolium* var. *rosulare* Schott

An unpretentious perennial from Transylvania, worth growing in the rock garden or the wild garden, it has rounded leaves and forms vigorous yellow-green mats. It needs a moist place in full or partial shade. Given such conditions it will soon carpet considerable areas and even medium-sized rocks. The flowers are inconspicuous, but the light-green mats are restful to the eye. It looks pleasing beside *Primula rosea* and the double yellow form of *Caltha palustris*.

### *Chrysosplenium tetrandum* (N. Lund) Th. Fries

From Scandinavia and Finland, it resembles *Chrysosoplenium alternifolium*.

## *HEUCHERA*

The species and varieties belonging to this genus are useful garden plants which flower for several weeks in the summer. There is hardly any part of the garden where they cannot be used, and they look presentable at all seasons. Their evergreen foliage is stiff and leathery, and often handsomely mottled, especially when young. The rosettes ultimately form dense mats. The long-stalked basal leaves are ovate or circular.

The panicles of red or pink flowers reach a height of 40–70 cm. Despite their height, they are so slender that they do not look out of place even in smaller rock gardens. They are also suitable for the wild garden, in sun or half-shade, but they do not flourish in deep shade. In such plantings they should be kept near the front. *Heuchera* is also useful for extensive level areas. Such plantings can be broken up by adding a few of the taller ornamental grasses such as *Molinia* and *Miscanthus*, and by dwarf conifers. *Heuchera* in its various forms is also used for edgings and cut flowers.

Most of the wild species have inconspicuously coloured flowers and are grown mainly by enthusiasts. However, they have given rise to numerous hybrids, raised by growers in England, France and Germany. Their work has given us brilliantly coloured flowers in robust panicles which stand up well to rain and wind.

All species and forms of *Heuchera* grow well in ordinary garden soil given a necessary minimum of humus and moisture. If the soil is very heavy some peat should be dug in. Though they prefer neutral soil, they will grow satisfactorily in mildly acid or mildly calcareous soils. They will flourish in sun or light shade but they must have some moisture and will not tolerate prolonged dryness. When choosing a place for them, the gardener must remember that they need some shelter. Although hardy, they must be given some protection with brushwood against prolonged frosts. This protection can equally well be achieved by planting them among conifers and evergreens which will shield them from winter sun.

## Species

### *Heuchera americana* L. (syn. *H. lucida* Schlecht.)

There is documentary evidence that this North American plant has been in cultivation since 1656. Height 50–60 cm. Leaves broad, resembling ivy in outline, long-stalked, flat and leathery, 5–7 lobed, with hairs on the lower surface. The leaf colour is dark green, with reddish veining and a general reddish tinge, especially when young. There is a selected garden form *H. americana* 'Purpurea' with more conspicuous brownish mottling, often incorrectly described as a species (*Heuchera rubescens*). The greenish white flowers appear in May—June, followed by the greenish fruits. The plant is grown not for its flowers but for the sake of the decorative leaves and is used for under-planting among shrubs.

### *Heuchera cylindrica* Dougl. ex Hook.

This species from western North America has been in cultivation since 1830 and is grown chiefly for the sake of its leaves. It forms tufts of lobed heart-shaped dark green leaves. The flowers are small and brownish. The white form *H. cylindrica* 'Alba' with creamy flowers is somewhat more attractive. The English plant-breeder Alan Bloom has selected two varieties: *H. cylindrica* 'Greenfinch' with huge sprays of greenish sulphur flowers up to 90 cm high, and *H. cylindrica* 'Hyperion' with shorter inflorescences of deep-pink florets.

### *Heuchera micrantha* Dougl.

This species comes from the western United States and was introduced in 1827. It has fine leaves with grey markings and numerous spikes, up to 90 cm high, of countless small reddish-white flowers in early summer.

### *Heuchera pilosissima* Fisch. et Mey.

From California. The entire plant is thickly covered with velvety hairs. The flower stems rise to a height of 45–50 cm out of the mass of delicate green leaves, carrying panicles of grey-white flowers with a reddish tinge. Seldom seen in Europe, it is of doubtful hardiness.

### *Heuchera racemosa* S. Wats.

(Some botanists put this in a separate genus: *Elmera racemosa* Rydb.) From western North America, this species is seldom seen in gardens. Airy panicles of pretty white flowers rise about 25 cm above the mat of leaves.

### *Heuchera sanguinea* Engelm.

From North America, chiefly New Mexico, Arizona and the northern parts of Mexico, it is known locally as 'Coral Bells'. In cultivation since 1882, it is low-growing, only 30–40 cm high. Leaves rounded or heart-shaped, with 5–7 shallow lobes, faintly toothed, dark green with inconspicuous markings. Extremely free-flowering, flower colour carmine-red. This species has been widely used for hybridization. Selected forms (not hybrids) include *H. sanguinea* 'Alba' with white flowers, *H. sanguinea* 'Robusta' with dark-red, somewhat larger flowers and *H. sanguinea* 'Splendens' with an enormous profusion of brilliant carmine-red flowers.

### Heuchera villosa Michx.

Another North American species, it has been in cultivation since 1812. Leaves are large, clear-green, lobed. It flowers rather late (August), with loose panicles about 60 cm high with numerous small creamy flowers. Valuable for its late flowering, it makes a good partner for the 'Willow Gentian'.

## Hybrids

### Heuchera × brizoides Lemoine

This hybrid arose in France and was the origin of most of the garden forms. It probably came from a cross between *H. americana* and *H. sanguinea*, though some authors state that its parents were *H. sanguinea* and *H. micrantha*. As the original hybrid is no longer extant, the point is not of much importance.

### Heuchera 'Bressingham Seedlings'

This is not a uniform clone, but an assortment of seedlings raised by Alan Bloom and displaying a range of colours from pink to dark red. They are about 50 cm high and most of them flower in June–July.

### Heuchera 'Carmen'

A new hybrid up to 50 cm high with dark-red flowers in May to July.

### Heuchera 'Feuerregen'

A very old French hybrid (Lemoine), it is sometimes offered under its original name ('Pluie de Feu'). About 40 cm high with numerous deep-rose-pink to bright-red flowers in June–July. The stems are robust and wind-resistant, and the flowers proof against rain and sun.

### Heuchera 'Firebird'

Growing to a height of 40–60 cm, it is more compact in habit than most hybrids, and extremely floriferous, with bright scarlet flowers in June–July.

### Heuchera 'Gracillima'

Raised by Arends in 1903, it has finely branched panicles about 50 cm high with numerous delicate pink flowers.

### Heuchera 'Lady Romney'

A new English variety with pale pink flowers on loose panicles about 60 cm high.

### Heuchera 'Pruhoniciana'

An old and well-loved variety about 50 cm high. It has compact inflorescences of pink flowers which turn red as they age. The foliage resists adverse weather well.

### Heuchera 'Rakete'

A widely grown variety raised by Frikart, it is vigorous and somewhat taller than most (60–70 cm), with brilliant vermilion flowers, later than other hybrids.

### Heuchera 'Red Pimpernel'

A very old variety, but still available. The compact panicles are 50–60 cm high, of bright-scarlet to coral-red flowers. A healthy and vigorous plant.

### Heuchera 'Red Spangles'

Raised by Alan Bloom. The compact panicles grow 50–60 cm high consisting of brilliant scarlet flowers. Early flowering.

### Heuchera 'Scintillation'

Also raised by Bloom, 50–60 cm high with brilliant pink flowers, each tipped with coral red. Many awards from the Royal Horticultural Society.

### Heuchera 'Silberregen'

About 50 cm high, with pure-white flowers.

### Heuchera 'Titania'

A very old variety, but still available, this is a vigorous plant with broad robust panicles of pink flowers with a salmon tinge. Flower stems 50–60 cm high, wind-resistant.

### Heuchera 'Weserlachs'

Raised by Junge. Salmon-pink flowers on sturdy stems 50–60 cm high occur in June–July.

### Heuchera 'Coral Cloud'

Raised by Bloom, it is taller than most other hybrids (60–70 cm), with large spreading panicles of small but numerous coral-pink flowers. Free-flowering.

Many other varieties are listed in the older literature, but most of them have been superseded and have disappeared from the catalogues. However, there is a steady flow of new varieties such as 'Pearl Drops', 'Sparkler', 'Oakington Jewel', 'Jubilee', 'Sunset' and 'Gloriana'.

## Intergeneric hybrids

The two genera *Heuchera* and *Tiarella* interbreed readily and the resulting intergeneric hybrids are called × *Heucherella* Wehrb. Their offspring have shoots which run along the ground and green foliage with a golden tinge. The young leaves often have brownish markings. The slender flowering stems, 20–25 cm high, carry carmine-pink flowers. They are reasonably robust, and the first variety in the list below is outstandingly valuable. They are all valuable perennials for the rock garden or for planting in semi-shaded spots, provided they are not too dry.

### × *Heucherella* 'Bridget Bloom'

A plant with luxuriant foliage and abundant flowers when grown in a suitable place. Each floret is partly pink and partly white, giving an overall pale-pink effect. The normal flowering time is May to June, but there is often a second flowering in September to October. Though relatively undemanding, the plant should be given an annual top dressing of rich soil or well-rotted manure.

### × *Heucherella* 'Alba' (Lemoine) Stearn

Raised in 1925, probably from a cross between a white-flowered Heuchera- × Tiarella cordifolia, it is only 20–30 cm high. Flowers are white. It does not produce runners.

### × *Heucherella tiarelloides* (Lemoine) Werh. ex Stearn

Raised in 1912 from a cross between *Heuchera* × *brizoides* × *Tiarella cordifolia*. The spikes of pink flowers are 20–30 cm high. It spreads by runners. The leaves are rounded or heart-shaped with coarsely indented margins.

## *LEPTARRHENA*

### *Leptarrhena pyrolifolia* (D. Don) R. Br.

This is the only species of any horticultural importance, a moorland plant from North America and north-eastern Asia, notably Alaska. It forms creeping overground stems, thickly covered with leathery dark-green leaves, spathulate to ovate in shape and 4–5 cm long. The flowering stems, 10–15 cm high, have only a few leaves, and in July they carry a compact panicle of small, white or pale-pink flowers. It is shy-flowering and is mainly useful for ground cover beneath rhododendrons or in similar situations. It will grow in full sun or half shade but needs some degree of moisture all the year round. As might be expected from its provenance, it flourishes only on peaty lime-free soils.

## MITELLA

These small perennials from North America, closely related to *Tiarella*, are for shady places. They spread by runners and soon cover the ground.

### Mitella breweri A. Gray

From British Columbia, evergreen, with small rounded deep-green leaves. The flower stems are 25 cm high, flowers small and greenish but not without a certain charm.

### Mitella caulescens Nutt.

Leaves heart-shaped, with irregular serrations. The entire plant is covered with coarse hairs. Flower stems are 10–15 cm, carrying inconspicuous pale-yellow flowers in a drooping panicle. Flowering time May.

### Mitella diphylla L.

From eastern North America, this is the most widely distributed species. The basal leaves are small, bright green, glossy, broadly heart-shaped, with 3–5 lobes. Flower stems are 20–25 cm high with two stem leaves and small greenish-white flowers appearing in April–May.

### Mitella nuda L.

A little known species from North America. The leaves are rounded and kidney-shaped, flowers greenish.

### Mitella pentandra Hook.

The basal leaves are kidney-shaped. Flower stems, 25–30 cm high, carry small yellowish flowers with plumed petals in May-June.

### Mitella trifida Grah.

Leaves heart-shaped. Flower stems 10–15 cm, carrying a dense one-sided cluster of small white flowers.

These species flourish on damp soil in a cool half-shaded spot. They make attractive ground-cover plants, and their flowers, though inconspicuous, are exquisite.

# *PARNASSIA* (GRASS OF PARNASSUS)

A genus of some 44 species from the northern hemisphere. Though of little importance to the average gardener, some of them are grown by enthusiasts who have moist spots in their gardens. It was felt useful to include *Parnassia* here, although the genus is nowadays usually placed in a separate family, Parnassiaceae.

### *Parnassia fimbriata* Koenig

From North America, this is one of the most useful species, somewhat larger than *P. palustris*. The flowers are white, with petals fringed at the edges.

### *Parnassia foliosa* Hook f. et Thoms

From Japan, China and northern India. The flower stems, about 20 cm high, have leaves arranged in such a way as to resemble a pagoda. The flowers are white with fringed edges.

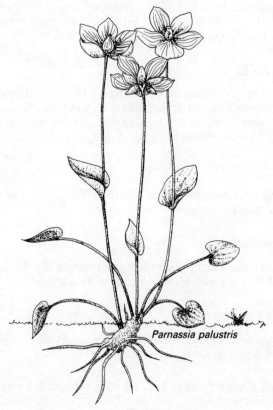

*Parnassia palustris*

Fig. 51

## Parnassia nubicola Wall.

From the Himalayas. Leaves ovate, dull green, on long stalks. Flower stems 15 cm, petals white with green veins. It is easier to grow than *P. palustris*.

## Parnassia palustris L.

Grass of Parnassus, native to Britain and Europe, is not easy to grow. The basal leaves are heart-shaped, forming a rosette. Each flower stem carries one leaf and a relatively large white cup-shaped flower. Height about 15 cm. It flowers from June to August. In the lowlands it grows in bogs but in alpine regions, where the atmosphere is more humid, it is found in drier habitats. This, the species most commonly offered, is often difficult to establish, possibly because of its sparse root system. In the garden it may be tried in a loamy hollow filled with earth from a bog. An alternative substrate is peat with a proportion of sphagnum. The site may be in sun or half-shade. A trough filled with a mixture containing some loam and placed in half shade might also be suitable.

## Parnassia parviflora D.C.

A North American species closely similar to *P. palustris*, but the white flowers have greenish or purple veins.

## TANAKAEA

### Tanakaea radicans Franch. et Sav.

The genus contains this species only. It is a woodland perennial from Japan and requires a lime-free growing medium of peat, humus and sand. Bark compost is ideal. It flourishes only in cool half-shaded places. The woody rhizomes emit numerous short runners carrying leathery evergreen rounded or heart-shaped leaves with toothed margins. The flower-stems, up to 20 cm high, have pyramidal panicles of small white flowers in June–July. The plant resembles a miniature Astilbe. In Europe it is not fully hardy and requires some shelter from early morning sun.

## TELLIMA

In all there are some 12 species from western North America, but for garden purposes the only one of any importance is *Tellima grandiflora* (Pursh) Dougl. ex Lindl. and its variety 'Rubra'. Though not a very striking plant, it is useful for under-planting in shady places and among shrubs. Given moderate soil moisture it will tolerate full sun. It grows readily and soon forms large stands. It is unaffected by polluted city air.

*Tellima grandiflora* occurs from Alaska to California. It is an upright plant reaching heights of 50–60 cm. The hairy leaves are heart-shaped and long-stalked, forming rosettes. In the winter they assume a brownish tinge. The flower stems carry numerous inconspicuous fringed hanging greenish-yellow bells in May–June. The variety 'Purpurea' (known in Germany as 'Rubra') has dark-green leaves which turn purple in winter. The flowers are pinkish-yellow and the whole plant is considerably lower.

# TIARELLA

The plants of this small genus flourish in cool half-shady places. One species (*T. polyphylla*) is a native of eastern Asia, and all the others come from North America. They are handsome low-growing perennials, flowering in spring or early summer. The leaves are mostly basal and long-stalked, lobed or palmately divided. The inflorescence is a simple or compound raceme.

### *Tiarella californica* Rydb.

Similar to *Tiarella unifoliata*, with white flowers on 30 cm stems. Seldom grown.

### *Tiarella cordifolia* L.

The best known and most important species, this is a woodland plant from North America which spreads by thin runners after flowering. Leaves light green, glossy, broadly ovate with 5 or rarely 3 lobes. They often have reddish markings and in the garden form *T. cordifolia* 'Purpurea' they have a purple tinge. The leaf stalk is long and hairy. The flower stem rises to a height of 15–30 cm depending on the situation. The white starry flowers are borne in long racemes from April to June. It is a plant for shady places where the soil is not too dry.

### *Tiarella laciniata* Hook.

An uncommon species with deeply divided leaves and small white flowers in a lax slender inflorescence.

### *Tiarella polyphylla* D. Don

From the Himalayas, China and other parts of eastern Asia. Leaves 3-lobed, toothed. Flower stems 30 cm with a simple raceme of small white flowers.

### *Tiarella trifoliata* L.

The small green leaves are divided into three segments, the middle segment having 3 lobes and the outer segments 2 each. Narrow inflorescences of white flowers on short stems.

### *Tiarella unifoliata* Hook.

Closely resembling *T. cordifolia*, it does not, however, emit runners. The leaves are heart-shaped or triangular, with a brownish tinge when young, later turning olive-green. Leaf margins indented. Flower stems 20–30 cm high, panicles coarser than those of *T. cordifolia*. The cream-white flowers appear in May. Not very vigorous.

### Tiarella wherryi Lakela (syn. *T. cordifolia* var. *collina* Wherry)

This plant from south-eastern North America is sometimes offered by nurseries. It does not put out runners. The leaves are ovate or heart-shaped, up to 8 cm wide, conspicuously 3-lobed, with brownish markings at the base and a reddish tinge in the autumn. Leaf stalks hairy, flower stems 15–35 cm high carrying racemes of white flowers with a pink tinge. Stamens orange. It has a delicate scent, reminiscent of annual mignonette (*Reseda*). It flowers in May–June.

Although the individual flowers are tiny, a large planting of *Tiarella* in a half-shady place can be extremely pleasing and the leaves are decorative at all times. They will grow in any good garden soil which is moderately water-retentive, but they flourish best in woodland soils. Intractable clays can be lightened by digging in peat and compost. They are well-suited for under-planting and beneath rhododendrons.

## TOLMIEA

### Tolmiea menziesii (Pursh) Torr. et A. Gray

The only species of the genus, formerly known as *Tierella menziesii*. A woodland plant from the north-west of North America, it is not uncommon there in the wet coastal woodlands. Related to *Heuchera*, it is distinguished from it by the numerous leaves on the flower stem and the laxer racemes, inclined to one side. It has a creeping root-stock. The leaves are long-stalked, heart-shaped, with irregularly double-toothed lobes. The basal leaves often carry adventive buds which develop into young plants. Flower stems 15–25 cm high carry panicles of small flowers in May.

The plant is easy to grow under the conditions which suit *Tiarella*. It can even be used as an indoor plant in cool rooms.

## PROPAGATION

### Astilbe

Propagation by seed is feasible only for the species; named varieties must be increased vegetatively. Like all members of the family, Astilbes have very fine seed. Depending on the species, 1 gram contains 15,000 to 20,000 seeds with an average germination rate of 50–60%. After sowing, the seed should not be covered with compost; it is enough to press it down gently. The seed pan must be kept uniformly moist, and should not be watered with a coarse hose, otherwise all the seeds will be washed into one corner. Some growers report that the seed needs a period of exposure to cold, while others deny this. When sown in the ordinary way it will sometimes germinate rapidly at +20°C, but sometimes fails. If it is to be exposed to frost it should be sown from December to March and later brought into a cold greenhouse, where it will germinate after about two weeks at +15°C. Normally it is sown in pots or boxes, but it can be sown in rows on a prepared seed bed out of doors. The fine seed should be mixed with sand or talc powder so as to ensure uniform distribution, and the rows should then be covered with sphagnum.

Division also gives a good rate of increase, and for the named varieties it is the only mode of propagation. When possible, division should be undertaken between November and March. The pieces should be potted up in a cold frame and planted out in May–June. Alternatively, the plants can be divided in April, and normally this should be done every three years to make them continue to flower freely. *Astilbe chinensis* 'Pumila' yields large numbers of divisions, but if great increase is required the runners can be treated as cuttings.

## Bergenia

*Bergenia* can be propagated by seed in much the same way as *Astilbe*. The seed is somewhat coarser, there being 4000 seeds to the gram, with an average germination of 75%. They should be sown from December to March and exposed to frost. When brought into a cold greenhouse they will germinate after about 20 days at +15°C.

The named varieties must be propagated vegetatively. Large clumps are best divided in March or April and the divisions can be planted out at once. When named varieties have to be propagated on a large scale, rhizome cuttings are taken from November to March. The cuttings are placed in weed-free compost in a box and the latter is left in a cold greenhouse or cold frame. After growth has started the cuttings can be potted up in March to May.

## Chrysosplenium

Propagation by seed is feasible, but hardly necessary as division is so productive and can be undertaken at any time of year. The small divisions should be placed in plastic pots and kept moist and shaded until they have rooted.

## Heuchera

These plants can be propagated by seed in the same way as Astilbe. There are about 25,000 seeds to the gram and the germination rate is 60%. Heuchera seeds require light for germination, but do not normally need exposure to frost. Once germination has taken place the seedlings should not be given too much light.

Division is normally undertaken in April–May, and the pieces can be planted directly in their intended sites. The end of August or beginning of September is also recommended as it is at this time that the woody roots are anchoring themselves in the soil. Cuttings can be taken in early summer, preferably with a heel.

## Leptarrhena

It can be propagated by division or seed.

## Mitella

Propagation by seed is feasible but hardly necessary. Plants can be divided at any time during the summer. One favourite method is to take offsets in September to November and to plant them straight into a well prepared nursery bed. They must be protected against hard frost and will be ready to transfer to their permanent positions in April–June.

## Parnassia

Division or seed.

## Tanakaea

Seed can be sown from January to April and should germinate in 20–30 days. The seedlings should be potted out when they are large enough. Division is also feasible.

## Tiarella

These plants can be propagated by seed, but it is hardly worth the trouble. Division can be undertaken at any time in the summer, provided robust plants are available. Rooted offsets can be taken in September–October and planted out of doors, but must be protected from severe frost. Cuttings of runners can be taken in September–October, placed in boxes in a greenhouse or cold frame and potted up in May–June.

## Tolmiea

Propagated by the small buds on the backs of the leaves. As a rule, large numbers of young plants will establish themselves around the mother plant, and need only be potted up.

# Saxifrages (listed) for special purposes

The following recommendations are intended to help those who require saxifrages for special purposes. They are not comprehensive lists.

Vigorous, easily available saxifrages, classified by month of flowering.

### Usually flowering in March:

S. × apiculata 'Gregor Mendel'
S. × elisabethae 'Carmen'
S. × eudoxiana 'Haagii'
S. × irvingii 'Walter Irving'
S. marginata 'Major'
S. × elisabethae 'Ochroleuca'
S. sancta ssp. pseudosancta var. macedonica

### Flowering at the end of March or beginning of April:

S. × boeckeleri 'Armida'
S. burserana
S. ferdinandi-coburgii
S. grisebachii
S. × kellereri 'Johann Kellerer'
S. oppositifolia in various forms
S. × rubella
S. × kellereri 'Suendermannii Major'

### Flowering from the second half of April:

S. arendsii hybrids
S. hypnoides var. egemmulosa
S. muscoides and hybrids

### Usually flowering in the first half of May:

S. × andrewsii
S. cuneifolia
S. × geum
S. granulata 'Plena'

### Flowering in the second half of May:

S. *paniculata* (syn. S. *aizoon*) in various forms and cultivars
S. *cochlearis*
S. *cochlearis* 'Minor'
S. *trifurcata*
S. × *urbium* (S. *umbrosa* of gardens)
S. × *urbium* 'Variegata'
S. × *urbium* 'Elliott's Variety'

### Usually flowering in July

S. *cotyledon*
S. *cotyledon* 'Caterhamensis'
S. *cotyledon* 'Pyramidalis'
S. *crustata*
S. *hostii*
S. *callosa*
S. *callosa* var. *lantoscana*
S. *longifolia*
S. *tenella*

### Autumn-flowering saxifrages:

S. *fortunei* and varieties.

Flowering times may be altered by unusual weather conditions.

A small collection for beginners

S. × *andrewsii*
S. × *apiculata* 'Gregor Mendel'
S. × *arendsii* 'Triumph'
S. *callosa*
S. *cochlearis*
S. × *eudoxiana* 'Haagii'
S. *hypnoides*
S. *paniculata*
S. *trifurcata*
S. × *urbium*

The most vigorous 'Kabschia' saxifrages

S. × *apiculata* 'Gregor Mendel'
S. × *borisii* 'Margarette'
S. × *boydii* 'Aretiastrum'
S. × *boydii* 'Pilatus'
S. × *edithae* 'Bridget'
S. × *elisabethae* 'Boston Spa'
S. × *elisabethae* 'Carmen'
S. × *elisabethae* 'Mrs Leng'
S. × *eudoxiana* 'Haagii'
S. × *stormonthii* 'Stella'

## 'Kabschia' saxifrages which should be in every collection

*S.* × *anglica* 'Cranbourne'
*S.* × *anglica* 'Myra'
*S.* × *hornibrookii* 'Riverslea'
*S.* × *irvingii* 'Jenkinsae'
*S.* × *kellereri* 'Johann Kellerer'
*S.* × *kellereri* 'Suendermannii Major'
*S.* × *mariae-theresiae* 'Theresia'
*S.* × *paulinae* 'Kolbiana'
*S.* × *petraschii* 'Kaspar Maria Sternberg'
*S.* × *pragensis* 'Golden Prague'
*S.* × *salmonica* 'Salomonii'

## 'Kabschia' saxifrages forming dwarf cushions

*S.* × *anglica* 'Cerise Queen'
*S.* × *arco-valleyi* 'Arco'
*S.* × *geuderi* 'Eulenspiegel'
*S.* × *irvingii* 'Gem'
*S.* × *megaseaeflora* 'Robin Hood'
*S.* × *petraschii* 'Affinis'
*S.* × *salmonica* 'Assimilis'
*S.* × *smithii* 'Vahlii'

## Miniature encrusted saxifrages

*S. cochlearis* 'Minor'
*S. paniculata* 'Baldensis'
*S. paniculata* var. *brevifolia*
*S. paniculata* 'Minutifolia'
*S. paniculata* 'Portae'
*S. paniculata* var. *sturmiana*
*S. valdensis*
*S.* 'Vreny'
*S.* 'Whitehill'

## Saxifrages of Sections Porophyllum and Euaizoonia which require acid soil

*S. cotyledon*
*S. florulenta*
*S. lilacina*

## Monocarpic saxifrages

*S. florulenta*
*S. longifolia*
*S. mutata*
*S. pasumensis*

## Saxifrages suitable for edgings

*S.* × *andrewsii*
*S. callosa*

*S.* × *geum*
*S. muscoides* 'Findling' ('Foundling')
*S. trifurcata*
*S.* × *urbium*

## Biennial saxifrages

*S. adscendens*
*S. cymbalaria* (often annual)
*S. hederacea* (often annual)
*S. petraea*

## Annual saxifrages

*S. tridactylites*
*S. sibthorpii*

## Unusual cultivars

*S.* × *arendsii* 'Biedermeier' (corrugated or frilled flowers)
*S.* 'Bob Hawkins' (greenish silvery variegated leaves)
*S.* 'Darlington Double' (double flowers)
*S. granulata* 'Plena' (double white flowers)
*S. moschata* 'Cloth of Gold' (yellow leaves)
*S. moschata* 'Variegata' (white variegated leaves)
*S.* 'Ruffles' (double white flowers)
*S.* × *urbium* 'Aureopunctata' (yellow spotted leves)

## Mossy saxifrages for holes in tufa

*S. cebennensis* (full shade)
*S. cuneata* (some sun)
*S. exarata* (full shade)
*S. presolanensis* (full shade)
*S. reuterana* (some sun)

## Saxifrages which are difficult to cultivate

*S. androsacea*
*S. chrysantha*
*S. conifera*
*S. flagellaris*
*S. pentadactylis*
*S. seguieri*
*S. tolmei*

## Saxifrages of doubtful hardiness which require alpine house cultivation

*S. camposii*
*S. corsica*
*S. demnatensis*
*S. erioblasta*
*S. flagellaris*
*S. globulifera*

S. *maderensis*
S. *maweana*
S. *oranensis*
S. *portosanctana*
S. *spathulata*
S. *trabutiana*
S. *vayredana*

# Sources of supply

The following list is intended to help gardeners in search of plants. It is restricted to firms known to the author and is hence not comprehensive. Nearly every nursery carries a small assortment of saxifrages, and beginners should start by visiting their local garden centres. All the firms listed below have more than 15 different saxifrages in their catalogues, and some of them offer more than 100. Because of the high costs (health certificate, carriage), not all firms are willing to execute small export orders.

## Great Britain

Little Heath Farm Nursery, Little Heath Lane, Potten End, Berkhamsted, Hertfordshire
Waterperry Horticultural Centre, Nr Wheatley, Oxford OX9 1JZ
C. G. Hollett, Greenbank Nursery, Sedbergh, Cumbria LA10 5AG
Oldfield Nurseries, Trowbridge Road, Norton St Philip, Somerset BA3 6NG
Reginald Kaye Ltd, Waithman Nurseries, Silverdale, Carnforth, Lancs LA5 0TY
Jack Drake, Inshriach Alpine Plant Nursery, Aviemore, Inverness-shire, Scotland PH22 1QS
W. E. Th. Ingwersen Ltd, Birch Farm Nursery, Gravety, East Grinstead, Sussex RH19 4LE
Robinsons Hardy Plants, Greencourt Nurseries, Crockenhill, Swanley, Kent BR8 8HD
Joe Elliott, Broadwell Nursery, Moreton-in-Marsh, Glos.
Barton Alpine and Hardy Plant Nursery, Barton House, Pooley Bridge, Penrith, Cumbria CA10 2NG
Hartside Nursery Gardens, Low Gill House, Alston, Cumbria CA9 3BL

Some of these firms require advance payment (about £1) for catalogues.

## Germany

### Nurseries

Georg Arends, Staudenkulturen, Monschaustr. 76, 5600 Wuppertal 21 (Ronsdorf)
Joachim Carl, Pforzheimer Alpengarten, Auf dem Berg, 7530 Pforzheim-Würm

Giessbeck, Alpenpflanzengärtnerei, Ramsbachstr. 129, 7060 Schorndorf
Hans Götz, Staudengärtnerei, 7622 Schiltach/Schwarzwald
Heinz Hagemann, Staudengärtnerei, 3001 Krähenwinkel b. Hannover
Kayser & Seibert, Odenwälder Pflanzenkulturen, 6101 Rossdorf b. Darmstadt
Heinz Klose, Staudengärtnerie, Rosenstr. 10, Gärtnersiedlung, 3503 Lohfelden-Kassel
K. H. Marx, Staudengarten, Bahnstrasse 36, 8602 Pettstadt bei Bamberg
B. Müssel, Alpinenanzucht, 8053 Heigenhausen
Margarete Scholz, Postfach 130173, 4800 Bielefeld 13
Dr Hans Simon, Gärtnerischer Pflanzenbau, Postfach 32, 8772 Marktheidenfeld (large range of saxifrages
F. Sündermann, Alpenpflanzengärtnerei, Aeschacher Ufer, 8990 Lindau-Bodensee (a large range of saxifrages)
Gräfin v. Zeppelin, Staudengärtnerei in Laufen/Baden, 7811 Sulzburg 2 (large selection of bergenias as well as saxifrages)

## Seed suppliers

Klaus R. Jelitto, Horandstieg 28, 2000 Hamburg 56
Kayser & Seibert, Odenwälder Pflanzenkulturen, 6101 Rossdorf b. Darmstadt
F. Sündermann, Alpenpflanzengärtnerei, Aeschacher Ufer, 8990 Lindau/Bodensee

## Switzerland

Correvon & Cie, Jardin Alpin 'Floraire' 1225 Chene-Bourg, Genève (large selection)
J. Eschmann, Alpengarten, CH 6032 Emmen (large selection)
Frei, Gärtnerei und Staudenkulturen, CH-8461 Wildensbuch/ZH (large selection)
Frikart Staudengärtnerei, Inh. Longin Ziegler, CH-8627 Grüningen-Oberzelg

## Austria

F. Feldweber, Baumschulen, Staudenkulturen, A 4974 Ort im Innkreis OÖ
F. u. M. Strohmeier, Wachauer Alpengarten, 3392 Schönbühel/Donau NÖ. (despatch within Austria only)

## Czechoslovakia

Frantisek Holenka, Na Sedlisti 777, 10200 Prag 10-Hostival ('Kabschia' saxifrages)

# *Garden societies*

The following societies include saxifrages within their scope. They offer contact with gardeners with similar interests, specialist literature and in some cases a seed exchange.

## Great Britain

Alpine Garden Society, c/o Mr E. M. Upward, Lye End Link, St John's, Woking, Surrey GN2 1SW
Scottish Rock Garden Club, c/o Mrs E. M. Bezzant, 24 North Grange Road, Glasgow G61 3QF

## Germany

Gesellschaft der Staudenfreunde, Justinus-Kerner Str. 11, 7250 Leonberg

## U.S.A.

American Rock Garden Society, Wm T. Hirsch, 3 Salisbury Lane, Malvern, PA 19355

## Canada

Alpine Garden Club of British Columbia, c/o Emmy Fisher, 2988 Starlight Way, Port Coquitlam, B.C./Canada

# Bibliography

Carl, J.: Miniaturgärten in Trögen, Schalen und Balkonkästen. Verlag Eugen Ulmer, Stuttgart 1978.

Encke, F.: Zwergsteingärten, Franckhsche Verlagshandlung, Stuttgart 1978.

Engler, A., and Irmscher, E.: Das Pflanzenreich, Saxifragaceae, Verlag Wilhelm Engelmann, Leipzig 1916.

Foerster, K.: Der Steingarten der sieben Jahreszeiten, Neumann Verlag, Radebeul 1954.

Harding, W.: Saxifrages. The Alpine Garden Society, London 1970.

Hegi, G.: Illustrierte Flora von Mitteleuropa. Band IV, Teil 2a. Verlag Paul Parey, Hamburg 1975.

Henshaw, J.W.: Wild Flowers of the North American Mountains. Robert M. McBride and Company, New York 1915.

Heynert, H.: Botanische Kostbarkeiten. Urania Verlag, Leipzig 1977.

Horny, Sojak and Webr: Zeitschrift Salnicky, Heft 1, 1974, Heft 4, 1974, Heft 2, 1975. Prag 1974/1975.

Ingwersen, W.: Manual of Alpine Plants. Will Ingwersen and Dunnsprint Ltd, Eastbourne, England, 1978.

Irving, W., and M., Reginald, A.: Saxifrages or Rockfoils. The Swarthmore Press Ltd, London (before 1914).

Jelitto, L., and Schacht, W.: Die Freilandschmuckstauden, Band 1. Verlag Eugen Ulmer, Stuttgart 1963.

Kohlhaupt, P.: Blumenwelt der Dolomiten. Verlagsanstalt Athesia, Bozen 1972.

Krüssmann, G., Siebler, W., and Tangermann, W.: Winterharte Gartenstauden. Verlag Paul Parey, Berlin and Hamburg 1970.

Madalski, J.: Atlas Flory Polskiej, XI/5 Saxifragaceae. Warszawa-Wroclaw 1962.

Schacht, W.: Der Steingarten. Verlag Eugen Ulmer, Stuttgart 1978.

Seyfert, W.: Stauden für Natur- und Steingärten. VEB Deutscher Landwirtschaftsverlag, Berlin 1965.

Thomas, G. S.: Plants for Ground-Cover. J. M. Dent and Sons Ltd, London 1970.

Tutin, T. G., ed.: Flora Europaea. Vol. 1. Cambridge 1964.

Weber, A.W.: Rocky Mountain Flora. Colorado Associated University Press, Boulder, Colorado 1976.

Wocke, E.: Die Kulturpraxis der Alpenpflanzen. Verlag Paul Parey, Berlin 1940. Nachdruck bei O. Koeltz, Königstein 1977.

Zander, Handwörterbuch der Pflanzennamen. Revised by F. Encke, G. Buchheim and S. Seybold. Verlag Eugen Ulmer, Stuttgart 1979, 11th edition.

## Nursery Catalogues

F. Sündermann, Lindau/Bodensee
J. Eschmann, Emmen/Schweiz
Frei, Wildensbusch/Schweiz
Dr Hans Simon, Marktheidenfeld

# *Index*